'Liz Carmichael recognizes that much of our religious talk about friendship or even love somehow misses the mark and threatens to become abstract. In this wonde[illegible]lth of scholarship and experience alike, t[illegible] and transforming category we need to [illegible] flesh out love in action, mindful of hov[illegible] of friendship and how theologians have thought about faith and love as friendship with God. This is a treasury of insight and resource.' Rowan Williams, Archbishop of Canterbury

'With this book Liz Carmichael takes us on an expedition into a forgotten land of Christian life and theology. The category of "friendship" throws a surprisingly new light upon our relationship with God, with Jesus, with the life-giving Spirit, with other people, with the whole creation community. Respect and affection, freedom and reliability, distance and closeness come together. The topic of this book is not only true, but also beautiful. We warmly welcome this intensive study and we are happy for the author who took this great step forward into a promising direction of Christian presence in today's world.' Elisabeth and Jürgen Moltmann

'This is a scholarly and persuasive rehabilitation of the love of friendship, which has much to offer us for living today.' Archbishop Desmond Tutu

'In a book both theologically astute and eminently practical, Liz Carmichael shows why Christian love is most fittingly understood as the love of friendship. Through a comprehensive and insightful analysis of how friendship has been understood in the Christian tradition, Carmichael demonstrates how friendship modelled on Christ can become a force for reconciliation and peace in the world. Beautifully written and inspiring, Carmichael's book is an important contribution to the tradition she so deftly explores.' Paul J. Wadell, St Norbert College, De Pere, Wisconsin

'I agree with Thomas Traherne, one of the many authors quoted in this fascinating book: "There is great talk of friendship. It is accounted the only pleasure in the world." Liz Carmichael shows us convincingly why friendship matters. She is readable yet profound, contemporary yet with a fine sense of history. A work of considerable (and considerate) scholarship.' Bishop Kallistos Ware

To the glory of God, eternal Friend,
and to all people,
made in the image of God.

Friendship: Interpreting Christian Love

E. D. H. (LIZ) CARMICHAEL

T & T CLARK INTERNATIONAL
A Continuum imprint
LONDON • NEW YORK

T&T CLARK INTERNATIONAL
A Continuum imprint

The Tower Building, 11 York Road, London SE1 7NX
15 East 26th Street, New York, NY 10010
www.tandtclark.com

British Library Cataloguing-in-Publication Data
A catalogue record for this book is available from the British Library.

ISBN 0 567 08072 2 (Paperback)
ISBN 0 567 08082 X (Hardback)

Typeset by Aarontype Limited, Easton, Bristol
Printed and bound in Great Britain by The Cromwell Press, Trowbridge, Wiltshire

Contents

Acknowledgements and Abbreviations

New Revised Standard Version Bible: Anglicized Edition, copyright 1989, 1995, Division of Christian Education of the National Council of Churches of Christ in the United States of America. Used by permission.

Quotations from Ambrose, *De officiis* (text, edited with introduction, translation and commentary by Ivor J. Davidson; 2 vols; Oxford: OUP, 2001) by permission of Oxford University Press; from Aelred of Rievaulx, *Spiritual Friendship* (trans. Mary E. Laker, S.S.M.D., intro. by D. Roby; CF 5; Kalamazoo: Cistercian Publications, 1977) by permission of Cistercian Publications; and from Thomas Aquinas, *Summa Theologica*, literally translated by Fathers of the English Dominican Province, 3 vols (London: Burns & Oates, 1947) by permission of Burns and Oates and the English Dominican Province.

Every effort has been made to trace owners of copyright material. Any omissions brought to the attention of the publishers will be rectified in future editions.

Abbreviations

CF	Cistercian Fathers Series
NPNF 1/2	A Select Library of Nicene and Post-Nicene Fathers, Series 1/Series 2
PG/L	Patrologia Graeca/Latina, ed. J.-P. Migne

Prologue and Introduction

This book has its roots chiefly in two places, one of action, the other of reflection. The action has taken place mainly in South Africa, the reflection in Oxford.

In June 1976, in a chilly southern winter, the school students of Soweto initiated the uprising that began the long painful death-throes of apartheid. On Wednesday 16 June a large demonstration was fired on, and all over the 'township' of two million, mayhem broke out. Smoke from a dozen burning government buildings made black pillars in the still air. Beneath, police and people milled in a confusion of fear and fury, and a trail of the wounded began arriving at the teaching hospital across the main road.

That weekend there was a knock on the door of our flat in the centre of Johannesburg. A young Sowetan, about my own age, came in and collapsed into an armchair. 'Everyone's all right', he said, 'I've been round and checked.' At that moment I knew that friendship was real and that it could be the shape of the future.

This young Sowetan worked as a car mechanic. I was a young British doctor at the Soweto hospital. I had met him and his wife and many of their friends through church contacts. They came to sing at my wedding to Michael, a South African Anglican priest, and we'd all become close over the previous eighteen months, just doing the normal things friends do together, having barbecues, playing volleyball, larking about in rowing boats on Zoo Lake. Apartheid made such friendship difficult. Most amenities were segregated. Sowetans could not stay overnight in a white area, and I was not supposed to be in the township without a permit. The vast majority did not try to know their neighbours, and racial communities remained ignorant and suspicious of one another.

On the evening of 16 June our Sowetan friend had reached home by dodging bullets. He didn't move out again until an eerie calm fell over Soweto that weekend, as if a great cry of anger had been followed by an exhausted, menacing silence. I had been due to visit him but could not. We had no means of knowing, until he came, who was safe or whether there was any reality, when it came to the crunch, in the ideals and examples of peace and reconciliation in Christ that had drawn me to South Africa.

What marked out those who lived in a manner that was significantly different from the pattern of apartheid society, was that they had taken trouble and risks to form and maintain friendships across the racial divides. Committed Christians, black and white, were among those most involved, most willing to pay the real cost in terms of courage and energy, time and money, of making and deepening the links of friendship. There was a clear integral link between these personal friendships, and wider love of neighbour in terms of a commitment to justice for all. Years later, the friendships the few had dared to make played a vital part in bringing the whole country through the turbulent transition period and to freedom in 1994. They were signs of the Kingdom of God, and the seed of a new, if inevitably still imperfect, society.

It seemed friendship was the shape that genuine love took, and that to be genuine, love could not be less than an offer of friendship. Yet despite the fact that Christians were among the foremost of such friends, it was rarely if at all that one heard this being explicitly discussed, explored, and encouraged in churches. The language of friendship did not feature in sermons. Instead there was the word 'fellowship', a vague and comfortable term, usually too remote to have any real effect. Friendship seemed to be, as it were, intellectually if not spiritually invisible. Why, I began to wonder, this apparent avoidance of an evidently significant reality?

Some years later, after the Soweto uprising and before the time of the transition, I was studying theology and I noticed on the one hand the relatively free use of the language of friendship by the patristic writers of the early centuries and some later systematic and mystical theologians – and on the other hand, particularly as one moved through the Reformation and towards the present day, the inhibition of its use.

A change was however just beginning. In particular Jürgen Moltmann, whose sympathy for the theology of liberation was much appreciated in South Africa, had recently suggested that Christ's three traditional titles as Prophet, Priest and King should be supplemented with a fourth and equally biblical title, that of Friend. He explored the implications for Christian love, showing how friendship makes it both a universal invitation to the messianic feast, and yet specifically personal and welcoming. That made sense in terms of my own experience and I wanted to know much more about those who might have explored this in the past and what support and insight they might have to offer. What were the positive reasons why we should use the language of friendship, and were there any conclusive arguments against? This became, for several years in the 1980s, the subject of my own theological research.

I found that the problems were varied, and sometimes contradictory. There was the overarching influence of the classical friendship-tradition of Greece and Rome, which in its final Ciceronian form reserves true friendship for a tiny minority of educated and virtuous males who enjoy and depend on each other's character. Such friendship elects with great care whom it will love and is partial, exclusive and contingent on worthiness, unlike the universal love commanded by Christ. Nevertheless classical friendship was sufficiently broad that New Testament writers drew on its language, and the great theologians of the fourth century who were still steeped in its traditions, integrated them into their understanding of love in Christ. Long afterwards, in the Cistercian abbey of Rievaulx in twelfth-century England, Aelred made a Christian version of Cicero's book on friendship; and Aristotle's philosophy of friendship was essential for Thomas Aquinas as he explored the Christian doctrine of love in the universities of Italy and Paris in the thirteenth century. But neither Aelred, nor Thomas on this subject, came to have a wide impact until the late twentieth century.

There was the problem of the suppression of 'particular friendships' in monastic life, either in favour of communal love, or out of fear: fear of cliques and sedition, distraction from inner calm, and other possible sins. Such suppression put friendship itself under a cloud. Despite this, a tradition of love as friendship persisted in the monastic setting and attracts strongly reawakened interest in the present day.

There was, again, the problem of understanding how love between humanity and God could be conceived of in terms of friendship, since friendship seemed to imply equality. In the early centuries it was natural to speak of serious Christians as 'friends of God' because the term primarily conveyed the sense of commitment. When, however, members of mystical groups in Germany in the Middle Ages applied it to themselves, they appeared to claim a special status and attracted the suspicion of church authorities. Finally, in later Roman Catholicism, 'friendship with God' became little more than a stock synonym for being in a 'state of grace'. But the great scholastic Thomas Aquinas had made friendship with God the basis for all our understanding of love, both for God and neighbour.

In the high Renaissance of the sixteenth century, classical friendship became for a time the preserve of scholars with pagan leanings, as a subject on which it was thought that Christianity, with its general love of neighbour, had nothing to say. The seventeenth-century Anglican Divine, Jeremy Taylor, knew how counter-cultural he was being when he said, and meant it, 'Christian love is friendship to all the world'. In the eighteenth century friendship somewhat lost the aura of strength that had graced it since the classical period and was seen quite differently, as a sentimental attachment that was the product not of rational choice but of irrational feeling. It was merely a love engendered by liking, having nothing in common with the command to love, and as such could be excluded from the sphere of ethics. Friendship and Christian love had drifted very far apart, although there were always a few spiritual writers who continued to revive a link between them; and in the nineteenth century in particular there was some rapprochement.

As the twentieth century dawned, the problem appeared in a new form in the study of biblical language. Protestant scholarship made a sharp distinction between the revealed Judaeo-Christian religion of the Bible and natural pagan 'Hellenism'. One focus of this distinction was found in the Greek of the Bible, and especially in its words for love. Classical Greek had chiefly used two words, *philia* (loosely translated as friendship) and *erōs* (desiring love). New Testament writers seemed to have decided on an almost completely new word, *agapē*, generally translated as *caritas* in Latin and 'charity' or 'love' in English, which must therefore denote a new kind of love, revealed and divine, and distinct from both *erōs* and *philia*. This trend of thought reached its zenith in the 1930s in Anders Nygren's highly influential work, *Agape and Eros*, in which 'Agape' is utterly altruistic love flowing down from God while 'Eros' is selfish, possessive, desiring love that seeks to climb up to God. Friendship became lost in the process, there being no room for relationship in this powerful dichotomy. His personal praxis as a teacher and bishop may have been very different, but in theory Nygren effectively dismissed *philia* as a subsidiary of 'Eros', as love that seeks reward. Ironically, following classical precedent friendship had been represented by Héloïse in the twelfth century as the love that does *not* seek reward but loves the other for their own sake!

In truth, as the critics of Nygren's stark Agape–Eros antithesis pointed out, the love of friendship alone gives a wholly satisfactory account of love precisely because it embraces both giving and receiving. More recently, friendship has come to the fore as a key paradigm of community and renewed human society, while the concept of friendship has been steadily evolving through the impact of personalism and of liberation and feminist theologies, themselves incorporating Gospel insights. The shape that love takes is significant for every aspect of Christian self-understanding, since love itself is so fundamental to it.

In all this it is clear that the word 'friendship' is commonly used in two senses, on the one hand to denote a reciprocal relationship and on the other, by transference, to convey the kind of love one associates with a friend. This book is interested in the latter sense. It seeks to explore the meaning of friendship-love, the love of a friend. Friendship as relationship models such love and enables us to observe its nature. My aim is to provide a composite picture of how we may conceive and exercise Christian love as the love of friendship in the twenty-first century and beyond, by bringing together the major, and some less well known, writings on friendship chiefly from the western Christian tradition. Writing on this topic has been more developed in the West, although as we shall see, some key insights into divine and human love have been best preserved in Eastern Orthodoxy. I begin with the pre-Christian classical discussion of friendship, because it remained influential through the centuries and some understanding of it is essential if we are to understand later writers. In the subsequent chapters we shall meet many who, in large and small ways, in their different contexts and with their diverse experiences, have reflected on Scripture and made contributions to the Christian theology of love as friendship.

You might perhaps be wondering what happened to that young Sowetan after that day in June 1976. A couple of years later friends made it possible for him to attend a short course at Ford in Daventry in England, and he came to know what apartheid did not intend him to know, that he could hold his own in a normal society overseas. He later moved to North Carolina in the USA to further his studies. After receiving a Ph.D. degree, he returned to a free South Africa where he became a Deputy Vice-Chancellor at an institution of higher learning in Durban.

Meanwhile in the early nineteen-nineties I had returned to Johannesburg, where I was ordained and had the immense privilege of being with South Africans of all races and backgrounds, together with personnel from the UN, Commonwealth and other international organizations, in the unique structures of the National Peace Accord. The Accord, which involved and empowered the people, and the simultaneous political constitutional talks, complemented one another in a twofold process to bring South Africa to its first democratic election in 1994. The grassroots work of the Accord was an experience of resolving what had remained a situation of desperate anger, violence and pain, and of creating friendship through intense and extraordinary encounters and vital common action. After the election the work of healing and forgiveness continued through the Truth and Reconciliation Commission, a part of the constitutional settlement.

More thanks than I can say to everyone who has made this study possible, by living the realities that it can only reflect, and by many kindnesses in helping to find or translate material. A special tribute to Michael Carmichael, without whom the project could neither have been begun nor ended! The errors that remain are mine, and I ask your forgiveness for so much as attempting to write on a topic that must, since love reflects God's own nature, forever remain above and beyond our human grasp. Love is nevertheless our calling, and in the end it is a matter of grace. The love revealed in Jesus Christ is God's love, given to us to practise in the power of the holy Spirit. The love of Christ on the cross is that of a friend who wills to draw all, through forgiveness and reconciliation, into friendship. Hence divine love can be described in terms of the love of friendship, and is creative of friendship. This study reveals the deep roots this way of understanding love has in Scripture and tradition, and its liveliness and potential for the present.

Liz Carmichael
St John's College
Oxford

Easter 2004

1

From classical friendship to New Testament love

The good person is a friend

Christian theologians have discussed love and friendship against a cultural background formed partly by Scripture, partly by the major Greek and Latin writers. The classical discussion ranged from love as cosmic unifying harmony to intimate personal friendship, described in terms easily recognizable to us today, as the focal example of human relationships.[1] In the Bible love becomes an increasingly central theme until when Jesus gives his 'new commandment' to 'love one another as I have loved you' (Jn 13.34; 15.12) that love has the shape of profound friendship.

The Bible and classical writings reach back to the beginnings of literature. Greek writing began with the epic poets and early philosophers, flourished in the golden age of Athens with Plato and Aristotle and expanded into the Hellenistic age, the two centuries before Christ when Greek culture spread widely around the eastern Mediterranean. The books of the Old Testament, the Hebrew Bible, acquired a Hellenistic Greek translation. Even after the rise of the Roman Empire and the beginning of Latin literature, the New Testament was composed entirely in Greek, in contact with the classical thought-world of international culture and learning.

The earliest poets and philosophers

Homer

Homer's two great epic poems the *Iliad* and *Odyssey*, from the eighth century BC, mark the dawn of European literature and were responsible, more than any other texts, for forming the classical consciousness. Set in vivid Mediterranean scenery, these poems portray the heroes of the late Bronze Age some five centuries earlier.

Homeric society can be understood as based on extended households, each headed by a 'good' or 'worthy' man and forming a friendly microcosm on which its members could rely in face of a hostile world.[2] Every thing and person in this microcosm, whether relative, comrade or neighbour, was 'beloved' '*philos*', the same word that came to mean 'friend'. The 'good man', Odysseus being a typical example, was under obligation 'to love' (*philein*) all within his household and any admitted as guests. Pacts of 'guest-friendship' were made with households in distant places where travellers might need to venture. Homeric love or friendship (the Homeric word is *philotēs*; the classical form *philia* appearing some centuries later) is thus comprised partly of feelings of affection, partly of obligations of duty. The word *philos* was still mainly an adjective but had already acquired the two meanings 'friend' has carried to the present day: the passive meaning, 'beloved', and the active, 'that which is friendly to me'.[3]

Certain forms of friendship stand out in Homer's legends. Warriors could feel intense loyalty to their comrades, Achilles and Patroclus becoming a much admired paradigmatic pair of friends. Penelope showed absolute faithfulness to Odysseus, and both sexes shared in the profound, and hereditary, obligations of hospitality and 'guest-friendship'. One line of the *Odyssey* became a proverbial expression of the view that friendship is the attraction of like for like:

> As always, god brings like and like together.[4]

Hesiod

The pessimistic **Hesiod**, writing his *Works and Days* in the peasant society of central Greece around 700 BC, expressed the opposite view, that likeness causes jealous strife:

> Then potter is enemy of potter, craftsman of craftsman,
> beggar is jealous of beggar, and singer of singer.[5]

Hesiod reflects an international scribal culture that stretched to the Near East, and like the biblical 'Wisdom' writers he gives advice on friendship in pithy 'gnomic' form. His view is narrow, reserving friendship strictly for those useful and friendly to oneself: 'give to whoever gives' but do not give to those who do not give (*W&D* 1.354). Retaliation is the order of the day: a friend who wrongs one should be paid back double, but can be reinstated if he offers reparation (1.707–14). Hesiod's universe had degenerated from its ancient golden age when men were friends or beloved (*philoi*) to the gods. Now he anticipates the imminent breakdown of society, when brothers will no longer be friends (1.184), and its final destruction by Zeus. *Philos* is now functioning clearly as a noun, as well as an adjective.

Hesiod's other poem, the *Theogony*, is a florid mythological account of primaeval history, using the word *philotēs* exclusively for sexual love between the many pairs of divinities whose unions create the cosmos.

Theognis

A third poetic source of 'wisdom' on friendship was a collection attributed to **'Theognis'**, probably compiled in Megara and Athens in the sixth to fifth centuries BC. Its tone is both intemperately passionate, and utilitarian. In this urbanized and bourgeois circle friendship is advantageous partnership and 'consequently no human quality is so strongly stressed as trustworthiness in friendship, meaning a readiness to stand by in difficulties and to repay in full the services done to oneself.'[6] Favours and disfavours are strictly reciprocated, betrayal is repaid with fury, open generosity and free forgiveness are unknown. Theognis advises a young man:

> never mingle with bad men; banish them far from your side, staying with good men alone. Always eat and drink in their company: sit with them always; make it your task to please those who have might in the land. You will learn good from the good; but once you mingle with bad men, even the wits that you had speedily vanish away.[7]

In Theognis the classical word for friendship, *philia*, made its first appearance, in its Ionic form *philiē*, when he claims the wicked are not wicked from birth but learn wickedness through *philiē* with the vile (l.305–6), curses someone who schemed to take advantage of his friendship (l.600), and laments a friendship destroyed by a third party (l.1102). A distinction between a rational, deliberately chosen friendship and an irrational passionate friendship associated with *erōs* also appears for the first time. The love-poems of 'Theognis' to Cyrnus begin by mentioning the *Maniai*, manic powers associated with unreason and frenzy, as the 'nurses' of *erōs*.

Pythagoras

Among the pre-Socratic philosophers, **Pythagoras** and his followers were strongly associated with friendship. The great mathematician lived on the island of Samos in the sixth century BC. His biography comes to us only from much later sources. The much-quoted maxim, 'friends have all things in common' (*koina tōn philōn*) and the alliterative equation of friendship with equality (*philotēs isotēs*) are attributed to him by Diogenes Laertius writing in the third century AD (D. L. VIII.10). Damian and Phintias, Pythagoreans who were willing to die for each other, joined Achilles and Patroclus as proverbial friends, and in the fifth century AD the pagan apologist Iamblichus claimed Pythagoras had been the first proponent of universal friendship. It is possible he was consciously setting up his hero and his community of disciples against the rival claims of Christians to be a loving community; or he may simply have wished to show how Pythagoras fulfilled the classical ideal.[8] He claims friendship ran through the whole of Pythagoras' teaching:

> Pythagoras handed on the clearest teachings on friendship of all for all: friendship of gods for humans, through piety and worship based on knowledge; friendship of one doctrine for another, and in general of soul for body and the reasoning part for the unreasoning, achieved through philosophy and the contemplation it entails; friendship of people for one another: fellow-citizens through a healthy respect for law, different peoples through a proper understanding of nature, a man with his wife and children and brothers and intimates through unswerving partnership; in short, friendship of all for all, including some of the non-rational animals through justice and natural connection and association; even the mortal body's pacification and reconciliation of opposite powers hidden within itself, through health and a lifestyle and practice of temperance which promotes health, imitating the way in which the cosmic elements flourish. All these may be summed up in that one word 'friendship', and Pythagoras is the acknowledged founding father of it all. He handed on to his followers such a remarkable tradition of friendship that even now people say of those who show each other unusual goodwill 'They belong to the Pythagoreans'.[9]

Empedocles

The other early philosopher who exercised a lasting influence on thought about love and friendship was the extraordinary **Empedocles**, who flourished in the Greek colony at Agrigento in Sicily in the mid-fifth century BC. Part natural philosopher, part magical healer, part poetical-mystical revealer through his two poems *On Nature* and *Purifications*, he claimed near-divinity and travelled across Italy and the Peloponnese suitably attired in purple cloak and Delphic crown, with a retinue of admirers. He established the doctrine of the four basic elements, earth, air, fire and water, which underpinned physical science until the modern era. Clement of Alexandria, Hippolytus and Eusebius among early Christian writers found him intriguing and quoted him.[10]

Empedocles taught that the entire universe, physical and spiritual, is governed by two opposing forces, hatred or 'Strife' (*neikos*) and Love or 'Friendship' (*philotēs*, becoming *philia* in later commentators). This world is subject to a process, cyclical and probably repetitive, in which each force in turn is in the ascendant, creating an oscillation between harmonious unity and discordant multiplicity, the One and the Many. Thus, after an original age of harmony our world is now under the sway of Strife: but each individual soul should ideally be ruled by *philotēs* and it is each person's task to discipline themselves to live according to friendship, avoiding bloodshed, giving help and healing, thus breaking free from the cycle of reincarnation in order to rejoin the blessed immortals.

Empedocles became identified with the view that like attracts like, although he also taught that unlikes are 'made like' by *philia*; while the doctrine of mutual attraction between unlikes was particularly associated with his contemporary, Heracleitus.[11]

Aristotle interpreted Empedocles as believing *philia* to be the cause of good, *neikos* of evil.[12] The characterization of *philia* as the force, both physical and moral, that binds and creates harmony throughout the universe remained deep in the consciousness of the ancient world. Dante's 'Love that moves the sun and the other stars' is partly traceable to Empedocles via Lucretius, the first-century BC Latin poet who wrote of Venus, bringer of peace and concord, as the counterpart to Mars, bringer of war.[13]

The Athenian golden age

Socrates and Plato

In an early dialogue, the *Lysis*, **Plato** (427–327 BC) shows **Socrates** (*c*.469–399 BC) chatting with a group of boys in their gymnasium and playing logical games with the language of friendship.[14] Here for the first time we encounter the foundational concept for un-possessive love when Socrates defines 'to love' (*philein*) as to desire happiness for the beloved (207D). For young Lysis happiness consists in growing up to be a trustworthy leading citizen. Hence, that is what his parents and friends desire for him.

But is 'friend' (*philos*) an active word, meaning one who loves, or passive, one who is loved? Either or both, decides Socrates, who never insists, as Aristotle would, that it is impossible to be a 'friend' outside a mutual friendship (212B–213C).

Must friends be like one another? Yes, in that both must be good to some degree, otherwise they would be a source of conflict and danger to each other. Therefore 'the good alone is friend to the good alone; the wicked does not enter into true friendship either with the good or the wicked' (214D).

On the other hand, surely the good are self-sufficient, so why would a good person need a friend? Does friendship derive from some deficiency, and reveal our desire for a greater good than we currently possess, perhaps for beauty or wholeness? And perhaps, unless there is to be an infinite progression of desires, there is some finally desirable object, a 'First Friend', in which all our desires for good can come to rest? If we seek what we need in a friend, then our friend must somehow 'belong' to us, fulfilling our need. Or is a friend someone already like me, homely and familiar? On this bemused note Socrates ends, saying to his young audience, 'we believe we are friends of one another – for I place myself among you – but we have not yet succeeded in discovering what the friend is!' (223B).

We have a rather stiffer portrait of Socrates from the military historian Xenophon. His Socrates, approaching friendship in a strictly practical manner, declares the gods to be friends of the 'noble and good' (*Symp.* V.49). The aspiration to have such friends is itself an incentive to virtue. He urges the advantages of spiritual over physical friendship (VIII.9; 18–36). In the *Memorabilia* he discusses the usefulness and choice of friends, remarking that although it is frequently said there is no better possession than a good friend, most people merely concern themselves with acquiring houses, fields, cattle and slaves. The virtuous man lives simply and shares generously; he is just, kind, able to control his anger, and resolves conflicts amicably. We must examine ourselves to see how good a friend we ourselves are. Virtuous friends should be capable of ruling the state together, sharing political honours without envy and for the sake of the common good. However, the eirenic effect is somewhat spoilt when Xenophon's Socrates sums up virtue as: to excel one's friends in well-doing and one's enemies in hostility (*Mem.* II.iv–vii).

Plato's developed thought on love is bound up with his theory of the Ideas and the ascent of the soul to the realm of pure Being. *Erōs*, the love of desire, powers this ascent. Plato sets friendship in the context of *Erōs* because his ascent commences with love for some particular human being, which in his case took the form of homoerotic attraction.

In Plato's *Phaedrus* Socrates attempts to praise the sober male friendship of which Xenophon would have approved. But he soon gives up and begins to praise *Erōs,* whose insanity, he declares, is not an evil but blessing. *Erōs* inspires our souls, which are immortal and of a complicated nature, like charioteers driving two winged horses (246A). Divine souls have well-controlled horses that draw their chariot effortlessly to the outermost rim of the revolving heavens, where the gods feast and become happy by gazing on the Ideas, the absolute realities of wisdom, goodness and beauty – the world's first revolving restaurant! (247D). Our own souls once rose and saw these realities, but then fell, became joined to bodies, and now struggle with two unmatched horses, one aspiring to goodness, the other dragged downwards by evil desires. Our wings, our most divine aspect, have shrivelled up. But whoever chooses to be 'a philosophical lover' (249A) will nourish their wings on beauty, goodness and wisdom, and prepare for upward flight.[15]

The ascent begins when the true lover glimpses beauty in a person, here assumed to be a young man, and falls in love. He reverences his beloved as he would a god, desiring to educate him so that he will achieve divine nobility (253A–C). The best lovers restrain their physical impulses. These are the philosophers, who having opposed physical consummation with 'modesty and reason' (256A) live in happiness, harmony, and self-control, giving free rein to virtue and restraining evil. They become light and winged, with two strong well-trained horses, flying upwards at death into the divine state (249A). Meanwhile their beloved, their 'friend by nature' (255A) will be astonished at the unique quality of *philia* experienced with such an inspired lover (255B). His own wings will grow, for he too is in love but does not realize it, believing it to be 'not love (*erōs*) but friendship (*philia*)' (255E). Plato portrays Socrates as such a philosopher – the laying aside of physical expressions of love in favour of a 'higher' spiritual love had its beginnings long before it flourished, partly under platonic influence, in Christian asceticism.

Physically consummated love would put the lovers on a lower plane where their wings only just start to grow. Not being philosophers, they love honour rather than wisdom. They live as friends, but less so than the others. Their upward journey has nevertheless begun and they will complete it together in continuing mutual friendship (255C–56D). Plato does not suggest friends are to be used selfishly as mere rungs on the ladder, and then discarded.

In Plato's *Symposium* the guests at a lively Athenian dinner party give a series of witty speeches in praise of *Erōs*. It produces excellence of character, and hence eternal happiness, in men and even women (178A–180B); it creates the state of *philia* described by Empedocles in which men converse with one another and are friends of the gods (186A–188E). Aristophanes contributes his comic myth that human beings were originally quadrupeds comprised of two male or two female halves, or one male and one female, and *Erōs* is literally the pursuit of our 'other half' so as to restore our original wholeness. In our present divided state the best course is to become friends with the god *Erōs* so we may each find our own true beloved (186A–193C). Agathon the host remarks *Erōs* must be a young god because he consorts with the young, and 'like always draws near to like', and moreover tales of ancient wars between the gods reveal there was a time before *Erōs* was born to secure peace and *philia* among them (195B–C).

Socrates comes in and questions whether *Erōs* is divine, for if he desires beauty and goodness he must be deficient in them (199C–200B). What the prophetess Diotima revealed to him is that *Erōs* is neither beautiful and good, nor ugly and evil, but 'in between'. So he is not a god but a *daimōn*, a spirit who communicates between mortal and immortal (201E–203A). Nor is he a beloved, but a lover, a needy schemer, desiring what is beautiful, good, wise and true: and therefore he is a philosopher, a 'lover of wisdom' (203B–204B). *Erōs* drives every human impulse towards the good and towards happiness (205D), things which are immortal and whose pursuit is the proper activity of the human soul: for love desires that the good should be one's own for ever (206A, 207A).

Diotima also revealed the method (*praxis*, 206B) of ascent. *Erōs* is not so much a direct love *of* the beautiful, but rather an engendering and begetting *on* the beautiful (206E). Human nature desires to beget, both in body and soul. Those 'pregnant in body' seek immortality by going to women and begetting children, or they perform deeds that will gain immortal memory (208D). Those 'pregnant in soul' beget virtues and are poets, craftsmen, inventors, and best of all statesmen who create temperance and justice. Such persons seek that which is beautiful, in which they may do their begetting. On meeting their beloved, beautiful in body and at least potentially in soul, they will converse about virtue and the qualities a good man should have. Such unions produce the greatest communion (*koinōnia*) and *philia*, and their offspring are great poetry, excellent laws, and deeds of virtue that remain for ever in the people's memory (209A–E).

Whoever wishes to proceed, 'as on the rungs of a ladder' (211D) on this ascent to Beauty must begin from youth to love beautiful bodies, starting with a single one and engendering beautiful conversation within it. Then he must understand that beauty is universal, so he can love all beautiful bodies and be less attached to any single one. After this he must learn to value beauty of soul above that of the body, loving it in all souls however little endowed. Then he will appreciate beauty in the abstract, in good customs and laws (210B–C). This spiritual beauty is a vast unity, to be found in the various areas of knowledge and the broad ocean of philosophy. Finally the vision of Beauty uniquely existing in itself, *auto to kalon*, is suddenly revealed, of which all transient beauties are now seen to partake (211B–E).

A person thus in contact with reality has passed beyond illusion and can bring forth true virtues: 'when he has begotten a true virtue and has reared it up he is destined to win the friendship of heaven (*theophilei genesthai*); he, above all men, is immortal' (212A). Since *Erōs* is man's greatest helper in his search for happiness and immortality, we should indeed praise him (212B). Plato and his later followers influenced the development of the Christian mystical tradition, in so far as it too embodies the contemplative desire for the good, beautiful, and true. Nygren was to complain that *Erōs* is human love striving upwards; yet as a gift empowering humans to rise beyond their natural capacity *Erōs* holds for Plato a position somewhat analogous to that occupied by divine grace in Christianity.

Aristotle

Plato's pupil **Aristotle** (384–322 BC), an independent, systematic and prodigiously learned thinker, came from northern Greece to study and teach in Athens; he carried out research on the coast of Asia Minor and stayed for a time at the court of Philip of Macedon, father of Alexander the Great. In his *Nicomachean Ethics* (*NE*), he became the first to investigate the nature and function of *philia* in the lives of individuals and the state. For the individual, a capacity for *philia* precedes fulfilment in the life of philosophical contemplation (*theōria*). For the community, *philia* holds the city-state (*polis*) together, being intimately related to concord and justice (1155a23–8). Thus it forms a link to the *Politics* in which Aristotle's virtuous politicians, working together for the common good, enable citizens to lead the happy life.

Ethics, according to Aristotle, concerns our attainment of happiness (*eudaimonia*) through achieving the 'good', for human beings, which is 'activity of soul in conformity with excellence' (or 'virtue', *aretē*) (*NE* I.1098a16–17).[16] It entails 'three objects of choice and three of avoidance, the noble, the advantageous, the pleasant, and their contraries, the base, the injurious, the painful' (II.1104b30–32). The *NE* consists, in its earlier Books, of an exploration of the virtues of justice, generosity, courage and all the other excellences of character which the human soul can choose, through its own inbuilt rational principle (*logos*), to develop. The treatment of *philia* suitably follows that of virtue, since Aristotle declares *philia* to be a proper subject for ethical discussion because 'it is an excellence or implies excellence (*esti gar aretē tis ē met' aretēs*)' (1155a3–4), it 'is a virtue or involves virtue'.

Philia is fundamental to life, since no one would choose to live without friends. The wealthy need friends on whom to practise beneficence. The less fortunate depend on friends. Friends guide the young and assist the old, while all our plans and activities benefit from friendly collaboration. We believe that the good are also friends, and we admire those who have many friends.[17] *Philia* is characteristic of all animate creatures, and particularly of the human race. We praise lovers of humankind (*philanthrōpoi*) and travellers remark how humans everywhere are homely and friendly to one another (1155a20–22).

Aristotle briskly examines the common usage of 'to love' (*philein*) and 'friend' (*philos*). *Philein* and other *phil-* words may be used to indicate a 'love' or liking (*philēsis*), even for inanimate things such as wine; but love for inanimate objects is not called '*philia*', for two distinct reasons: there is no return of love and no wishing well to the object for its own sake. We do wish good to a friend 'for his sake (*ekeinou heneka*)' (1155b31) and this is only possible with a human being. Plato had already said to love is to desire the other's happiness (*Lysis* 207D), but here we have the first explicit expression of the concept of loving others 'for their own sake', and clearly underlying it is the intuition that only a human being can be loved 'for their own sake' because only a human person can be, not only the *object* of love but also a *subject* in their own right; but neither Aristotle nor any other ancient writer made this intuition explicit.

Although he declined to speculate on any cosmological role *philia* might play, Aristotle's thoughts are still coloured by the Greek cultural understanding of *philia* as the unifying principle of relationship and harmony, 'wide enough to include all relations in which things come together'.[18] It naturally follows that he presents mutual friendship as its central case. He is adamant that he will only call people 'friends' where they are 'mutually recognized as bearing goodwill and wishing well to each other' (1156a3–5). Friendship exists where each wishes well to the other for their own sake, and is willing to act on that goodwill, and is aware of the goodwill of the other; and a 'friend' is a person involved in such a relationship. 'For many people have goodwill to those whom they have not seen but judge to be good or useful, and one of these might return this feeling ... but how could one call them friends when they do not know their mutual feelings?' (1155b34–56a3). The *Lysis* had allowed a variety of answers to this question but Aristotle allows only one. He gains in logical neatness, but at the price of absolutely limiting 'friend' to the consciously mutual situation. Even so, he will turn out not to be entirely consistent. Socrates and Plato were perhaps rightly unwilling to make this move and common usage of the word 'friend' has never fully accepted it. I may be a friend to someone, or recognize someone as a friend, long before a mutual relationship has been established.

Aristotle distinguishes three kinds of *philia*, which we shall discuss below. He then discusses friendship between equals, quoting the proverb 'equality and likeness are friendship (*hē d' isotēs kai homoiotēs philotēs*)' and adding, 'especially the likeness of those who are like in excellence' (1159b2–4). Friendship between unequals is also possible provided each makes an 'equal' response, albeit one that is different in kind. Such sharing illustrates the truth of another proverb, 'what friends have is common property (*koina ta philōn*)'; indeed friendship consists in community (*koinōnia*) (1159b31–2). Friendship with gods is impossible, their superiority and remoteness being too great (1159a2–6) – although later Aristotle does allow a *philia* of humans towards the gods analogous to that of child towards parent (1162a5–6). He concludes Book Eight with sections on political, social, and family relationships and a note on the close connection between *philia* and justice.

Book Nine examines the relationship between friendship and self-love, to which we shall return. It also treats unequal social relationships; goodwill (*eunoia*) as leading towards friendship; concord (*homonoia*, unanimity) as 'political friendship' and as perfect between the good; the intense love of parents and benefactors; whether the happy person needs friends and if so how many, and whether they are most needed in good or bad fortune or, as Aristotle believes, their presence is desirable at all times.

Koinōnia and the three kinds of friendship

Before examining Aristotle's famous three-fold definition, we should notice that he will mention an essential ontological precondition or ground for friendship, the sharing in some kind of 'communion' (*koinōnia*), which of itself engenders friendship between its participants. Simply to be human is such a ground. Kinship, citizenship, and common enterprise constitute further grounds. 'Friendship depends on community (*en koinōnia gar hē philia*)' (1159b31–2). Aristotle significantly remarks that because of the *koinōnia* of humanity one can befriend a slave *qua* human but not *qua* slave in which capacity he is a mere tool (1161b5). *Koinōnia* would acquire fresh significance in the New Testament and become a key concept in Aquinas's doctrine of Christian love (*caritas*) as friendship.

Aristotle categorizes his three kinds of friendship teleologically, according to three desirable goals: 'the good, the pleasant, and the useful' (1155b19), exactly the same ends on which his whole ethical system depends.

Perfect, complete friendship (*teleia philia*) is contingent on virtue in both partners, who will be 'alike in excellence; for these wish well to each other *qua* good, and they are good in themselves' (1156b7–9). Such persons embody moral excellence to such a degree that it is the same thing to love them '*qua* good ', and 'for their sake', and 'by reason of their own nature' (1156b8–10). Because virtue is a stable state, friendship based on it will have the perfection of permanence. In theory, then, perfect friendship is grounded in what the person essentially *is*, but only to the extent that they instantiate excellence, not simply because they are a fellow human being.

Friendships merely for advantage or pleasure are imperfect in that the partners love each other, not for themselves but 'in virtue of some good which they get from each other' due to some incidental quality attaching to the beloved (1156a10–16). The exchange of goodwill is directed, not to the character of the friend, desiring their excellence to increase, but merely to the increase of those accidental qualities that please me or supply my need. Such loves are impermanent, lapsing when partners cease to be useful or pleasing, whether they themselves, or their friends' tastes and needs, undergo change.

Utility friends include business partners, and may not find each other pleasant. They do not necessarily spend time together. Pleasure friends do wish to 'spend their days and lives together' (1156b4–5).[19] They are often young persons, led by emotion, who 'pursue above all what is pleasant to themselves and what is immediately before them', they 'quickly become friends and quickly cease to be so' (1156a34–5). Aristotle places *erōs* here, ignoring the divine role Plato gave it and bringing it down to earth with a thump: 'Young people are amorous (*erōtikoi*) too; for the greater part of the friendship of love (*tēs erōtikēs*) depends on emotion and aims at pleasure; they fall rapidly in and out of love' (1156b1–3).

Perfect friendship embraces the advantages of the two imperfect kinds, because the virtuous are also useful and pleasant. The good person derives pleasure from contemplating his own and his friend's virtuous activities, which 'are the same or like' (1156b12–17). Such happy contemplation is mutually fulfilling, for self-sufficiency does not in fact isolate us but inherently requires the full actualization of our social nature.[20] The best love and friendship is found between such 'lovable' persons (*philētoi*); but since they are rare, and familiarity requires time for growth, perfect friendships are few (1156b23–33).

Aristotle's central case of love is perfect friendship between good individuals. The many relationships to which we give the name *philia* deserve it by virtue of partial resemblance to this central ideal (1157a1–2). John Finnis gives a particularly clear summary of Aristotle's position which he, writing as a legal philosopher, has adopted and developed as the central case for his own exploration of community and the common good:

> In the fullest sense of 'friendship', A is the friend of B when (i) A acts (or is willing to act) for B's well-being, for the sake of B, while (ii) B acts (or is willing to act) for A's well-being, for the sake of A, (iii) each of them knows of the other's activity and willingness and of the other's knowledge, and (iv) each of them co-ordinates (at least some of) his activity with the activity (including acts of friendship) of the other so that there is a sharing, community, mutuality, and reciprocity not only of knowledge but also of activity (and thus, normally, of enjoyment and satisfaction).[21]

The love of friendship as virtue

In Christian understanding love would itself become the greatest virtue; and despite his teleological definitions Aristotle has much to contribute to this idea. He begins by stating that *philia* is a virtue or implies virtue (1155a4), but then rather than probing further into how it might be virtue he draws back to the position that *philia* is a relationship involving or implying virtue. As already foreshadowed in earlier writers however, it turns out that friendship 'implies virtue' in two distinct ways.

Teleologically, it is motivated by the attractiveness of goodness: I am attracted by my friend's character, and they become my friend in a passive sense. It is equally clear, however, that for Aristotle a good person is a friend in the active sense: it is the inherent nature, and in that sense the duty, of a virtuous person to love and be a friend. This is another sense, which we shall call 'deontological', in which friendship 'implies virtue'. Friendship-love in Aristotle is both teleological (love as attraction) and deontological (love as right action). Virtue is, to employ Aristotelian terminology, simultaneously the final cause (goal) and efficient cause (originating force) of being a friend. While Aristotle's discussion emphasizes the teleological, the fact that *philia* appears under both aspects goes a long way to explaining why Aristotelian friendship has encountered both strong approbation and complete rejection from Christian writers.[22]

Aristotle defines a 'virtue' as an excellence of character, moral or intellectual, developed by early training or mature choice; it is a habit or state, existing on the level of reason as distinct from passion (*NE* II.1105b19–06a13). When he places *philia* on the level of virtue, but *philēsis* (liking or affection) on that of irrational passion, he again verges on identifying *philia* as a virtue:

> Now it looks as if love (*philēsis*) were a passion, friendship (*philia*) a state; for love may be felt just as much towards lifeless things, but mutual love involves choice and choice springs from a state; and men wish well to those whom they love, for their sake, not as a result of passion but as a result of a state. (1157b28–32)

Aristotle draws a metaphysical parallel between virtue and friendship in that virtues are states which embody potential that can be realized in activity, and 'so too in the case of friendship': when friends are asleep or temporarily separated their friendship still exists in potential; when they get together again its activity recommences (1157b5–11). Virtue and friendship are, moreover, intrinsically connected because friendship as a state depends precisely on the exercise of virtue for its actualization. The potential state of the virtuous man is that of being a friend in both passive and active senses: 'we think it is the same people that are good men and are friends' (1155a31); the good man 'does many acts for the sake of his friends and his country, and if necessary he dies for them' (1169a9–11).

Aristotle again suggests that the love which characterizes *philia* is itself a virtue when he says that friendship 'seems to lie in loving (*to philein*) rather than in being loved' and 'since friendship depends more on loving, and it is those who love their friends that are praised, loving (*to philein*) seems to be the characteristic excellence of friends' (1159a27, 33–35). The emphasis on active love is notable, and here the verb *philein* displays its fullest classical meaning, encompassing both affection and active well-doing. It is 'only those in whom this is found in due measure that are lasting friends' (1159b1).[23] Remarkably, Aristotle's example of this virtue is a maternal love that is courageous, altruistic, unpossessive and non-mutual, granting complete freedom:

> But it (*philia*) seems to lie in loving rather than in being loved, as is indicated by the delight mothers take in loving; for some mothers hand over their children to be brought up, and so long as they know their fate they love them and do not seek to be loved in return (if they cannot have both), but seem to be satisfied if they see them prospering; and they themselves love their children even if these owing to their ignorance give them nothing of a mother's due. (1159a 27–33)

Despite this moment of admiration, however, Aristotle normally allows only domestic virtues to women. In a household 'the man rules in accordance with merit, and in those matters in which a man should rule, but the matters that befit a woman he hands over to her' (1160b32–5). Reasonable as this may seem, it is the dangerous doctrine of 'separate but equal' in which one side sets the rules and the full humanity of the other will inevitably be denied. Aristotle does not mention, and is unlikely to envisage, friendship between men and women apart from marriage, nor does he explicitly touch on friendship between women. Marriage, however, given the caveats above can be a true friendship, for *philia* exists between man and woman by nature, disposing them to form couples in a friendship of utility and pleasure which 'may also be based on excellence if the parties are good; for each has their own excellence and will delight in the fact' (1162a25–7).

Two early passages in the *Nicomachean Ethics* reveal how Aristotle was confronted by a simple linguistic problem: the lack of a noun to name the excellent love that exists in friendship. The problem emerges while he is expounding the nature of moral virtue as 'a mean between two vices, the one involving excess, the other deficiency . . . its character is to aim at what is intermediate in passions and in actions' (II.1109a20–4). In the case of the virtue of congenial behaviour or 'pleasantness',

> the man who is pleasant in the right way is a friend (*philos*) and the mean is friendship (*philia*), while the man who exceeds is an obsequious person if he has no end in view, a flatterer if he is aiming at his own advantage, and the man who falls short and is unpleasant in all circumstances is a quarrelsome and surly sort of person. (1108a26–30)

Examining this virtue in more detail, he adds that it implies principled behaviour in which the giving or withholding of pleasure is regulated by 'what is noble and expedient', and 'no name has been assigned' to it 'but it most resembles *philia*. For the man who corresponds to this middle state is very much what, with affection (*to stergein*) added, we call a good friend' (1126b20–29). In his *Eudemian Ethics*, *philia* makes a similar appearance as the habit of self-control and right action, tempering irrational passion, producing behaviour that is the virtuous mean between flattery and dislike (*EE* II.1121a7).

Aristotle points to the candid positive regard, the reliable love, that grounds true friendship. He recognizes it as virtue, but what to call it? He verges on recruiting *philia*, but cannot because he reserves '*philia*' to define the state of mutual love. *Philēsis* will not serve because it denotes passion and not rational commitment. He does not attempt to coin a new noun. At one point he makes do, as we have seen, with the verb *philein*. Without naming it, Aristotle points to the as yet unnamed virtue of love and builds up a picture of it as the reliable behaviour of an excellent friend.

Understanding self-love

During his discussion of *philia*, Aristotle initiated what was to become the perennial debate about self-love and its role in love for others. Self-love was not yet construed as a problem in itself. Classical tradition assumed we naturally love our selves, sharing with animals a morally neutral instinct of self-preservation. As rational creatures, however, humans face the moral difficulty of knowing how to love self rightly; and the pursuit of virtue was understood to constitute right self-love. The possibility of an absolutely disinterested love, refusing all reward, was not seriously suggested prior to Abelard (AD 1079–1143).[24]

Aristotle makes two points. First, love of others is like love for one's self (1166a2–3; b1–2); second, there are two distinct kinds of 'self-love', one wrong, which makes *philia* impossible, and one right, without which it cannot exist (1168a29–69b3). A dual conception of the ethical self is implicit here, comprising the mind (*nous*) as the subject of rational choices and desires, and the 'self' that is loved, 'a persona constructed by forming desires and making choices'.[25]

On his first point Aristotle writes, 'friendly relations with one's neighbours, and the marks by which friendships are defined, seem to have proceeded from a man's relations to himself' (1166a1–2). His meaning can be argued in two, not necessarily mutually exclusive ways: that self-love is the exemplar for all other loves, or that all love is fundamentally self-love. The exemplary meaning is foremost when he says that very strong friendship 'is likened to' one's friendship for one's self (1166b1–2).

A good person who wishes well to his higher, intellectual self and enjoys his own company, will treat a friend in the same way, for a friend is another self (*allos autos*) (1166a32). Life can be shared to such an extent that 'I may, as a matter of virtuous love, allow my friend to do an action that I might have done, or I may die so that he may live and continue to act' (1169a18–34).[26]

The other mode of interpretation, that love of others is an extension of, or participation in, love of self, is illustrated by the strong affection of parent for child, or craftsman for their creation. 'Parents love (*stergousi*, feel strong affection for) their children as being part of themselves', and they love more than they are loved because 'the originator is more attached to his offspring than the offspring to their begetter' (1161b18–22) and children are 'a sort of other selves' (28–9). Similarly benefactors, craftsmen and poets love their creations because men love their own existence, and existence consists in activity, and 'the handiwork *is*, in a sense, the producer in activity . . . for what he is in potentiality, his handiwork manifests in activity' (1167b17 ff.).

In either case, capacity for friendship depends on right self-love, which is free of selfishness in that the good I will for myself is the good of virtue, and the virtuous person is free of self-seeking passion, and acts according to intelligent reason (*nous*). 'To love a person in himself is to love him for what he quintessentially is, i.e., a rational being and a virtuous agent' and this love is *ipso facto* disinterested, because 'one cannot love virtue and rationality for one's own exclusive sake'.[27] 'Therefore the good man should be a lover of self (*philautos*) (for he will both himself profit by doing noble acts, and will benefit his fellows), but the wicked man should not; for he will hurt both himself and his neighbours, following as he does evil passions' (1169a11–15). The evil person (who has in effect failed to become fully actualized as a moral self) is not even a friend to himself. That wretched state should be avoided by striving for goodness, 'for so one may be friendly to oneself and a friend to another' (1166b28–9).

In perfect friendship the apparent object of love is the goodness which the excellent person instantiates; and goodness is universal – and yet, as Suzanne Stern-Gillet reflects, Aristotle insists on love and loyalty to our friends as actual concrete persons with whom we share life's experiences. The universality of goodness does not in effect make virtue-friends merely interchangeable.[28]

The *Nicomachean Ethics* does not appear to have been widely known in antiquity, the partially similar *Eudemian Ethics* being much better known. Cicero barely mentions its existence (*De Fin.* V.12). It was only fully translated into Latin in the thirteenth century, when its exploration of friendship was immediately introduced into theological discussion. Since when it has held pride of place among classical contributions.

Hellenistic and Roman thought

At the end of Aristotle's life the conquests of Alexander the Great inaugurated the Hellenistic age. Two new philosophical schools, Stoic and Epicurean, emerged in Athens to join Plato's 'Academy' and Aristotle's 'Peripatetics'. From now on intellectual life was largely driven by developments within, and debate between, these major schools. The Stoics proved the more generally influential, particularly in the Roman period. Politico-social changes meant that the Athenian ideal of friendship between equal citizens was supplemented, if not entirely replaced, by the realities of unequal relationship between wealthy patrons and their clients, which could be genuine friendship provided there was mutual frankness, and the absence of fawning and flattery.[29]

Stoics

The **Stoics** took their name from the 'Painted Stoa', a colonnade on the Athens agora decorated with paintings of Athenian victories, where Zeno began to teach about 300 BC. Human excellence was summed up for them in the ideal 'Wise Man' who, in theory, is wholly self-sufficient. Yet his lack of need does not in practice exclude his participation in relationships. Indeed, the good alone can be true citizens, friends, or even kindred,[30] and the ideal human community, now conceived as worldwide in scope, would be a friendship of the wise:

> In the ideal world the state withers away because each sage is self-sufficient and his own authority (*SVF* iii.617). But he is united with his fellows by the bond of friendship, for all wise men are friends to each other and it is only between them that friendship in its true sense can exist (*SVF* iii.625). A communal way of life which dispenses with all distinctions based on sex, birth, nationality, and property – this is the pattern of social behaviour. The theory is utopian and was recognized as such.[31]

The ecumenical breadth of this way of thinking was necessarily restricted by another Stoic conviction, that the wise man is a rarity. We have only fragments of the writings of the early Stoic philosophers, but their belief that friendship is inherent in the true nature of things, and is inseparable from virtue, became an all-pervasive influence.

Epicureans

Epicurus (341–270 BC), founder of the other major Hellenistic philosophical school, came from Greek-speaking Asia Minor to share a life of philosophical retreat in a garden house in Athens with his closest disciples. For them, to retreat from public affairs and live simply and frugally, studying philosophy with a trusted master and congenial companions, was itself wisdom; and since Epicureans had no intention of being active in political life, their community did, at least at first, include some women.

Epicurus' aim seems to have been to achieve inner peace and equanimity, 'undisturbed-ness' (*ataraxia*) by engendering a feeling of safety in mind, body, and soul. His teaching is summarized as the 'fourfold remedy': 'the gods are not to be feared, there is no risk to run in death, the good is easy to obtain, the bad easy to endure with courage'.[32]

Of Epicurus' voluminous works only three letters, two collections of sayings, and a few fragments remain. He wrote no book on friendship and only 11 of his 121 extant sayings mention it, tending simply to praise it: 'Of all the things which wisdom acquires to produce the blessedness of the complete life, far the greatest is the possession of friendship'.[33] Just to have friends lessens our anxiety: 'it is not so much our friends' help that helps us as the confidence of their help'. 'Friendship goes dancing round the world proclaiming to us all to awake to the praises of a happy life'.[34] Although he himself mentions 'friends' only rarely, it is clear from the lifestyle and writings of Epicurus and his followers that the ministrations of friends and the feeling of trust between them contributed significantly to the Epicurean sense of safety.

Some Epicureans probably continued to share a common life, although according to Diogenes Laertius, Epicurus 'did not recommend them to put all their belongings into a common stock, as did Pythagoras, who said that "friends have all in common". For to do so implied distrust: and distrust could not go with friendship.'[35] Philodemus of Gadara, a first-century BC Epicurean teacher in Herculaneum where many fragments from his library have been excavated, took up a friendship theme in exploring the pedagogical role of candid speech (*parrhēsia*) between teacher and disciple, and among disciples themselves.

In his desire to eliminate fear Epicurus preferred to depict the gods as living far away in their own utterly untroubled state, not interfering in human affairs. But Philodemus, while otherwise rejecting friendship language as inapplicable between worshipper and divinity, allows that when the sage joyfully strives in prayer to draw close to the divine nature and be transformed by it, we can in a contemplative sense call 'wise men the friends of the gods, and the gods friends of the wise.'[36]

Epicurean literature reflects a strong consciousness of friendship among themselves. However, Epicurean friendship was certainly not universally admired, and they cannot be said to have copyrighted the idea of friendship, nor does it seem they designated themselves technically as 'friends' in any unique sense.[37] Stoic friendship was based on virtue and consisted in mutual appreciation among the wise, but Epicurean friendship was the clubbing together of vulnerable human beings for mutual support. It was an alternative view of friendship, based on human needs and feelings rather than on absolute integrity. The majority classical view was always that true friendship rests on virtue, while friendship for pleasure or advantage is only partially worthy of the name. Not surprisingly, mutual incomprehension arose, not only between Stoics and Epicureans but between Epicureans and virtually everyone else. Epicureans were attacked as hedonistic drop-outs, incapable of true friendship because lacking in virtue. Epicurus appears to be defending himself against charges of utilitarianism when he explains: 'All friendship is desirable in itself, though it starts from the need of help.'[38] Cicero's Epicurean friend Torquatus admits that friendships may well originate in attraction to pleasure, but love (*amor*) will then grow 'strong enough to make us love our friends for their own sake, even though no practical advantage accrues from their friendship'.[39]

Cicero's 'De amicitia'

Born near Rome just a century before Christ, Marcus Tullius **Cicero** (106–43 BC) was a prominent public figure throughout the turbulent final years of the Republic. A practical philosopher and an important transmitter of Greek thought to the Latin-speaking West, he hammered out his understanding of friendship and its duties in the midst of active political life. His dialogue on friendship, *Laelius, de amicitia*, was one of several works produced during a brief period of retirement in 44 BC shortly before his assassination.

As a philosopher Cicero aligned himself with the 'New' Academy, which allowed him to be eclectic: 'it is within my right to defend any theory that presents itself to me as most probable.'[40] There are reminiscences of Xenophon's Socrates in Cicero's practical tone and behind his remark about friends and possessions.[41] He had acquired from Stoicism a profound sense of virtue and natural law and his writing on friendship breathes this atmosphere; he considered the Epicureans superficial by comparison. Moral questions concerning friendship appear in his *De officiis* ('On Duties'), which he patterned on a book by the Stoic Panaetius of Rhodes. In it he refers his readers to the *De Amicitia*, written at about the same time (*De off.* II.31). He depicts himself borrowing commentaries on Aristotle from a friend's library, and mentions the *Nicomachean Ethics* with approval (*De fin.* III.10; V.12), but it is uncertain whether he had read it. He did almost certainly know a three-volume work 'On Friendship' by Theophrastus, the less profound thinker who had succeeded Aristotle.[42] But he made no use of Aristotle's threefold division of friendship, reportedly preserved by Theophrastus,[43] perhaps because it does not coincide with the twofold Stoic pattern of the right and the expedient that structures his own moral thought.

Friendship fits our nature

The conversation on friendship is set in 129 BC, in the ideal republican Rome that Cicero so cherished. The wise Gaius Laelius is reminiscing with his two sons-in-law about his friend, the great general Scipio Africanus the Younger who has just died:

> . . . still such is my enjoyment in the recollection of our friendship that I feel as if my life has been happy because it was spent with Scipio, with whom I shared my public and private cares; lived under the same roof at home; served in the same campaigns abroad, and enjoyed that wherein lies the whole essence of friendship – the most complete agreement in policy, in pursuits, and in opinions (15).[44]

So rare is this that throughout the ages scarcely three or four pairs of friends have been named; but now he hopes Scipio and Laelius will join them.[45] The young men ask him to share his wisdom on what friendship is and how to practise it. After disclaiming any theoretical knowledge, for which they must turn to the Greeks, Laelius begins.

We should, he says, value friendship above all other human things, because it perfectly fits our nature, adapting to all our circumstances in good or evil fortune. But it is impossible except among the good, those who, while not necessarily paragons of wisdom, are good in a practical sense, 'who so act and so live as to give proof of loyalty and uprightness, of fairness and generosity; who are free from all passion, caprice, and insolence, and have great strength of character' (18–19).

A natural bond (*societas*) unites the human race. It is more strongly felt towards those closer to us, and friendship is a concentrated form of *societas* in which love (*caritas*) is joined only between two or a few, and which requires goodwill (*benevolentia*) over and above closeness or relatedness. So Cicero advances his famous definition: 'For friendship is nothing else than an accord in all things, human and divine, conjoined with mutual goodwill and affection.' '*Est enim amicitia nihil aliud nisi omnium divinarum humanarumque rerum cum benevolentia et caritate consensio*' (20).

With the exception of wisdom, nature and the gods have given us no better gift than friendship. People seek their 'highest good' in many places, in health, wealth or power; but it lies best in virtue, which engenders and preserves friendship and without which it cannot exist at all. Friendship affords the joy of goodwill and sharing in good times and bad, it 'adds a brighter radiance to prosperity and lessens the burden of adversity by dividing and sharing it' (22). Empedocles sang that the universe is 'united by friendship and scattered by discord'; and because friendship is so built into nature, to risk danger to help a friend always wins praise. When the theatre audience applauds Orestes and Pylades as each offers to die for the other, they reveal their innate sense of the fundamental nature of things, judging the action to be right even though they could not rise to it themselves (24). Love (*amor*) from which *amicitia* is derived, brings goodwill in its train (26).

Since it is natural to love, true friendship originates from nature rather than from need, from an inclination of soul joined with a feeling of love rather than from calculation of gain (27).[46] Even animals love their offspring, and love (*caritas*) exists between parents and children. We naturally feel attracted to anyone 'whose habits and character are congenial with our own; because in him we seem to behold, as it were, a sort of lamp of uprightness and virtue. For there is nothing more lovable than virtue, nothing that more allures us to affection (*ad diligendum*)' (28). Love is bound to spring up when similar souls encounter each other and delight in one another's goodness and capacity 'to return love' (here Cicero coins a new verb, *redamare*) (49). The good display a kind of necessary goodwill, which nature itself has made a fount of friendship (50). When goodness rises up and makes its light shine, and sees and recognizes the same in another, then love and friendship will burst into flame (100). Elsewhere Cicero says that likeness of character among the good brings about what Pythagoras required of friendship, that many become one (*unus fiat ex pluribus*) (*De off.* I.56).

Virtue is lovable even in those we have never seen, even in enemies, but closer familiarity increases love until it becomes 'a marvellous glow and greatness of goodwill' (29). Only goodness lends permanency to friendship. If advantage were the cementing factor and it were removed, friendships would dissolve, but nature is unchanging, therefore 'real friendships are eternal (*verae amicitiae sempiternae sunt*)' (32).

Cicero's argument from nature against utilitarianism is Stoic and anti-Epicurean; and when he says friendship has a noble origin and is not 'the daughter of poverty and want' it appears he is also distancing himself from Plato's friendship based on *erōs*:

> If this were so, then just in proportion as any man judged his resources to be small, would he be fitted for friendship; whereas the truth is far otherwise. For to the extent that a man relies upon himself and is so fortified by virtue and wisdom that he is dependent on no one and considers all his possessions to be within himself, in that degree he is most conspicuous for seeking out and cherishing friendships (29–30).

The friendship between Scipio and Laelius brought great advantages but these were not its cause: they had no *need* of each other. The entire profit (*fructus*, fruit, enjoyment) of love lies in the love itself (31). The Epicurean opinion that friendship springs from need would imply that those who are the least strong in mind and body would most desire friendship and consequently, that helpless little women (*mulierculae*) rather than men, the poor rather than the rich, and the suffering rather than those who are deemed to be happy, seek its shelter (46). And yet, fortunately, even the most virtuous and self-sufficient friends do have needs: 'wherein, for example, would my zeal have displayed itself if Scipio had never been in need of my advice or assistance?' (51). In fact, proud refusals of help, relying solely on one's own power, wealth or resources, avert love and prevent friendship (52–4).

Good friends, reverencing one another, will grow in goodness: 'friendship was given to us by nature as the handmaid of virtue, not as a comrade of vice' (83). Virtue achieves its full potential only in relationships, thus through friendship come fame, glory, joy and tranquillity of mind, and in short, the happy life (*beata vita*) (84). Goodness is evidently present even among the masses, because they can recognize and applaud it; and virtue is neither proud nor inhumane but serves the welfare of entire nations, 'which she certainly would not do if she disdained the affection (*caritas*) of the common mass' (50).[47] Reciprocal friendship does it seems, in this wider sense, embrace the many and not just the few.

If the good do have needs, and virtue and the happy life require friendship for their full flowering, what remains of the concept of the self-sufficiency of the wise? Certainly Cicero takes it to be necessary that goodness should be expressed outwardly. In 'On the Nature of the Gods' he says, once more against the Epicureans, that if we refer the profit of friendship to ourselves and not to those we love, it will not be friendship but trade in self-interest like a trade in cattle – and, he continues, if human *caritas* and friendship can in this way be gratuitous and disinterested, how much more is that of the gods who, needing nothing, yet love one another and care for humans. How could their *sanctitas* (holiness, moral integrity) itself exist, if the gods took no care for human affairs?[48] The state of virtue is not then sufficient in itself, but must activate itself in practical love.

Ethical difficulties

Having established the significance of friendship Laelius addresses its ethical problems. Must we do anything a friend asks? (36). No, for only if a friend were absolutely wise and virtuous, an ideal person such as does not in practice exist, could one resolve to do all they might ask (40). If we commit treason 'it is no justification whatever of your sin to have sinned on behalf of a friend'. Moreover, if friendship rests on virtue alone, sin destroys it (38). The practical rules are: 'neither ask dishonourable things, nor do them, if asked'; and, 'ask of friends only what is honourable; do for friends only what is honourable and without even waiting to be asked' (44).[49] Later, however, Cicero allows that if a friend requires help in a matter that touches his life or reputation but is not entirely honourable, some deviation from the straight path may be permissible 'provided, however, utter disgrace does not follow'. Thus we may bow to expediency, but there are limits. Our reputation and the affection (*caritas*) of the people, won by our virtue, are not to be lightly thrown away (61).

Our friend's need should however take precedence over our own feelings and passions; we should not for example, through intemperate 'goodwill', hold a friend back from a necessary journey because we fear being temporarily separated (75).

It is vital to friendship that superior and inferior stand on a par with each other (*superiorem parem esse inferiori*) (69), but for Cicero such equality is not so much a prerequisite as a consequence of friendship. It is the responsibility of the superior to ensure it comes about. Scipio did not stand on his own dignity but enhanced that of all his friends:

> And this course every man should adopt and imitate, so that if he is endowed with any superiority in virtue, intellect, or fortune he may impart it to his relatives and share it with his next of kin (70) ... As, therefore, in friendship, those who are superior should lower themselves, so, in a measure, should they lift up their inferiors (72).

The well-endowed must help their friends to the greatest of their ability, giving as much as the one who is loved and assisted has capacity to receive. This whole passage reflects Cicero's social context in a class that 'will have been well provided, singly and collectively, with the noble protectors – *patroni* or, more tactfully, "friends", so vital to success in the Roman world', where social structure and individual morality were intertwined with 'a firm nexus of obligations and dependencies, created by military service, representation in the courts, marriage and so on'.[50] The giving and receiving of frank advice goes with such friendship. Those who merely flatter or cannot hear the truth or whose reputation for virtue rests on flattery, cannot be friends, for friends must be able to give and take advice unhesitatingly, openly and without hypocrisy (91):

> dare to give true advice with all frankness, in friendship let the influence of friends who are wise counsellors be paramount, and let that influence be employed in advising, not only with frankness, but, if the occasion demands, even with sternness, and let the advice be followed when given. (44)

In this connection Christian writers frequently quote Proverbs, 'the wounds of a friend are better than the kisses of an enemy' (Prov. 27.6). Cicero quoted Cato: ' "Some men are better served by their bitter-tongued enemies than by their sweet-smiling friends; because the former often tell the truth, the latter, never"' (90). Truthful sharing is essential: 'for in friendship, unless, as the saying is, you behold and show an open heart', you will have no loyalty (*fides*), nothing proved and sure, nor the experience of loving or being loved, since you do not know what that really means (97).

Laelius urges real involvement with friends, in contradistinction to 'some Greeks' – the Epicureans – who say one should avoid too much concern and intimacy in order to enjoy a tranquil life. Cicero will have none of that. To avoid friendship in the name of *securitas* is to refuse the most joyful gift the gods have given, indeed it is to abandon practising virtue itself. Friendship must involve pain, but 'that mental anguish ... which must often be felt on a friend's account, has no more power to banish friendship from life than it has to cause us to reject virtue because virtue entails certain cares and annoyances' (47–8).

Choosing and losing friends

Spontaneous though love may be, Laelius counsels care in selecting friends. 'We ought, therefore, to choose men who are firm, steadfast and constant', choosing them by a conscious and deliberate act. How strange that many know the number of sheep they own but are uncertain how many friends they have (62).[51] In a passage reminiscent of Lk. 16.9, 'make friends for yourselves by means of dishonest wealth', Laelius remarks on the foolishness of using one's resources to acquire material goods that are insecure, in preference to loyal friends who are life's best and most beautiful furnishing (55). Friendships should normally be decided at a mature age, on the basis of settled likeness in character (*mores*) and interests (74). Enthusiasm is best kept in check while we observe the character of a new friend, for such is the power of money and rank that those who put friendship first are few: 'they either hold a friend of little value when their own affairs are prosperous, or they abandon him when his are adverse'; a steady friend is 'exceedingly rare ... almost divine' (64). Loyalty (*fides*) ('faith' in later Christian discussion) gives *amicitia* its firm foundation (65).

Laelius tells his young interlocutors to seek out friends who are open, sociable, sympathetic to their own feelings and ideas, who will 'neither take pleasure in bringing charges against you nor believe them when made by others'. A friend is free of hypocrisy, not suspicious, and can temper their *gravitas* with relaxed geniality. Finally, satiety is never reached in friendship so there is always room for new friends, without displacing old ones whose worth is known and whose pleasantness matures like wine (65–7).

The friendships of the wise may be eternal, but 'ordinary' friendships may prove more transitory. Cicero lists some reasons for breakdown: people change, patterns of mutual advantage shift, jealousy or political disagreement may appear (33–35). If our friend adopts a mild vice we may withdraw gradually; if more severe, immediately (76). Friendship should be always dissolved without recrimination, and if enmity emerges one should if possible endure it without retaliating: 'such respect is to be paid to the old-time friendship that he may be in the wrong who committed the offence and not he who suffered it' (78).

Joy in an 'other self'

As he draws to a close Cicero is at his most philosophical, reflecting on the intimate relationship between friendship, happiness and the fulfilment of human nature in goodness. The full joy of friendship can only be experienced when we seek it in and for itself, not for any ulterior motive. We naturally love ourselves, simply because we are dear (*carus*) to ourselves, not because we expect to gain from that love (*caritas*). We shall never find a true friend unless we transfer that same attitude to friendship, for a true friend 'is, as it were, another self (*tanquam alter idem*)' (80). Cicero's language is analogical: in a true friend I contemplate a likeness (*exemplar*) of myself (23), and the love I bear towards my friend is like, not an extension of, the love I bear myself. We may experience a fellow feeling for the ancient Romans when we hear Cicero commenting that our self-esteem is often lower than it should be, and one of the duties of a good friend is to arouse us to a better estimate of our own worth (59).

If love of self and longing for community are built into animal nature, how much more into that of human beings, who can love themselves and search out another whose soul they may so mingle with their own as almost to make 'one out of two (*unum ex duobus*)' (81). 'And since the effect of friendship is to make, as it were, one soul out of many (*ut unus quasi animus fiat ex pluribus*)', it can only exist between those of stable and integrated character who are always 'one and the same (*unus animus . . . idemque semper*)' within themselves (92). Right self-love, for Cicero as for Aristotle, consists in determining to be ruled by virtue and free from passion, and the way to friendship is first to become good, then seek out another like oneself (82), one of those rare people who are worthy of friendship because they bear within themselves the reason why they should be loved (*ipsis inest causa cur diligantur*) (79).

Friendship being essential, and the most joyful gift, 'they seem to take the sun out of the universe when they deprive life of friendship' (47). Everyone thinks friendship necessary to the life of freedom (86). The greatest delights require someone to share them, nature dislikes solitariness, and the most delightful support is a dear friend (88). We 'must ever be on the search for some person whom we shall love and who will love us in return'; for if *caritas* and goodwill are taken away, 'every joy is taken from life' (102).

Laelius enjoyed all this with Scipio, finding 'agreement on public questions; ... counsel in private business, ... a leisure of unalloyed delight' (103). 'I exhort you both', he ends, 'so to esteem virtue (without which friendship cannot exist), that, excepting virtue, you will think nothing more excellent than friendship' (104).

Narrow though its view is, Cicero's *De amicitia* paints a compelling portrait of friendship grounded in virtuous love. Copies circulated widely, and until the translation of the *Nicomachean Ethics* in the thirteenth century it remained the major source on friendship in the Latin West.

Seneca

Lucius Annaeus **Seneca** the Younger (4 BC–AD 65), a contemporary of Christ, was born at Córdoba in Spain. Trained in Stoic and neo-Pythagorean philosophy, he led an active legal and political life in imperial Rome where among other precarious achievements he was tutor to the young Nero. His philosophical writings and dark tragedies form part of the intellectual furniture of Mediaeval and Renaissance Europe.

Three of his *Letters to Lucilius*, expounding Stoic ethics, are on friendship (*Epp.* 3, 9, 35) and it is an important theme in others, notably 'On Master and Slave' (*Ep.* 47).[52] Seneca contributed to the deposit of wisdom on friendship by saying that the wise man is self-sufficient in the sense that he *can* survive without friends; but he would never *wish* to do so. 'Self-sufficient though he be, [he] nevertheless desires friends if only for the purpose of practising friendship, in order that his noble qualities may not lie dormant'; 'in order to have someone for whom I may die, whom I may follow into exile, against whose death I may stake my own life, and pay the pledge too' (9.5, 8, 11).

Friends must be actively made. Seneca approves Hecato's advice: 'if you wish to be loved, love (*si vis amari, ama*)' (9.6) and in general lays notable emphasis on friendship as active love. Friendship is love that kindles the soul with desire to possess its object for its own sake; and it hopes for mutual love (*caritas*) – and even the self-sufficient may legitimately desire something for its own sake (9.11,12). Friends trust one another completely: 'if you consider any man a friend whom you do not trust as you trust yourself, you are mightily mistaken and you do not sufficiently understand what true friendship means' (3.2). Friendship perceives the real person, not just the outward appearance; and therefore, strange though it may seem, it is good and rewarding to live on terms of friendship with one's slaves. All humans are equal before Fortune, and a slave may be more free inwardly than a 'free' man (47.17). Friendship with God is also possible: 'Men', says Seneca, 'are the children of God' (*De Prov.*1; *De Benef.* 2), 'beloved of Him as a father loves' (*De Prov.* 2), 'like to Him and capable of His friendship' (*De Prov.*1).[53]

Epictetus

Epictetus (*c.* AD 50–130), a freed slave, taught as a Stoic philosopher in Rome and Greece. He was markedly religious and understood God as personal. For him '*philos tou theou*' means 'friend of God' in the fullest substantive sense, as one enjoying a free inter-personal relationship: 'I am a free man and a friend of God, so as to obey Him of my own free will'.[54]

Epictetus' discourse 'On Friendship' (*Peri Philias*) again stresses the activity of virtue in the loving friend, rather than the attractiveness of virtue in the beloved. Where virtue and moral purpose exist, so does the ability to *be* a friend. Whenever people place their interest in moral good, not in 'the flesh' (*en sarki*) nor in externals, then 'though this is the only knowledge you have concerning them, you may confidently declare them friends, just as you may declare them faithful and just' (II.xxii.19, 29). To value material things is to be prey to jealousy and intrigue, therefore anyone who desires to have or to be a friend should cultivate moral virtue and detachment from the desire for external goods, so finding peace within himself and with all others:

> . . . in relation to his comrade, he will be always straightforward to one who is like himself, while to one who is unlike he will be tolerant, gentle, kindly, forgiving . . . But if you fail to do this, you may do everything else that friends do – drink together, and share the same tent, and sail on the same ship – and you may be sons of the same parents; yes, and so may snakes! But they will never be friends and no more will you, as long as you retain these brutish and abominable judgements. (II.xxii.36–7)

Plutarch

Plutarch (*c.* AD 50–120) criticized both Stoicism and Epicureanism, reflecting earlier Greek ideas and forging his own independent thought. His *Moralia* includes a 'Dialogue on Love' in which he examines the relationship between desire (*erōs*) and friendship and concludes that friendship can include one's wife, for if union between males does not destroy a lover's tenderness, how much more will *erōs* according to nature, between men and women, be conducive to the development of *philia* (751C–D).

The women in his group 'were apparently expected to have a good deal of literary and philosophical culture', allowing them at least into the fringes of male philosophical friendship.[55]

Plutarch's 'On having many friends' questions whether such polyphilia is laudable? He objects that 'a strong mutual friendship with many persons is impossible' because our capacity to love 'if portioned out among many persons becomes utterly enfeebled' (93F); and besides, duties as well as rewards attach to friendship (95C).[56] In 'On brotherly love' he cites Theophrastus, that if friends hold possessions in common they should also hold their friends in common, and he urges brothers to cement their bonds by sharing both friends and enemies (190E–F). In 'How to tell a flatterer from a friend' (48E–74F) when Plutarch contrasts honesty and affectation: 'the general sense is that a friend praises or blames the *action* of a friend, while the flatterer heaps praise or blame on the *person*.'[57] Such objective truthfulness again links friendship with frank speech, constructive use of which marks out a true friend from a flatterer or enemy.

The classical legacy

The classical world bequeathed an understanding of *philia* and *amicitia* that ranged from the cosmic harmony of Empedocles to the exclusiveness of Cicero's virtuous male pairs.

Three ways of grounding friendship have emerged. Ontologically it requires, and can be engendered by, participation in some common mode of being. Teleologically, true friendship is motivated by the attractiveness of a good character. Deontologically, it is the expression of virtue in that being a good person implies being a friend to others – but not to the wicked. 'Perfect friendship' is mutual relationship combining all three grounds.

The love found in friendship has acquired a definite shape as the activity of all the virtues, expressed collectively in the character of the good person and seen paradigmatically in 'true' friendship. It is possible for this love to exist even when not reciprocated. It is not a prerequisite that friends should be equal in all respects. The presence of goodness in one friend can and should engender excellence in the other. But the love of friendship has not yet acquired a name nor been unequivocally defined as, itself, 'a virtue'; and the possibility that friendship might be an open offer of love, extended even to the wicked without prior conditions, has not yet become thinkable.

Classical thought has persisted, resurfacing and resonating down the ages in philosophical and theological debate, and providing starting points for anthropologists and social psychologists. New developments have taken place above all within the Christian experience of God's love in Christ, to which we now turn.

Love and friendship in the Bible

From now on we shall be hearing from those who, down the Christian centuries, have meditated on love in Scripture and wrestled with its meaning. In preparation, we briefly orient ourselves to this theme in the Bible, and view what happens to the language of love in New Testament Greek.

The history of salvation recounted in the Hebrew Scriptures enshrines the mystery of merciful love at every moment. As Creator, God imparts goodness to creation and draws from that creation human beings in God's own image, for friendship with himself and one another. We see human beings falling from that intimacy and God drawing us back, covenanting steadfast love to individuals and groups that respond and unite themselves to him. The notion of 'covenant' has overtones of political and lord–vassal friendships, but also embraces individuals. Abraham, Moses, and seekers after divine Wisdom enter God's friendship. 'In every generation she [Wisdom] passes into holy souls and makes them friends of God, and prophets' (Wis. 7.27). Through the Psalms, Proverbs, and the Wisdom of Solomon and of Ben Sirach (Ecclesiasticus), the Wisdom tradition imparts nuggets of advice on friendship, human and divine.[58] Ruth and Naomi, David and Jonathan, Job and his 'comforters', become paradigmatic friends.

Divine love is revealed in a new way in the incarnation, life, crucifixion and resurrection of Jesus Christ. Jesus summarizes the Law in the twofold love-command: to love God, and your neighbour as yourself.[59] He gives the new commandment, to 'love one another as I have loved you' (Jn 15.12). For Paul and John, to know God is to discover an inconceivable height and depth of love (Eph. 3.14–21). 'God is love' (1 Jn 4.8,16); 'God's love has been poured into our hearts through the Holy Spirit' (Rom. 5.5). The mystery of love within God as Trinity begins to unfold.

Agapē and friendship: biblical Greek and Anders Nygren

The word for 'love' used in the verses just quoted above was a new word, *agapē*. The meaning of Christian love is bound up with what *agapē* means in the New Testament. What does its appearance signify?

Agapē was unknown in classical Greek and its first appearances in writing occur in the Septuagint (LXX), the Hellenistic Greek translation of the Hebrew Scriptures made in the two centuries before Christ. The word became a theological issue in the early twentieth century, when German theology perceived a sharp dichotomy between the Hebraic and Hellenistic thought-worlds, and Greek words for love were placed on one or other side of this divide. *Agapē* together with its related verb 'to love', *agapan*, became identified with the biblical, Hebrew thought-world, and were considered to have been deliberately chosen by the Septuagint translators to denote God's strong, revealed divine love, which is wholly generous and unmotivated. By contrast, *philein* and its cognate words must denote weak, motivated, earthly love.

The high point of this anti-Hellenistic polemic came in the late 1930s with Anders Nygren's *Agape and Eros*, His 'Agape' is God's freely given love; 'Eros' is the possessive, calculating love exhibited by human beings. Philia is really a subset of Eros: 'egocentric desire is the basis of friendship'.[60] 'Eros is acquisitive desire and longing', wrote Nygren, 'Agape is sacrificial giving.'

> Agape is God's way to man, and descends; Eros is man's way to God, and strives upwards. Agape is grace, bringing about salvation; Eros is man's effort to win his own salvation. Agape is unselfish, 'seeks not its own', gives itself; Eros is egocentric self-assertion. Agape is wealth and plenty, it lives the life of God, therefore it freely gives and dares to 'lose' its life; Eros seeks to achieve immortality. Agape is not determined by its object but is spontaneous, unmotivated, and creates value in its object; Eros is determined by the beauty and worth of its object, loving it because it recognizes value in it.[61]

Behind Nygren lay the Lutheran understanding of justification by faith alone, by God's action and not by human striving.[62] 'Agape' and 'Eros' are different kinds of love, and function as 'fundamental motifs' permeating and controlling two contrary worldviews. According to Nygren, 'Agape' was taught in its purity by Paul and is discernible in the first three Gospels (Synoptics); but when John speaks of Christians loving one another he 'weakens down' unmotivated 'Agape', contaminating it with 'Eros'.[63]

Nygren's thesis, although quickly recognized as extreme, was immensely influential. 'The centre of biblical religion lay in *agape*. Everyone who knew anything about theology knew this.'[64] It could still be said in 1983 that 'its ideas have become part of our mental furniture' and 'its influence on less technical Christian moral thought seems to continue unabated.'[65]

More objective scholarship suggests that the appearance of *agapē* is to be attributed, not to theological motivation but to the natural evolution of the Greek language. The New Testament was written in the 'common' Greek of the late Hellenistic period, into which the new word *agapē* had been born, not as a completely fresh coinage but evolving within the semantic family of the verb *agapan*, which was in full classical use. In the Hebrew Scriptures, loving is mainly conveyed through verbs, so the noun 'love' occurs only about forty times in the Septuagint translation. It is usually rendered by *agapēsis*, 'affection', including erotic affection; but the shorter form *agapē*, used as a synonym for *agapēsis*, appears fifteen times. In the New Testament *agapēsis* has completely disappeared and *agapē* becomes the usual noun for 'love', occurring one hundred and sixteen times, mainly in Paul and John.

'Friendship', *philia*, occurs just once in the New Testament, and in a manner that opened it to anti-Hellenistic disapproval. 'Do you not know that friendship with the world (*philia tou kosmou*) is enmity with God? Therefore whoever wishes to be a friend of the world becomes an enemy of God' (Jas 4.4). The anti-Hellenists took this as confirmation that *philia* possesses an inherently 'bad' nature: 'The word *philia* is only once used in the NT and there it is in a bad sense'; '*philia* appears only once, Jas 4.4, and significantly with a negative sense'.[66] But as his early readers will certainly have understood, 'friendship' here implies commitment to certain values and James is simply applying a 'two ways' pattern of ethical thought, setting 'over against one another as radically antithetical, "friendship with the world" and friendship with God.'[67] Since he has just positively praised Abraham as a 'friend of God' (2.23), he hardly supports the conclusion that New Testament writers shunned *philia* and adopted *agapē* because 'friendship' was an inherently worldly, self-seeking love.

A similar cloud of suspicion still faintly hangs over the alternation of the verbs *agapan* and *philein* at Jn 21.15–17. Are two different kinds of love meant here, one weak and human, one strong and divine? The risen Jesus asks Peter 'Do you love me?' (*agapais me*?) and Peter twice responds 'Yes, Lord, you know that I love you' (*philō se*). When Jesus asks a third time he switches to *philein*: 'Do you love me?' (*phileis me*?) Had he been attempting to raise Peter to the level of 'agapeic' love, but found himself forced to accommodate to his disciple's earthbound understanding?

What we know of *philein* may incline us to doubt that interpretation; and Robert Joly and James Barr have shown that both verbs had in fact been well established in classical use, with widely overlapping meanings. Over the centuries a slow evolution has taken place until in modern Greek *agapan* is the sole verb 'to love' while '*philein*' means simply 'to kiss'. New Testament Greek represents a stage in this evolution where the two verbs were synonyms with little or no differentiation, except that *philein* already included 'to kiss'. *Agapan* predominates in the New Testament (one hundred and forty-one occurrences against twenty-five for *philein*) but the two verbs are close and interchangeable: those who 'love' front seats do so with *agapan* at Lk. 11.43 but *philein* at Mt. 23.6. In the case of Jn 21.15–17, as Barr points out, both the Septuagint and the first-century AD Jewish historian Josephus alternate the verbs for purely stylistic reasons, and style is the most likely reason here. If there are any added nuances, he concludes, they would have to do with different ranges, not kinds, of love.[68]

The word 'friend', *philos*, has not in the main attracted controversy. In the Gospel of John, Jesus calls Lazarus 'our friend' (11.11) and the disciples 'my friends' (15.15). John the Baptist styles himself 'friend of the Bridegroom' (Jn 3.29), and Pilate is threatened with losing his status as 'friend of Caesar' (19.12), a clear case of political client–patron friendship with perhaps the ironic implication that Pilate must choose between friendship with Caesar or Jesus. The third Johannine letter ends: 'the friends greet you. Greet the friends' (3 Jn 15).

Luke, author of the Gospel and Acts, was comfortable with literary Greek and well versed in the 'topos' of friendship, the cluster of ideas and words constituting friendship's traditions and discourse. He is responsible for many (eighteen) of the twenty-nine New Testament occurrences of 'friend'. Once, Jesus calls his disciples 'my friends' (Lk. 12.4); he tells the parables of the 'importunate friend' (11.5–8) and of the man and woman who, finding something that was lost, call their friends to celebrate (15.6, 9; cf. 29), and advises his followers to use their money wisely to 'make friends' (16.9). But friends and relatives may become betrayers under persecution (21.16), and Herod and Pilate become 'friends', whether political or personal, by agreeing on Jesus' death (23.12). Paul is assisted by 'friends', Christians or others, in Ephesus and Sidon (Acts 19.31, 27.3).

The most significant passage in Acts appealing to the traditions of friendship is Luke's description of the early Jerusalem Church: 'Now the whole group of those who believed were of one heart and soul, and no one claimed private ownership of any possessions, but everything they owned was held in common.' (Acts 4.32). Monasticism took inspiration from this ideal, which also sets a standard for Christian unity; and as a modern commentator suggests, Luke was stating the fundamental Christian belief that humanity was 'capable of receiving the grace of the Holy Spirit in ways that overcame external social differences and shaped it into a viable *koinōnia*': Luke is inviting the Christian community to 'reimagine the relationship between rich and poor'.[69]

Centrally significant, too, is the insult that Jesus was 'a friend of tax collectors and sinners' (Mt.11.19; Lk. 7.34), understood as revealing the ironic truth that his love is indeed that of a friend, but far outrunning the limits of classical friendship. The same transcendence of past ideas lies behind Paul's amazement that Christ died for us when we were still sinners, when it is hard enough for anyone to pass the ultimate test of classical friendship, that of willingness to die for a good person (Rom. 5.6–7). Paul only rarely employs the specific vocabulary of friendship but he frequently, as here, implies its 'topos'.[70]

John's Gospel gives the love of friendship an explicitly central place:

> No one has greater love (*agapē*) than this, to lay down one's life for one's friends. You are my friends if you do what I command you. I do not call you servants any longer because the servant does not know what the master is doing; but I have called you friends because I have made known to you everything that I have heard from my Father. (Jn 15.13–15)

Here *agapē* is the love of a true friend, setting these verses at the heart of the interpretation of Christian love as friendship.

Significant developments were indeed taking place, and they do arrive at an intense focus in the noun *agapē*, a hinge on which hangs the continuity and discontinuity between the classical and Christian worlds. First, the New Testament use of *agapē* shows that its meaning, originally close to that of *agapēsis*, had expanded and was still expanding to cover a much wider semantic field. One important aspect of this expansion was that *agapē* was becoming capable of filling the gap identified centuries earlier by Aristotle. It was acquiring the capacity to name the love given by a good friend. If *agapē* leaps with force out of the pages of the New Testament it is not least because the concept of virtuous love has finally acquired a name. By contrast to *philia* which, as Aristotle had insisted, always primarily denoted relationship and not love itself (although it could in a transferred sense denote friendship-love) *agapē* simply and unconfusedly denotes 'love', whether prior to, or within, or beyond, an established relationship. *Agapē* could, and in the New Testament unequivocally did, denote 'good' love, the outward expression of goodness. '*Agapē* is the fulfilling of the Law' (Rom. 13.10); 'God is *agape*' (1 Jn 4.8, 16). As 'good' love, *agapē* is not different from, nor opposed to, friendship, but denotes the very love that makes true friendship possible.[71]

At the same time, the conventional limits of love and friendship were being transcended through the life and actions of Jesus. Friendship found itself transformed by grace. God in Christ extended friendship to all human beings, and to be a 'friend of sinners', hitherto a genuine insult or impossible paradox, now becomes thinkable and possible.

Within a relatively short space of time, *agapē* had emerged in Greek, its meaning had expanded to fill the gap identified by Aristotle, and through Christ the love that it signifies was transfigured. These three developments converge in the use of *agapē* in the New Testament. In Latin *agapē* would become *caritas* (and *dilectio*); in older English 'charity', and in modern English simply 'love'.

2

Ambrose, Cassian and Augustine

Caritas 'is the great and true virtue'

Early Christianity inherited the strongly familial terminology of Scripture. God is our Father and in Christ we are adopted and restored to our true relationship as 'sons' or children of God. But the language of friendship also makes appearances and the 'topos' of friendship continues to be pervasively present within and alongside the familial imagery.

Luke addresses his Gospel and Acts to '*Theophilos*'. He possibly had a specific individual in mind, but this name is also capable of being understood generically, as 'beloved', 'lover' or friend of God: 'For the gospel was written to Theophilus, that is to him who loves God. If you love God, it is written to you.'[1] Reciprocally, '*philanthrōpia*', the Stoic ideal of universal love for humankind, is ascribed to God in the Letter to Titus (Tit. 3.4) and taken up in the eucharistic liturgy of the Eastern Church, which repeatedly addresses God as '*philanthrōpos*', 'lover of humankind'. Visitors to Jerusalem can see early Byzantine mosaic inscriptions at the Dominus Flevit church on the Mount of Olives, and in the Rockefeller Museum, that describe priests and benefactors of churches as '*philochristos*', 'one who loves Christ'. The Italian translation at Dominus Flevit renders this '*Amico di Cristo*', Friend of Christ. Such compound *phil-* words are not always exact synonyms with 'friend of', but the fields of meaning overlap. They are part of a thought-world that was comfortable with the ideal of friendship with God and could conceive of it, not only as a 'political' affiliation but also, in equally biblical terms, as having either an ethical or mystical basis.[2]

Early writers used friendship language infrequently but with ease.[3] In the second century AD 'friends of Christ' and 'friend of God', appear in **Justin Martyr** (*c.*100–*c.*165).[4] **Clement of Alexandria** (*c.*150–215) made greater use of these terms, asserting for example, that if philosophers had said that all things belong to the wise because the wise are friends of God and 'friends hold things in common', then those who become friends to God through the mediation of the Logos do indeed possess all things in common with God.[5] **Origen** (*c.*185–*c.*254) reflects that Christ once as shepherd led his sheep to pasture, but now as friend calls his friends to the eternal table: '"I no longer call you servants, but friends." The fear of God makes us servants, but knowledge of the mysteries of God makes us his friends.'[6]

A golden crop of classically-educated theologians graced the late fourth century when Christianity became the religion of the Roman Empire: the Cappadocians Basil of Caesarea, his brother Gregory of Nyssa and friend Gregory of Nazianzus; John Chrysostom; Ambrose, Jerome, Augustine and their many correspondents. It was natural to all of them to blend their theology with the cream of their classical learning, and they were steeped in the traditions of friendship.[7] There is for them no opposition between 'friendship' as merely worldly love and '*agapē*' as Christian. We must include, not exclude, friendship language when seeking to understand love in all these writers.[8]

The Jewish scholar Philo of Alexandria (*c.*20 BC–*c.*AD 50), well known to Christians in this period, had shifted the philosophical ground of true friendship from human virtue to shared faith in God.[9] It now becomes axiomatic that friendship between Christians is grounded in common commitment to Christ, a paradigm shift that widens the community of friendship from the select few to the entire committed Church, including women. For **Gregory of Nyssa** (*c.*330–95) Christ is our true friend, wounded with love yet loving those who wound him, so that his wounds 'are better than the kisses of an enemy'; and we all, like Moses, should long to be 'known by God' and 'become his friend'.[10] **Gregory of Nazianzus** quotes the father in the story of the prodigal son, 'All that is mine is yours' (Lk. 15.31), commenting that friends share everything because of the fellowship (*koinōnia*) of the Spirit and the *agapē* that unites them.[11]

We have two short works on friendship from this early period, by Ambrose and John Cassian.

Ambrose

Ambrose (*c.*339–397), Bishop of Milan from 374 to 397, commands attention as one of the Latin 'Fathers of the Church' and the bishop whose sermons attracted Augustine to orthodox Catholic Christianity. He was Augustine's role model, first as a Christian writer, then as bishop. He composed the first Christian passage on friendship, in an exhortation to his clergy at the close of his book 'On Duties', *De officiis*.

Ambrose had presided over the Church in Milan for ten years when Augustine arrived, a young intellectual seeking wealth and fame. Milan was then the political centre of the Western Roman Empire, the base of the imperial court. One of Augustine's tasks as professor of rhetoric was to contribute to imperial public relations by writing speeches in praise of the Emperor. Within two years he tired of creating elegant distortions of the truth, and realized his arrival in northern Italy had really meant something quite different to him: 'I came to Milan, to Ambrose the Bishop, known throughout the world as among the best of men, devout in your worship.'[12] The Bishop had welcomed him warmly. He went to hear his sermons because he found their style interesting. Then he began to listen more deeply and was drawn in.[13]

Ambrose had become a bishop rather suddenly, elected in 374 by the people of Milan where he was provincial governor. He was from a devout Christian family but as was then often the case, he was not yet baptized. Within a week he was baptized, ordained and enthroned. His father had held a high administrative position and his own education in Rome had prepared Ambrose for similar government service. He had good Greek and Latin and had studied law; but he had never intended to be a theologian and, in the fully creative sense, he never was. But he did become a vigorous theological teacher and a polemicist for Nicene orthodoxy. He helped develop Latin into a theological language. He remained a political figure, developing a prominent role for bishops and clergy in public life.

Ambrose had grown up under the influence of the strongly ascetic form of Christianity that swept through the Mediterranean world during the fourth century. Marriage was good but virgins could win a greater crown, and he encouraged celibacy. His elder sister Marcellina took vows as a dedicated virgin. He and his brother Satyrus never married. Many celibates and widows continued living in their own homes, but this movement was promoting the growth of monastic communities. Ambrose founded a men's community outside Milan. He was highly impressed by a women's community numbering about twenty at Bologna, recognizing that their lifestyle expressed the friendship that had hitherto been a male preserve: 'Not being of the sex which lives in common', they bear fruit to 'an hundredfold, leaving their parents' dwelling they press into the houses of Christ ... singing spiritual songs, they provide their sustenance by labour, and seek with their hands supplies for their liberality.'[14]

Doubts are often voiced as to the extent to which this austere and combative bishop was himself inclined to personal, as opposed to political, friendship.[15] There are indications of affection in a few of Ambrose's letters, but no substantial letters of friendship to or from him, and little record of strong friendships in his life. Augustine was never able to enlist him in his intense debating circle. He had no time; he gave short interviews and used any breaks for quiet study in his house, where Augustine had to be content with watching him read when what he really wanted was to unburden his soul to him. Instead, Augustine went to pour out his heart to Simplicianus, a senior priest and Ambrose's own instructor in the faith. When Augustine describes Ambrose as truly loving Simplicianus 'as one loves a father', we get a rare glimpse of the bishop's hidden side.[16] A letter of Ambrose also reveals appreciation of this older priest's friendship and fatherly kindness.[17]

Ambrose was close to his sister Marcellina, whom he kept well informed of his doings, and their brother Satyrus gave up his own career to live in Milan and manage Ambrose's affairs. Lamenting his untimely death, Ambrose mentions friends and acquaintances with whom they shared confidences, and their meals with friends.[18] Ambrose probably found it easiest to be intimate with his close family. Then he discovered that in Christ a new, eternal, familial relationship could be enjoyed with others. He addresses his clergy as his beloved 'sons' whom he has chosen and tested, the language of choosing friends.[19] Certainly Ambrose was private and uncompromising, and it is hard to penetrate behind his public persona; but there is no compelling evidence that he regarded himself as exempt from his own advice to his clergy to practise true friendship. Since he was known as a good man who took his dedication to Christ with profound seriousness, it would probably be right to look there for his closest friendship, while not disregarding his human relationships.

Duties and virtues

When Ambrose was made bishop he was, as he put it, pitched into learning and teaching at the same time. An assiduous reader of Scripture and its Greek commentaries, he relayed this information in Latin books and sermons. He took it as axiomatic that all real wisdom comes from God and therefore theology should incorporate the best from philosophy while illuminating and correcting it from Scripture. In this spirit he composed, probably around 386–91, a three-volume work 'On Duties', *De officiis*, later known as *De officiis ministrorum*, 'On the Duties of the Clergy', for the priests and other clerics he was training in Milan. He explicitly models it on the well-known *De officiis* which Cicero wrote for his son Marcus, itself modelled on a Stoic work by Panaetius of Rhodes. Cicero had discussed the practice of the four major virtues, prudence, justice, fortitude and temperance, in public leadership.[20] Ambrose writes on clerical 'duties' in terms of the same virtues, now illumined by Christian teaching and lavishly illustrated from Scripture. These new young leaders should receive a no less thorough formation than their pagan predecessors. Ambrose's style is homiletic, he is 'a spiritual teacher articulating *ad hoc* practical advice, not an ethical theorist developing a careful intellectual case.'[21] He conforms to Cicero's structure with increasing imprecision and finally diverges altogether to conclude his work with an exhortation to friendship, where his plundering of Cicero's *De amicitia* will have been obvious to his hearers.

The goal for human beings, both authors agree, is 'the happy life' or, as Scripture calls it, 'eternal life' (II.1), which results from right action flowing from moral goodness. The virtue of 'prudence', practical wisdom, means the search for truth, upon which alone right action can be grounded. For Ambrose, practical wisdom is Christianity put into action: ' "Not everyone who says to me, Lord, Lord, will enter the kingdom of heaven," but only the one who does those things that I say.' (I.125; Mt. 7.21). Courage, for the clergy, is the mental strength to stay constant and to do what is just and right, as when Moses rescued his fellow-Hebrew (I.179). 'Temperance' is moderation and self-control, 'preserving due measure and proper order' in speech and action, calming anger and promoting tranquillity and gentleness (I.115). So fundamental is this virtue to Ambrose's clerical *modestia* or seemliness, that he opens his treatise with a homily on keeping silent, not returning abuse for abuse, but awaiting an opportune moment to speak (I.5–22). Later he illustrates temperance with the different reactions of 'three types of persons' to being subjected to injustice. The first type nurse resentment, are unwilling to forgive, demand 'eye for eye', and repay abuse with abuse. The second are making progress and refuse to retaliate, keeping silence. The third type are the perfect (but Ambrose quickly disclaims perfection, saying 'the truth is, I am weak') who embody Paul's words ' "We are cursed, and we bless" (1 Cor. 4.12)' and have taken to heart 'the One who says: "Love your enemies, pray for those who slander and persecute you." (Mt. 5.44)'. (I.233–5). Perfection will at least be reached in the world to come. Meanwhile in this life there is growth through grace.

Specific links between the virtues and the capacity to love are becoming more and more evident. They are most obvious in the case of *justitia*, 'justice' or 'righteousness' which embraces goodwill (*benevolentia*) and its outcomes in well-doing (*beneficentia*), generosity (*liberalitas*) and mercy or kindness (*misericordia*). Cicero had summarized the requirements of justice in a twofold rule: do no harm, and do good wherever opportunity occurs. For Ambrose, justice directs our natural love first to God, then towards our country, our parents, and finally to all, and from this is born *caritas*, Paul's *agapē*, 'which puts others before itself and does not pursue its own interests; this is where justice has its primary seat.' (I.127). One biographer of Ambrose, writing in 1935, equated Christian love with altruism and found it here. 'Justice, in short, is transfigured into altruism, charity. Although this supreme virtue of Christianity is not, under its own name, classed among the cardinal virtues, yet, under the name of justice, it receives full recognition.'[22]

In Latin translations of the Bible, *agapē* had been rendered by two broadly interchangeable words, *caritas* and *dilectio,* the latter being a post-classical coinage from the verb *diligere*, 'to love' with overtones of choosing or regarding the beloved above others. *Caritas*, *dilectio* and *amor* would all be used by theologians down the centuries as close or exact synonyms, with *caritas* alone gaining the honour of use in an exclusively 'good' sense and becoming the primary term for Christian love.[23] In Ambrose's works as a whole *caritas* far outweighs the other two words, not because it was yet recognized as a technical term but because of Ambrose's fondness for quoting certain verses that feature it, either from the New Testament or Song of Songs: God is love; love is a fruit of the Spirit; love is the fulfilling of the law; thinks no evil; covers a multitude of sins; love is greatest among faith, hope and love; it is universal since we must love even our enemies. 'Love is stronger than death'; 'order love in me'; 'I am wounded by love'.[24] But in *De officiis,* under Cicero's influence, the balance of Ambrose's language shifts. His discussion of Christian love in this work is signposted not only by the relatively infrequent occurrences of *caritas* but by all the justice-related words mentioned above and, crucially, by his explorations of friendship, *amicitia.*[25]

'*Caritas*' and 'goodwill' accompany one another in Cicero's definition of 'friendship' (*De am.* 20). In Ambrose these three words interpenetrate in meaning. Goodwill, as the orientation of our heart, occupies much of the semantic space later given to *caritas* or 'love'. Ambrose cheerfully transfers to it several of the accolades originally coined by Cicero for friendship. Thus goodwill now becomes 'the common parent of us all', faithful in counsel, joyful in prosperity, sad in times of sorrow.[26] 'Remove goodwill from human behaviour, and it will be as if you had taken the sun from the world'.[27] 'Since goodwill is the source from which friendship springs, a friend will not hesitate to risk great dangers to life for a friend's sake. "And if dreadful things befall me on his account", he will say, "I bear them"' (Sir. 22. 25–6).[28]

> Goodwill also tends to wrench the sword of anger from our hands. Goodwill makes wounds inflicted by a friend more beneficial than kisses given freely by an enemy [Prov. 27.6]. Goodwill makes those who were many become one, for though friends may be many they do become one, with one spirit and one mind [cf. Acts 4.32]. We see, too, that even rebukes are agreeable when they are delivered in the context of friendship, for while they carry the power to sting, they do not carry real pain. We are stung by the critical words, but we are pleased by the thoughtfulness and goodwill which lie behind them. (I.173).

Goodwill flourishes in the Church, the new quasi-familial community of the baptized (I.170). Almsgiving and hospitality extends it throughout the Christian community and towards strangers.

Cicero had advised his son that it is both more expedient and honourable to seek the love (*caritas*) of the people than to instil fear. We all, he adds, need friends who value us, and if a public figure is regarded with goodwill, he will attract friends.[29] Conversely, Ambrose suggests that when people see their leader has friends, they will feel persuaded of his trustworthiness and lovability. 'How could anyone not have loved him [David], seeing how dear he was to his friends?' (II.36).

> As we can see, it is the greatest possible incentive towards being held in popular affection (*caritatis communis*) if a person shows love in return to those who love him . . . and makes it clear by exemplifying faithful friendship . . . No wonder the wise man says: 'Lose money for a brother and a friend' [Sir. 29.10]. And in another passage: 'I will not blush to greet a friend, and I will not hide myself from his face' [Sir. 22.25], since in a friend there is 'the medicine of life and of immortality', as the words of Ecclesiasticus testify [Sir. 6.16]. (II.37)

The clergy should aim to be wise counsellors, just and hospitable to all, but love will be their chief recommendation, attracting even strangers to entrust themselves to their care 'when they see that you are dear to so many' (II.39). When Ambrose finally exhorts his clergy to be friends to one another he has already made clear how, in this further manner, friendship is integral to the lifestyle of a Christian minister.

'The friendship you have entered into'

The 'Duties' is concerned with ethical tensions that arise between what is absolutely honourable in theory (the '*honestum*') and what is expedient in practice (the '*utile*'), and it is Cicero's discussion of conflicting loyalties concerning friendship that provides Ambrose the opportunity to conclude his own work with an exhortation to friendship.

His point of departure is Cicero's ruling that 'a good man will never for his friend's sake do anything in violation of his country's interests or his oath or his sacred honour (*religio et fides*).'[30] The same rule appears in

De amicitia, where friendship also requires '*fides*' in the sense of fidelity (*De am.* 65, 97). Ambrose completely agrees: 'It is never right to break faith for the sake of friendship. No one can be a true friend to man if he has been unfaithful to God' (III.133). '*Fides*' is acquiring theological signification as commitment to God, and virtue and friendship will become fruits of such commitment.

The story of Esther, telling how her royal husband 'Ahasuerus', Xerxes I, executed his 'chief friend' Haman for plotting to exterminate the Jews, illustrates the priority of faith (III.124). Conversely, as demonstrated by Jonathan and Ahimelech, true friendship arises from goodness and supports it, taking precedence over wealth, honours and power (III.125, cf. 1 Sam. 20.17; 22.17). Scripture abhors giving false witness against a friend (Prov. 25.18) but true witness on their behalf must certainly be given. We may neither collude with a friend in evil, nor undermine one who is innocent (III.127). Ambrose recruits Matthew's teaching on church discipline: if we notice some fault in a friend we should first speak to them privately, and then if they fail to listen, rebuke them publicly (Mt.18.15–17). Friendly correction is painful but good: ' "the wounds of a friend are more bearable than the kisses of flatterers" ' (Prov. 27.6). Frank speech taken in good part, makes constancy in friendship possible – and we should not be so childish as to change friends with every passing whim (III.128; cf. *De am.* 91).

'In friendship', Cicero wrote, 'unless, as the saying is, you behold and show an open heart, you can have no loyalty or certainty' (*De am.* 97). Ambrose exhorts: 'Open your heart to your friend so that he will be faithful to you, and so that you will know joy in your own life from him: For "a faithful friend is the medicine of life, the grace of immortality" ' (Sir. 6.16; III.129). Defer to your friend as an equal, do not be embarrassed to be the first in doing kindness, for there is no pride among friends. Never fail your friends, for friendship is life's support. 'This is how we bear one another's burdens, as the apostle taught us to do – for his words are addressed to those who have been embraced by the same love (*caritas*)' (Gal. 6.2; III.129). Be ready to endure hardship and enmity on a friend's behalf (Sir. 22.26), for that is proof of real friendship; 'when things are going well everyone seems to be your friend' (III.130). Reproof is best given in good times, sympathy in bad, as Job so beautifully puts it: 'Have pity on me,' you are attacking 'someone for whom you ought to show sympathy in times of trial: that is what friendship is supposed to be about.' (III.131, Job 19.21).

> So, my sons, take good care of the friendship you have entered into with your brothers: in the whole range of human life, there is nothing more wonderful than

> this. It really is a comfort in this life to have someone to whom you can open your heart, someone with whom you can share your innermost feelings . . . in whom you can confide the secrets of your heart; to have at your side a man who will always be faithful to you, someone who will rejoice with you when things are going well, sympathize with you when circumstances are hard, and encourage you in times of persecution. (III.132)

Good friendship was shown among the three young Hebrews who found themselves together in the fiery furnace (Dan. 3), and by David to Saul and Jonathan (2 Sam. 1.23) (III.132). Friendship makes 'the superior prove himself equal to the inferior, and the inferior equal to the superior', its kindness or grace (*gratia*) overcomes the differences and pride that otherwise prevent friendship:

> The inferior must not lack authority if the occasion demands, and the superior for his part must not lack humility. He needs to listen with the attitude that the inferior is just as significant as he is himself, that he is an equal, and when the inferior voices words of warning and makes critical observations he needs to do it with the air of a friend, motivated not by a desire to score points, but by genuine concern and real love (*affectu caritatis*). (III.133, cf. *De am.* 69–73)

How interesting it would be to know whether Ambrose's clergy tested him on this! Ambrose moves on, praising friendship in a passage full of Ciceronian echoes:

> What is a friend, in fact, but a partner in love (*consors amoris*)? You unite your innermost being to his, you join your spirit to his, you blend so thoroughly with him that your aim is to be no longer two, but one. You entrust yourself to him as to another self; you fear nothing from him; and you do not ask anything dishonourable from him for your own ends. (III.134)

'For friendship', Ambrose claims, 'is a virtue (*virtus est enim amicitia*).' (III.134) Whether he realized it or not, he was breaking new ground, since no previous extant writer had unequivocally called friendship, or love in any form, 'a virtue'. He believes friendship qualifies as a virtue because it consists in freely showing honour and kindness, not in a desire for material gain. It is created, not by the offer of reward but 'by the one endeavouring to outdo the other in the display of goodwill' (III.134).

Cicero believed there were many honest poor but he did not proceed to Ambrose's conclusion that friendship is frequently more genuine and extensive among the poor than the rich: 'There are lots of people ready to fawn upon the rich . . . but no one makes any pretence with somebody who is poor' (III.135).[31] While discussing justice Cicero had accorded priority to our obligations to family and state while encouraging a degree of generosity to the poor as fellow human beings. Everyone should of course share commodities such as water which are the common property of nature, or assist travellers with advice: and Cicero even applies the proverb 'friends have everything in common (*amicorum esse communia omnia*)' to this universal sharing (Cic. *De off.* I.51). Ambrose instead quotes Jesus' injunction to 'make friends for yourselves by means of dishonest wealth' (Lk. 16.9). Who are these friends? They are not as we might expect the direct beneficiaries of our goodwill, but the inhabitants of heaven, whose friendship our generosity attracts:

> Mercy (*misericordia*) . . . makes people perfect, in imitation of this perfect Father. . . . it must be shown towards the poor: you should treat nature's produce as a common possession . . . You should give what you can to a person who is poor, and offer assistance to one who is by nature your brother and your fellow . . . In return for your help, he confers more upon you than you do upon him . . . If you take a stranger under your roof, or if you help somebody in need, such a person brings you the friendship of the saints and the tabernacles that are eternal. (I.38–9)

This interpretation of Luke now recurs: 'Is there anything more precious than friendship? It is shared by both men and angels. So the Lord Jesus says: 'Use unjust mammon to make friends for yourselves, so that they will receive you into their eternal tabernacles'. (III.136).[32] Most wonderfully, God makes us his friends, from being his lowliest servants. 'He says himself: "Now you are my friends, if you do what I command you"' (Jn 15:14; III.136).

In another work Ambrose affirms that we, like Abraham, become God's friends through obeying him but thereafter we obey as a friend out of love, not from fear like a servant. Obedience is at first the condition for divine friendship, then becomes consequential upon it.[33] Further light is cast on Ambrose's understanding of divine friendship by his concept of 'counsels of perfection', which he bequeathed to Western moral theology. He developed this by an association of ideas. Cicero had defined moral duties as 'ordinary' (or 'middle', *medium*) when merely adequate reasons can be given for an action, but 'perfect' when the reason rests on absolute moral principle (Cic. *De off.* I.8). Ambrose associated the 'ordinary' level with the 'precepts' or commandments applicable to everyone. When Jesus spoke to the rich young man, however, he revealed a level of perfection above the Ten Commandments: 'If you would be perfect, go, sell what you possess and give to the poor, and you will have treasure in heaven; and come, follow me' (Mt. 19.21; I.37). In one of his earliest works, Ambrose linked this story with Paul's words: 'concerning virgins I have no command (*praeceptum*) of the Lord, but I give my opinion (counsel, *consilium*)' (1 Cor. 7.25). If a command exists on the 'ordinary' level, then 'counsels', in this case Paul's exhortation to celibacy, must relate to perfection. Moreover, whereas commands are given to subjects, 'counsel is given to friends', counsel implies freedom: 'A commandment is given to enforce what is according to nature, a counsel to incite us to follow grace.' (*De vid.* 72).

Friendship with God was thus beginning to acquire an enduring link with the 'perfection' of a life of poverty and celibacy. With this new ideal came a new kind of exclusiveness, although indeed for Ambrose all genuine Christian commitment implied celibacy. But there remains the perfection to which all Christians are inescapably called, the requirement to 'love our enemies', to pray for those who slander and persecute us, and 'bless those who curse us' (Mt. 5.44; I.37).

Jesus, in saying 'You are my friends if you do what I command you . . . I have called you friends, because I have made known to you everything that I have heard from my father' (Jn 15.14–15), 'has given us the pattern of friendship we should follow': to do the will of our friend, open whatever secrets we have in our hearts, and know what is in theirs: 'A friend hides nothing then, if he is true, he pours out his heart, just as the lord Jesus poured out the mysteries of the Father' (III.136). This challengingly intimate sharing, implying a search for oneness yet potentially more open and dynamic than Cicero's already-established mutual agreement (*De am.* 20), was becoming the central definition of Christian friendship. To do God's will is to be 'of one mind' or 'one in spirit' (*unanimis*) with him, as friends should be (III.137).[34] '*Unanimis*' reminds Ambrose of the psalmist's cry of pain at betrayal by his table-companion 'who was one with me in spirit' (Ps. 55.13 *Vet. Lat.*), a verse understood as prophecy:

> So, when the Lord confronted the one who betrayed him, this was the thing he found worst of all about his treachery, this was the crime he condemned most of all – the man had shown no gratitude at all for all that he had received, but had mixed his evil poisons while sitting at the very table of friendship. (III.137)

So close should be the unity of friends that Jesus can, Ambrose suggests, say 'I am not the one who is betrayed: you have betrayed yourself, for you have betrayed a man who was one with you in spirit.' (III.137).

A superhuman capacity for forgiveness is needed if such intense friendship is to be sustained, so Ambrose appropriately closes on the note of divine forgiveness imparted through Job's prayers to his misguided friends. 'The Lord . . . chose to pardon them when their friend interceded for them, so that friendship's voice might secure the remission of sins . . . Arrogance did them nothing but harm; friendship brought them nothing but good.' (III.138, cf. Job 42.8–9).

According to Ambrose then, Christians should display the virtue of friendship and be par excellence potential friends to all. A Christian friend is faithful to God and hence wholly trustworthy in everything that accords with God's will. She will stand by you in trouble and difficulties even at the risk of hardship, even at the cost of incurring enmity against herself. She will open her heart to you and listen as you open yours, honour confidences and not betray you, sympathize in time of trouble, correct you when necessary, and encourage in time of persecution. She stands equal with you through friendship, above any differences of age or social standing. She will forgive you, and pray for God's forgiveness and restoration.

Dudden, who discerned Christian love in Ambrose's 'justice', had seen his interest in friendship as an almost curious survival from classical modes of thought:

> Finally, it is interesting to observe the importance attached by Ambrose to the virtue of friendship. This is a virtue of pagan antiquity. In the early days of Christianity the special intimacy of friends was, to a great extent, superseded by an all embracing charity. In modern Christendom love has taken the place anciently occupied by friendship. Ambrose, however, speaks of friendship with something of the old pre-Christian enthusiasm.[35]

More recently, by contrast, White suggests Ambrose 'is able to assimilate the pagan view and to see Christian love largely in terms of the traditional idea of friendship.'[36] Classically, as we have seen, a discussion of virtues is suitably crowned with a description of their outcome in friendship. Equally, in Ambrose's Christian context his moral dissertation appropriately culminates in an exhortation to love.[37] Ambrose does not simply repeat classical teaching. The true friendship that is the perfection of Christian love springs from faith and involves forgiveness and renewal. Ambrose expects it to be common, uniting not just the few but all whom *caritas* embraces together. In principle and in potential, the loving goodwill and forgiveness that extends to all should draw all humanity into this new community of friendship.

Finally, Ambrose was the first to collect together in one place the obvious biblical material on friendship. His *De officiis* was the first sustained treatise on Christian ethics and pastoral theology. It was soon superseded, by Augustine on moral thought generally and by Gregory the Great's *Regula Pastoralis* on pastoral theology. The *De officiis* enjoyed wide distribution nonetheless. Eight centuries later, it became Aelred's point of departure for a much fuller exploration of 'spiritual' friendship.

Desert interlude: John Cassian

The Christian asceticism that inspired Ambrose and Augustine had been pioneered by the men and women who became hermits in Egypt, Syria and Palestine. These desert 'fathers' and 'mothers' increased greatly in number after the mid-fourth century, when hermit life was supplemented with that of organized monasteries.

Cassian (*c.*360–435) probably came from a land-owning family near the Black Sea, in Dacia, modern Romania. Fluent in Latin and Greek he became the chief transmitter of desert wisdom to the West. As a youth he left home with his friend Germanus to become a monk in Bethlehem, from where they made two long pilgrimages to Egypt to sit at the feet of well-known 'fathers'. Eventually they turned homewards as far as Constantinople, where John Chrysostom ordained Cassian deacon and sent the friends on a deputation to Rome. There Cassian was made priest, and about the year 415 he founded two monasteries near Marseilles. He wrote two Latin works, the *Institutes* which gives rules, customs and advice for monastic life and the *Conferences* which conveys practical wisdom through twenty-four talks by various Egyptian fathers. Western monasticism absorbed these into its soul, with Benedict making specific mention of them in his Rule.[38]

For a talk on 'Friendship' Cassian goes to Abba Joseph in his hermitage in the Nile delta. Joseph lives near two other holy hermits, amid a ruined town where an earthquake some years earlier had reduced the fertile land to salt marshes. Joseph asks Cassian and Germanus whether they are brothers? No, they explain, their unity lies in 'spiritual brotherhood' and the 'indissoluble bond' of common commitment. Joseph takes this as his cue for a homily on the practicalities of living in love and peace, whether in pairs or in the common life.[39]

Friendship (*amicitia*) is the expression of shared *agapē* (*caritas* or *dilectio*), which Cassian defines as a virtue and a gift. The 'virtue of love' (*virtus caritatis*) is so great that John declares it not a divine possession but God himself: *Deus caritas est* (1 Jn 4.16). Paul's statement that *caritas* is diffused in our hearts by the Holy Spirit (Rom. 5.5) is therefore tantamount to saying God himself comes to be within us (xiii). Much of Abba Joseph's advice will concern self-control, but he is ultimately talking about divine love and how to facilitate its expression amid the scratchiness of everyday common life.

Like his classical predecessors Joseph remarks on the many kinds of friendship and association that unite human beings. We enter compacts of *caritas* and bonds of *amicitia* through chance meetings, or links of business, art or study, or on shouldering family responsibilities. All these, however, are common to good and bad alike, and are merely bonds of necessity, lust, financial gain or kinship, easily dissolved by separation in place or time or the pressure of affairs (ii). There is, however, one indissoluble kind of love, the one that is grounded solely in likeness in virtue and grows 'by means of the double perfection and goodness of friends'. Neither time, space nor death can dissolve it (iii).[40]

We need also to distinguish between 'love', '*caritas* which is called *agape*' and 'affection', '*diathesis*, that is *adfectio*' (xiv). *Caritas* can be shown by all to all; *adfectio* is felt for those more closely united to us. We feel it in different ways for parents, spouses, siblings and children, but virtue evokes the most intense affection. Jacob loved all his children but had a deeper affection for Joseph 'because he was a type of the Lord'; Jesus loved all his disciples but had a 'superabundant' love for John because of his purity and virginity.[41] 'This', says Cassian, 'is true love set in order, which, while it hates no one, yet loves some still more by reason of their deserving it' (xiv). Augustine would propose a more elaborate 'order' of love. Its various orderings in early writers are all inspired by the verse: 'he set in order love in me (*ordinavit in me caritatem*)' (Song 2.4).

Where parity in goodness is the bond of friendship, perseverance in virtue will preserve it. Friends must continue in equal and zealous love for Christ, or the failures of one will finally break the other's patience. The verse that says the Lord 'makes men to be of one mind in a house' (Ps. 67.7 Vulg.), suggests to Cassian that love is permanent where there is a single purpose 'to will and refuse the same (*unum velle ac nolle*)'[42] (iii). To achieve unity by ridding ourselves of vices and mortifying our self-centred will is to fulfil the psalm: 'Behold how good and joyful a thing it is for brothers to dwell together in unity' (Ps. 132/3).

Joseph gives six rules for common life, introducing them as the 'foundation of true friendship (*verae amicitiae*)' (vi). First, be completely detached from worldly goods so as to put nothing before loving your brother. Second, do not prefer your opinion above your neighbour's, insisting on the superiority of your own wisdom and experience. Third, realize that everything, even the apparently useful and necessary, must take second place to the good of love and peace. Fourth, never be angry for any reason, good or bad. Fifth, try to heal your brother of any vexation he may feel against you, even if it arose for no cause. Sixth, remember we shall be leaving this world and therefore it is pointless to persist in any vice, whether it be some inward indignation or possessiveness or actual sin. Joseph dwells on the call to love, quoting 'Now the whole group of those who believed were of one heart and soul' (Acts 4.32) and 'By this everyone will know that you are my disciples, if you have love for one another' (Jn 13.35).

The greatest threats to love are anger and resentment, and Abba Joseph dwells on how we can control them and 'not let the sun go down' on our anger (Eph. 4.26) (vi). Quarrelling can arise from heresy and disagreement on points of theology. Desert monks, as Cassian would have been well aware, had experienced violent controversies over the opinions of Origen and Arius. Frank sharing, always central to friendship, now also serves to maintain a common mind and avert heresy. New thoughts and bright ideas, particularly about the interpretation of Scripture, should be shared in general discussion and submitted to healthy correction by our peers and elders. Thus friendship serves to reduce error and assure our salvation (x).

Most commonly, anger arises from hurt feelings. Joseph amusingly sketches the monk who takes his ruffled feelings with him as he goes to sing psalms, vainly imagining his bitterness will melt. In truth he is nursing his pride, refusing to communicate with the person with whom he has fallen out. A humble effort to make up, with well-timed expressions of regret, would cure bruised feelings on both sides. Jesus warned that anger will be judged, and commanded us to be reconciled before offering gifts at the altar (Mt. 5.22–4) (xv). A monk should not therefore offer prayer 'until by kindly amends you have removed from your brother's heart the vexations arising from whatever cause', even the trivial or unfounded (xvi). Supposing the wrong was substantial, then a monk must not refuse to accept an apology from a brother monk, which they would have accepted from a heathen or lay person, on the ground that such behaviour in a monk is truly unforgivable (xvii).

Patience and control of anger demand much more than mere silence and a sullen look. They require a heart free from resentment and, if appropriate, the courage to speak the truth in love (xviii). Angry monks have been known to refuse food for days, as it were feeding on their anger. Such fasting is blasphemous, offered to devils rather than God (xix). Some have even incited their fellow monks to violent anger against them, imagining they are creating an opportunity for themselves to advance in patience by 'offering the other cheek' (Mt. 5.39) (xx). Rather, what the gospel requires is 'inward tranquillity of heart' (the Greek term, well known in the desert, is *apatheia*, inner freedom from passions) which guards us from anger and empowers us to calm it in others. 'Do not be overcome by evil, but overcome evil by good.' (Rom. 12.21) (xxii). Patience must be genuine. Hearts narrowed by impatience or cowardice are easily overwhelmed by sudden storms of passion, so 'be enlarged in your hearts, receiving the adverse waves of anger in the wide gulf of that love which "suffers all things, bears all things"' (1 Cor. 13.7) (xxvii).[43]

If a weaker person needs pampering and insists on his own way it will sometimes help if the stronger makes concessions even in significant areas, just to bear with and heal the other's weakness (Rom. 15.1; Gal. 6.2). But despite the magnanimity and patience of the stronger partner, the weaker may eventually do something truly intolerable, or may realize they have been put up with for long enough, and leave (xxiii–xxvi).

Joseph sounds a final note of warning. Friendships begun for reasons of conspiracy (*coniuratio*, 'plotting together') will not last, unlike those based on desire for perfection and the authority of apostolic love. Whatever Joseph means by this, the fear of seditious factions would become one cause for looking askance at monastic friendships.

Cassian tells us this 'spiritual talk on friendship' inspired him and Germanus with 'a more ardent desire to preserve the *caritas* of our fellowship (*sodalitas*) as a lasting one.' (xxviii). Christian love should, according to this talk, be expressed in friendship, and close friendship based on virtue should be a normal part of monastic life. Abba Joseph has not however examined how personal friendships relate to, or what problems they might pose to, general friendship as the goal of the whole community.

Augustine

Ambrose had still fitted his theological ethics into the ancient mould of the cardinal virtues, but it was his own catechumen Augustine (354–430) who would do more than any other Western writer to establish the primacy of love in Christian ethical and theological discourse. Augustine's writings were in practice a source for the friendship tradition, and yet as we shall see his doctrine of love is not wholly hospitable to friendship.

Augustine was born to a devout Catholic Christian mother and semi-pagan father, minor landowners in the small agricultural town of Thagaste in Numidia in Roman Africa (Souk Ahras in modern Algeria). Having studied in Carthage he moved to Rome to teach literature and public speaking. A rising star, he was appointed to Milan in 384 as the city's professor of rhetoric. He had been attracted into Manichaeism, a gnostic sect that taught the dualism of good and evil, matter and spirit, but in Milan under Ambrose's influence he was reconverted to Catholic Christianity and baptized at Easter 387. He immediately began to develop into a prodigiously active and original theological writer, relinquishing secular ambitions and wanting only to retire into a shared life of Christian philosophical reflection.

Back in Thagaste he embarked on this life in a small ascetic community with like-minded friends. Mindful of what had happened to Ambrose he carefully avoided going anywhere that lacked a bishop! But in 391 while visiting a friend in the port city of Hippo he was seized by the bishop and congregation and ordained priest. He moved his community to Hippo where five years later he became bishop, serving from 396 until his death in 430. Its mix of priests and odd characters made his episcopal monastery very different from the congenial group of educated young men who had returned from Milan to Thagaste.

Augustine's writing and correspondence continued on a vast scale. The Western Roman Empire was now failing. Rome was sacked by the Goths in 410. Nineteen years later as Augustine lay dying, the town of Hippo was crammed with refugees from outlying towns and villas, and about to fall to the Vandals. Augustine's almost one hundred works of theology survived to accompany the Western Church into its wholly uncharted future. It is no exaggeration to say that the essential philosophical framework of Western Christianity for at least the next thousand years is owed to him.

Friendship in Augustine's life

Augustine's childhood was spent in the semi-rural, small town society of Numidia where surviving inscriptions tell of a preoccupation with pride and reputation, likely to engender quarrels and fiercely loyal friendships. 'No thinker in the Early Church was so preoccupied with the nature of human relationships; but then, few environments would have impressed their importance upon Augustine so vividly as the close-knit world in which he had grown up.'[44] Having absorbed Cicero, he entered a public world where the patronage of influential friends was vital. Finally, for more than four decades he lived the new ideal of Christian friendship.

His autobiographical *Confessions* reveals his longing 'to love and be loved' and shows the significant part friendship played in his youth.[45] Crucially, we also begin to see how this experience was ambivalent, affording joy but also pain and confusion. Friendship led him once to share with other boys in vandalizing a neighbour's pear tree. Why? 'Friendship can be a dangerous enemy, a seduction of the mind lying beyond the reach of investigation.'[46] As a young man in Thagaste he had a close friendship 'sweet to me beyond all the sweetnesses of life that I had experienced' and was devastated when his 'other self' suddenly died. 'I was in misery, and misery is the state of every soul overcome by friendship with mortal things and lacerated when they are lost.'[47] In grief 'The lost life of those who die becomes the death of those still living.'[48] He felt this despite having acquired a concubine while studying in Carthage, a woman whom he never names yet deeply loved, who was utterly loyal, the mother of their son Adeodatus – but never his intellectual friend.

He found solace from his grief by returning to Carthage and his young Manichaean friends. To share in conversing and laughing, reading and debating, mutual kindness and hospitality, to miss friends when absent and joyfully greet their return, 'these and other signs come from the heart of those who love and are loved and are expressed through the mouth, through the tongue, through the eyes, and a thousand gestures of delight, acting as fuel to set our minds on fire and out of many to forge unity.'[49]

From this circle, Alypius, Nebridius and others followed him to Milan, where they devised plans to retire into the country and live the philosophical life. Thoughts of marriage deterred them, but after their conversion to ascetic Catholicism they did retire, first to a villa near Lake Como and then to Thagaste. For the rest of Augustine's long life he was engaged with others through common life, pastoral care, preaching and writing. He corresponded with numerous male and female friends some of whom, like Jerome in Bethlehem and Paulinus of Nola near Naples, he only met through letters.

In 412, writing to Proba, a rich widow who had fled to North Africa from the advancing Goths, he praised the comfort provided by good friends in adversity. Indeed, in any circumstances 'there is nothing truly enjoyable without a friend'. But, 'how rarely is one found in this life about whose spirit and behaviour as a true friend there may be perfect confidence!' No one knows another as intimately as they know themselves, 'and yet no one is so well known even to himself that he can be sure as to his own conduct on the morrow'.[50] Years earlier, Augustine had confidently said 'no one is known except through friendship'.[51] Now, only God truly knows the human heart. Augustine's warmth had made him very vulnerable. He has been well described as 'delightfully and tragically exposed' to the one thing he found unfathomable, friendship.[52]

The same juxtaposition of enthusiasm and misgiving appears in Book Nineteen of the *City of God*, in a passage composed in 425 near the end of Augustine's life: 'what consolation have we in this human society, so replete with mistaken notions and distressing anxieties, except the unfeigned faith and mutual affections of genuine, loyal friends?' Yet the more friends we have, the more our anxiety mounts. We hear of their falling ill, 'afflicted by famine, war, disease or captivity' or more bitterly their friendship may turn into treachery and 'who, except one who has this experience, can be aware of the burning sorrow that ravages our hearts? Certainly we would rather hear that our friends were dead, although this also we could not hear without grief.'[53] As to friendship with the angels, here at least we have 'no manner of fear that such friends may bring us sorrow, either by their death or by their degradation'. However, that 'they do not mix with us on the same familiar footing as do men ... is one of the disappointments involved in this life'. Moreover Satan may disguise himself as an angel of light, and those philosophers who claimed the gods as their friends had obviously fallen in with malignant demons.[54]

Human friendship is also a potential distraction from loving God. Although 'a nest of love and gentleness because of the unity it brings about between many souls', it is merely an earthly beauty and hence 'at the bottom end of the scale of good' and a possible cause of sin if, through desire for it, anyone abandons 'the higher and supreme goods, that is you, Lord God, and your truth and your law'.[55]

Christian friendship and Christian love as friendship

There is however another kind of friendship, true friendship, integrally linked to the 'higher and supreme goods'. As his thought developed Augustine remained steeped in the classical language of friendship but gave it new Christian meaning. The transition is beautifully illustrated in Letter 258 to Marcianus. Augustine rejoices that his old friend has become a catechumen, because now their friendship, previously based on the sandy foundations of a purely mortal relationship, will be real and lasting in Christ. He reflects that before his own conversion he could have had no true friend, because no one who wished for him the things he then wished for himself, would have been a true friend. As the verse 'Whoever loves iniquity, hates his own soul'(Ps. 10.6 Lat.) indicates, he was then not even a friend to himself.

Cicero, he tells Marcianus, correctly defined friendship as 'agreement in all things human and divine, together with *caritas* and *benevolentia*'.[56] But agreement in falsehood cannot be true friendship. The real truth about divine things is found in Christ. Therefore true friendship must be grounded in agreement in Christ, and agreement in human matters will follow. 'Now we have agreement in things human and divine, with benevolence and love, in Christ Jesus our Lord, our most true peace.' Christ commands us to love God, and our neighbour as our self. 'If, together with me, you hold most firmly to these two, our friendship will be true and eternal; and it will bind us together not only with one another, but with the Lord as well.'[57] No one, Augustine writes elsewhere, can truly be a friend to man who has not first become a friend to truth.[58] Friendship 'can only be faithful in Christ, in whom alone it can be eternal and happy'.[59]

Augustine's vision of true friendship ideally embraces all the redeemed in Christ. One of his repeated themes is that an unlimited number can share in love for God, and in the peace of God. Not only does he feel no envy towards others who love God's beauty, but the more they share with him in that love, the more they are his friends.[60]

For Ambrose the hallmark of Christian friendship is intimate sharing on the pattern of Jn 15.15. Such unanimity was an intense reality for Augustine. We do, he says, talk freely with friends, agreeing and disagreeing without rancour as if in debate with our own self; a friend is indeed another self, one soul in two bodies.[61] The downside is neatly suggested in Peter Brown's acerbic comment on Augustine's youthful relationships: 'Augustine was an imperialist in his friendships. To be a friend of Augustine's, meant only too often becoming a part of Augustine himself.'[62] But he was no doubt capable of applying to himself what he often quoted: 'Rebuke a wise man and he will love you' (Prov. 9.8) or, as quoted to Jerome, 'the wounds of a friend are better than the kisses of an enemy' (Prov. 27.6).[63]

Augustine expected his clergy in Hippo to dispose completely of personal possessions and share a monastic household with him, after the example of the Early Church: 'Now the whole group of those who believed were of one heart and one soul, and no one claimed private ownership of any possessions, but everything they owned was held in common' (Acts 4.32). The same verse inspired the women's community Augustine founded at Hippo under his sister, and is the basis of his simple monastic *Rule*. He also applies it to marriage, despite harbouring continuing doubts about the capabilities of women as friends.[64]

Augustine wrote in a remarkable way about Christian love in friendship in a set of answers to various questions which he completed at about the time he became a bishop. He explores Paul's injunction: 'bear one another's burdens, and in this way you will fulfil the law of Christ' (Gal. 6.2). That 'law' is to love one another, which to Augustine means friendship. But how can we love people as they really are, a mixture of good and bad? Like Christ who emptied himself (Phil. 2.4–8), and who said that the sick, not the healthy, have need of a physician (Mt. 9.12), we too should be the humble healers of our friends, bearing with their faults and anger. No one who offers friendship is to be rejected simply because we are prone to notice their bad points first, or to consider ourselves superior. If we hold a superior position, and see someone too timid to approach, we should descend to them and offer friendship. We should not judge, but seek the good in each person and know that everyone has something to offer that we lack. Christ does not love us because of some good in us, but in order to heal us.[65] God's love for us was shown in Christ 'when we were still sinners'. In the same way a steady friend does not break off friendship when their love is not equally returned, but continues to care even while it is not possible to enjoy their friend.[66]

Preaching at the wine harvest in Hippo, around the year 424, Augustine famously commented that when Jesus picked his friends he chose 'not senators, but fishermen' (*non senatores sed piscatores*). Christ shows how little value we should place on friendship for social advantage, or for feeding the pride of whoever thinks themselves chosen for their wealth or prestige. Christ chose one with no education or standing, a sinner whom he could fill with grace and make a divine orator. He chose the weak to confound the strong.[67] Augustine had once devoted his afternoons in Milan to cultivating useful friendships. Now he has encountered spiritual riches in rustic workers, and the reversal of values is complete.[68]

Increasingly, Augustine speaks of the divine gift of *caritas* as the foundation and essence of Christian friendship. Reflecting on his early experiences of friendship and loss he concludes that true friendship is impossible 'unless you bond together those who cleave to one another by the love which is "poured into our hearts by the Holy Spirit who is given to us" ' (Rom. 5.5).[69] Few biblical passages became more formative for him than that verse. Grace, not nature, now creates friendship.[70] Writing to Proba about the comfort a good friend brings, he says it is God who acts through them by the goodness his Spirit has created in them.[71] To Jerome he describes how when he sees someone burning with Christian love he considers him a faithful friend, feeling that if he confides in him, he confides in God, for 'God is love, and those who abide in love abide in God, and God in them.' (1 Jn 4.16).[72]

Just as friendship unites many souls in one, so *caritas* mingles all Christian hearts and souls in the one soul of Christ (*anima una Christi unica*).[73] All Christians should share the experience of the Apostles at Pentecost when, like gold melting into a single mass in fire, the Holy Spirit fused their hearts into one by the flame of spiritual love.[74] 'Love, and do what you will' (*dilige, et quod vis fac*) said Augustine: whether you are silent or speak, whether you correct or spare, let the root of love (*dilectio*) be within you, for nothing but good can spring from this root.[75]

In order to understand the second commandment, to love our neighbour as our self, Augustine as we have seen adopted the classical teaching that love, and not least the love of friendship, entails desiring good things for the other for their own sake. If the one good that affords ultimate happiness to every human being is to love God, then loving our neighbour as our self means desiring that they too love God. In this essential respect then, there is no difference between loving a friend or neighbour. Augustine believed our neighbour is every human being and in principle 'all other men are to be loved equally' although in the lottery of earthly life we can only help those who happen to come within reach.[76] The basic identity between love for friend and neighbour enabled him to advise Proba that *amicitia* itself is not to be restricted, but extended to all humanity:

> it [*amicitia*] embraces all to whom love and kindly affection (*amor et dilectio*) are due, although the heart goes out to some of these more freely, to others more cautiously; yes, it even extends to enemies, for whom also we are commanded to pray. There is accordingly no one in the whole human family to whom kindly affection is not due by reason of the bond of a common humanity (*communis naturae societate*), although it

> may not be due on the ground of a reciprocal love. But in those by whom we are requited by a holy and pure love, we find great and reasonable pleasure.[77]

Similarly, when commenting on the Sermon on the Mount he simply says 'where there is goodwill, there is friendship';[78] and on the first Letter of John he comments that we must love all with 'a certain friendship of goodwill'.[79]

In May 411 Augustine was preaching in Carthage on the eve of a tense meeting with the breakaway Donatists. He exhorts his Catholic hearers to be inseparable friends of peace, a friendship in which, he points out, an infinite number of people can share. Moreover 'the true lover of peace is a lover of his enemies'. They are to keep silence when taunted, praying inwardly: 'Don't repel with abuse someone showering you with abuse, but pray for him.' Inwardly through prayer they are to be 'a good person' (*bonus*) – a recent translator construes this as 'a good friend' – on their opponent's behalf.[80] Christian friendship to all can be lived inwardly in prayer: but its outward expression has then to be worked out on personal, social and political levels – and in the end Augustine supported state coercion against the Donatists, while still agonizing over it.

Brotherhood can coexist either with enmity or friendship. Augustine never presumed that all who called themselves Christians had chosen friendship. Indeed he knew many had not, no doubt one good reason why he addressed his congregation as 'brothers', not 'friends'. But friendship is to be steadily offered, until Christian brotherhood and friendship become synonymous. Marcianus is both 'brother' and eternal 'friend' in Christ (*Ep.* 258). 'Love all men, even your enemies, not because they are your brothers, but that they may be your brothers; that you may at all times be on fire with brotherly love, either towards him who has become your brother, or toward your enemy, that ... he may become your brother. Whenever you love a brother you love a friend.'[81]

The perspective of eternity, the blessed life to come, is vital to Augustine's understanding of Christian friendship. In Christ friendships are eternal and death brings no permanent loss: ' "Happy is the person who loves you" (Tob. 13.18) and his friend in you, and his enemy because of you (Mt. 5.44). Though left alone, he loses none dear to him; for all are dear in the one who cannot be lost.'[82] Universal friendship becomes reality in heaven, the 'perfectly ordered and completely harmonious fellowship in the enjoyment of God, and of each other in God.'[83] There we shall see each other full of God, for God will be all in all. 'Who', Augustine asks, 'does not long for that city, from which no friend leaves, into which no enemy enters?'[84] There all our loves, too often one-sided or painful in this life, are fulfilled in eternal friendship and true peace.

Friendship with God

Augustine, with all his contemporaries, considered 'friend of God' a normal description of a fully committed believer. He hails Moses as such, and John the Baptist as friend of the Bridegroom, Christ.[85] The *Life of Anthony* had a great impact on him when he was considering baptism. In it he learned that a monk adopts his way of life 'so that, obeying the Lord's commands, he might begin to be his friend rather than his servant'.[86]

When Augustine uses this language he is frequently concerned with the polarity between friendship and enmity. Conversion means turning from friendship with the devil or 'mortal things', or even from courtly status as a 'friend of the Emperor', to friendship with God.[87] The Church and the world presently contain a mixture of people who, while they may not yet realize it, will at the last judgement be revealed as enemies or 'predestined friends' of God.[88] God, infinitely superior to us as our judge and yet never ceasing to love humanity, stoops down in Christ, approaches us who were his enemies, and 'changes us into friends'.[89] God has loved his saints from the beginning of the world, and that a just person 'begins to be a friend of God' means they, not God, have changed.[90]

Augustine is awed at God's love for us, and rejoices in the warmth and sweetness of discovering God inwardly. Yet he does not seriously explore our reciprocal friendship with God. Burnaby wrote, 'what we miss in Augustine is a full sense that God's creation of man in His own likeness is the great token of His love, *because* it is the creation of children destined for love's fellowship with their Father'. He attributed this lack to Augustine's deep sense of divine self-sufficiency, together with his difficulty in seeing human beings as free agents; and besides, Ciceronian friendship grounded in likeness in virtue was a model that 'could for him have no place in the relations of man and God'.[91] Nowhere indeed does Augustine insist more adamantly on the absolute priority of grace than in his brief lectures on Jn 15.14–16, where the sole point he drives across is that only God's action in us can cause us so to serve God as to enter his joy and become, in some astonishing but real way, his friends.[92]

Friendship within the Trinity?

Ambrose had happily drawn analogies between human friendship and Trinitarian relationships. If Scripture says human believers had 'one soul and one heart', how much greater is the unity of Father and Son; the three Persons, one in substance, 'agree in what to will and to refuse'; if a human friend is a 'second self' (*alter ego*), how much greater must be the unity of substance between the Persons of the Trinity.[93]

Augustine neither denies nor promotes this analogy but effectively sidelines it. In 'On the Trinity' (*De Trinitate*) he argues that it is the distinctive *relation* of 'Father' to 'Son' and 'Son' to 'Father' that distinguishes those persons, and he rhetorically contrasts these relationships with that of friends, whose relationship indicates sameness.[94] His object was not to rule out friendship within the Trinity but to discern the distinctiveness of the Persons, for which purpose friendship (if it implies sameness) 'does not provide a particularly apt model'.[95] Again, in developing his doctrine of the Holy Spirit he argues that the Father and Son have the Spirit in common, since it is the love between them, and 'this consubstantial and coeternal communion, if it can suitably be called *amicitia*, let it be so called; but it is more aptly called *caritas*. And this too is substance, because God is substance and it is written: "God is *caritas*" (1 Jn 4.16)'.[96] Here his interest lay in demonstrating from Scripture that the Spirit is of the same substance as the other Persons and hence equally divine. Once again he does not exclude *amicitia* but sets it aside for the purpose of this particular argument. Had he sought, as he did not, to present the Spirit more strongly as Person, relating in love with the other two Persons, Augustine might have made much more of the mystery of *amicitia* within the Trinity.

Caritas *as love of God*

Despite all he has to say on friendship, Christian love as Augustine bequeathed it to later ages did not, at least so far as this earthly pilgrimage is concerned, have the shape of dynamic mutuality. His primary legacy was his powerfully unified doctrine of *caritas* as '*amor Dei*', 'love of God' in the objective sense of love directed towards God, a profound orientation of our heart, to which our love of all else must be aligned or 'ordered'.[97] Thus depicted, love appears as having a strongly linear profile.

His scheme of love begins to take shape in an early work *The Customs of the Catholic Church*, begun soon after leaving Milan.[98] While returning to the Catholic fold in Milan he had been much attracted to Plotinus' Neoplatonism, of which the organizing theme is *erōs*, the longing for truth and beauty which draws souls upwards to union with the One, the divine. Augustine accepted this as reasonably close to Christian thought. From now on his life, while always spent in communion with others, became centrally focused on desire for God.

Addressing his educated non-Christian readers, he assumes they will agree that rational people should direct their love (*amor*) towards possessing happiness. Scripture teaches us to love God alone as our ultimate good, and that to love virtue is to love God in Christ who is 'the virtue of God, and the wisdom of God' (1 Cor. 1.23–4).[99] It follows that we love our selves rightly through loving God, and since to love our neighbour as ourself means wishing the same good for them as for ourselves, we must draw them, too, to love God. Neighbour-love is ideally mutual, so we should hope our neighbour will be equally concerned that we love God.[100] Since love of our neighbour involves renouncing harm and doing good, it is 'a kind of cradle' of our love of God.[101] In a platonic phrase that he uses only here Augustine describes love of neighbour as the best 'step' (*gradus*) to the love of God.[102] Wisdom and goodness are on the other hand divine gifts, so both loves, of God and neighbour, will increase together. The preponderant message, however, is that love for God is primary, and love for our neighbour is aligned with that love.

Caritas as love of God for God's own sake and of all else for God's sake, became the organizing theme of Augustine's theology. By incorporating all legitimate loves within love for God, he will achieve a synthesis between his single-minded desire for God, and Christ's twofold love-command. By the year 396 he had completed his scheme, balancing *caritas* with its polar opposite, *cupiditas*:

> I call *caritas* the motion of the soul toward the enjoyment of God for his own sake, and the enjoyment of one's self and one's neighbour for the sake of God; but *cupiditas* is a motion of the soul toward the enjoyment of one's self, one's neighbour, or any corporal thing for the sake of something other than God.[103]

In *City of God* Augustine contrasts the 'heavenly city', the Church on its earthly pilgrimage, with the 'city of this world'. These two cities derive from two kinds of love: 'the earthly city was created by self-love (*amor sui*) reaching the point of contempt for God, the Heavenly City by the love of God (*amor Dei*) carried as far as contempt of self'.[104] Here the two loves form a simple choice between love for God, and selfishness. Finally in his work 'on Christian education', *De doctrina christiana*, he lists four legitimate objects of love: God alone is to be loved for his own sake, while our self, our neighbour as equal with us, and our body below us, are all to be loved for God's sake.[105] This is the true 'order of love' implied in the verse 'he has ordered love in me (*ordinavit in me caritatem*)' (Song 2.4).

To explain the meaning of loving an object 'for its own sake' or 'for the sake of' something else, Augustine experimented briefly but seminally with the terms 'use' and 'enjoyment': 'To enjoy (*frui*) something is to cling to it with love for its own sake. To use (*uti*) something, however, is to employ it in obtaining that which you love.'[106] We 'use' a person or thing when our love ultimately flows to something beyond it and is 'referred' to obtaining the 'enjoyment' of that ultimate object. God alone is finally real and eternal, and hence to be enjoyed for himself and sought for his own sake. Hence created things are to be 'used' with reference to the enjoyment of God, so all loves are rightly 'referred' to the love of God. In practice this means we love a person or beautiful scene not as ends in themselves but as creatures of God transparent to God's goodness, not seeking to possess them but to find God beyond them and serve God through them. 'He truly loves his friend who loves God in his friend, either because He is in him, or so that He may be in him.'[107]

It is, Augustine admits, debatable whether human beings, including our own selves, can be 'enjoyed' as well as 'used' but he tends to conclude: 'I think that man is to be loved for the sake of something else' because 'In that which is to be loved for its own sake the blessed life resides', which will only be fully true of humans in heaven. Meanwhile, in this uncertain life, ' "cursed be the man that trusts in man." ' (Jer. 17.5)[108] Someone must have protested at not being loved for themselves, since Augustine adds that if we love our own selves on account of God, 'no other man should feel angry with you if you love him also on account of God'.[109] Once, later in life, he allowed when writing to Proba that we may pray for health and friendship, as good things, for their own sake.[110] But he quickly adds that everything in this world is uncertain, and the one thing Proba should ask above all is 'to dwell in the house of the Lord' through constant inner prayer. Augustine soon ceased employing the language of 'use' and 'enjoyment', but the popularity of *De doctrina christiana* ensured its persistence within the philosophical deposit he bequeathed to the Middle Ages.

Caritas *is the great and true virtue*

While working out his doctrine of love, Augustine brought about a Copernican revolution in the relationship between love and virtue. When he expounded the four virtues in *The Customs of the Catholic Church* he did not follow his predecessors and present love, in the form of friendship, as virtue's fruit. Instead he linked virtue with love in a new way:

> As to virtue leading us to a happy life, I hold virtue to be nothing else than perfect love of God. For the fourfold division of virtue I regard as taken from four forms of love . . . The object of this love is not anything, but only God, the chief good, the highest wisdom, the perfect harmony. So we may express the definition thus: that temperance is love keeping itself entire and incorrupt for God; fortitude is love bearing everything readily for the sake of God; justice is love serving God only, and therefore ruling well all else, as subject to man; prudence is love making a right distinction between what helps it towards God and what might hinder it.[111]

Until now, the love shown by a good friend has been the collective function of the virtues. Augustine inverts and reorients the ancient system, making the virtues functions of our love for God, which itself becomes 'the great and true virtue (*magna et vera virtus*)'.[112] '*Caritas* is the virtue by which we desire to see and enjoy God'.[113] 'It seems to me that a brief and true definition of virtue is "rightly ordered love"'.[114]

Augustine's treatment of love began a new chapter in ethical history. *Caritas* is 'the principle of first importance in Augustine's mind' and 'the introduction and spread of this specifically Christian doctrine marks the decisive break between antiquity and the Middle Ages'.[115]

The dilemma and the hope of friendship

Augustine's legacy with regard to friendship was at once powerful and ambivalent. He was a warm and engaging person for whom friendship was an ever-present fact. His most-read book, the *Confessions*, arose within the context of friendship, as his self-revelation to God before the interested audience of his friends.[116] Yet he did not make *amicitia* an important theological theme, and he never urges us to welcome and celebrate friendship in Christ on earth as a foretaste of the eternal 'enjoyment of God and of one another in God' in heaven.

One issue is the sheer fickleness and mortality of human nature. Augustine's awareness of the griefs of earthly attachment even for a Christian are prominent in the works everyone read, the *Confessions* and *City of God*. He never went as far as Jerome who once, albeit perhaps as a rhetorical flourish, virtually counselled the abandonment of human friendships as almost always self-seeking, in favour of God's friendship.[117] Nevertheless, so intense are Augustine's descriptions of the pains and anxieties attendant on friendship, that they could be taken as a positive disincentive to close earthly relationships. His vivid descriptions of their power to distract must have reinforced monastic doubts about the value of particular friendships. These tensions, as Katherine TePas has pointed out, reach back into Scripture. The Old Testament, especially Wisdom literature, 'is filled both with praise for the blessings of the faithful friend . . . and warning against false friends. On several occasions Scripture explicitly warns against trust in another human and against efforts to please a fellow human.'[118] Ambivalence results: the Christian spiritual tradition is capable of holding 'side by side, even within works of the same author, praise and gratitude for one's friends as a help and consolation in the spiritual life and warnings against human friendship and marriage'.[119]

Most importantly, however, Augustine's formal doctrine of love subsumes human friendship within the ordered love that effectively draws all our powers into a strongly one-way love for God. Good so far as it goes, this is not yet an adequate account of our love-relationship with God as known in Christ. Nor does it do justice to love of neighbour.

Augustine's theory and practice do not sit entirely comfortably with each other. He desired balance in the Christian life: 'For no one ought to be so leisured as to take no thought in that leisure for the interest of his neighbour, nor so active as to feel no need for the contemplation of God.'[120] But if *caritas* is a linear and 'vertical' love it will risk being a neo-Platonic flight of the alone to the Alone. If we must 'use' our neighbour with reference to our 'enjoyment' of God, it will be little surprise if loving God through the neighbour, or even effectively bypassing the neighbour, will tend to eclipse loving our neighbour or friend in God, let alone with or from God.

One last picture from Augustine. He suggests to a correspondent that, like our bodily eyes which do not see each other but are united in gazing in the same direction, the hearts of friends separated by distance are joined by their common focus on the light of truth.[121] He speaks similarly of married couples who journey side by side, looking where they walk.[122] It is unlikely that Augustine, who valued his friends' presence and his interactions with them, intended this as a wholly adequate account of Christian friendship! But arguably the pattern of common pilgrimage towards God, accompanying and helping but not necessarily contemplating the other, came to obtain widely in Christian thought and not least in monasticism.

On the positive side of Augustine's ambivalence lies his experience of reciprocal love in Christ, and the hope for real and eternal friendship, contingent upon the transformation of character through grace, the 'love that is poured into our hearts through the Holy Spirit which is given to us' (Rom. 5.5). As 'the greatest gift of the Holy Spirit' *caritas* inherits the accolade Cicero conferred on friendship itself: the 'greatest divine gift'.[123] James McEvoy reflects that Augustine, by effectively making friendship a mystery of grace, made it 'a matter always of three persons and not simply of the two human partners'.[124] As a mystery of grace, friendship is decoupled from any pride that would have accompanied it as the mutual admiration of human virtue; and moreover virtue is now modelled on Christ, with his humility and forgiveness:

> Where humility is regarded as a notable, or even as the supreme virtue, and pride, on the contrary, as a sinful illusion – the sin of Lucifer – there repentance for offences committed, the readiness to forgive and to accept forgiveness, the bearing of one another's burdens and the extension of pardon even to the enemy, when taken all together, suggest that friendship does not come about only, or even for the most part, as the sequel of perfect equality.[125]

God's grace, McEvoy continues, can now be 'the origin of friendship between parties who do not at the very outset resemble each other', but may come to do so through 'the Spirit of God's working redemption within their souls'. Where the offer of friendship is reciprocated, 'Caritas is the perfect unity of minds in true wisdom and of wills in true benevolentia, willing the good of each other for eternity, and not solely for this life.'[126] The development of this aspect of Augustine's thought would, after more than eight centuries, come to occupy the minds of Aelred and Thomas Aquinas.

An Eastern approach: Maximus and John Damascene

While the doctrine of love in Western Christianity took the Augustinian trajectory, the Greek-speaking East perceived love in more relational terms. **Maximus the Confessor** (580–662) speaks of the inter-relatedness of love for God, self, and others, in a way that would only rarely be made so explicit among Western writers.

Perhaps originally from Palestine, Maximus makes his first appearance as a well-read theologian and spiritual father living, in his forties, in a monastery near Constantinople. There he wrote a *Letter on Love* to a friend at court, and four sets of one hundred short paragraphs or '*Centuries on Love*'.[127]

While Augustinian thought caused a deep awareness in the West of the rift between 'nature' and 'grace', 'in Greek patristic terminology, and particularly in St Maximus, "nature" presupposes divine presence in man, that is, "grace". No opposition between "nature" and "grace" is therefore possible.'[128] Redemption is a process of 'deification' (*theiōsis*) in which our nature, marred by the Fall, is renewed from within in God's image. The whole work of God incarnate in Christ makes deification possible: Christ emptied himself and took on our humanity so that we may be incorporated by the Spirit into the divine life. The transformation starts with baptism and continues, aided by prayer and sacraments, through the ascetic struggle to empty ourselves of the unruly passions of self-love and to learn love for others, until we come to perceive this world from God's perspective and finally to experience God in a constant state of inner prayer. 'Love', writes Maximus, 'is a holy state of the soul, causing it to value knowledge of God above all created things.'[129] But the authenticity of the transformation is attested by our actual participation in God's universal love:

> And the interpretation of love is: to love the Lord God with all the heart and soul and power, and the neighbour as oneself. Which is, if I might express it in a definition, the inward universal relationship to the first good connected with the universal purpose of our natural kind . . .This we know as love and so we call it, not divisively assigning one form of love to God and another to human beings, for it is one and the same universal: owed to God and attaching human beings to one another. For the activity and clear proof of perfect love towards God is a genuine disposition of voluntary goodwill towards one's neighbour.[130]

We are transfigured inwardly into the relational love of God, and love others in and with God's love. Christians wholly focused on God are thereby empowered to express their true human nature made in the image of God. Natural love is perfected in divine love.

> The person who loves God cannot help loving every man as himself, even though he is grieved by the passions of those who are not yet purified. But when they amend their lives, his delight is indescribable and knows no bounds.[131]

The 'deification' of human nature begins now. The pilgrim is already in some sense standing in Jerusalem. The divine life is within us and we can already in some way experience Augustine's heavenly 'enjoyment of God and of one another in God', and minister this love to one another. Maximus wrote to his friend John,

> ... I know quite certainly that your holy soul is indissolubly bound to my wretchedness in the spirit through love, having the law of grace as a bond of friendship, in accordance with which you invisibly embrace me, making my sinful shamefulness vanish in comparison with your own excellence. For nothing is more truly Godlike than divine love, nothing more mysterious, nothing more apt to raise up human beings to deification.[132]

A few years later, **John of Damascus** (*c*.655–*c*.750) developed, from the thought of the Cappadocians, the concept of '*perichōrēsis*', the dynamic mutual indwelling of the Three Persons of the Holy Trinity. This dynamic doctrine became known in the West, rendered as 'circumincession'; but in the main however Western theology continued to be more aware of the Oneness, the unity of God, expressed as the unity of Father and Son in the love of the Holy Spirit, and less aware of the mystery of the triune relationship of Father, Son and Spirit.

No extended reflections specifically dealing with Christian love in relation to friendship seem to have been elaborated in the East, with the exception of **Florensky**'s thoughts in 1914 on the complementarity between the agape of the whole Church, and intimate 'philia' between friends.[133] But in recent years the West has regained contact with Eastern Orthodoxy's more 'social' understanding of the Trinity, its greater confidence in the continuing goodness of creation, its doctrine of 'deification' and the ethos of *koinōnia* within which the loves of God, self and neighbour form a dynamic unity rather than being ordered in linear form. These, as we shall come to see in our final chapter, lend themselves to a vision of love as present communion and deep friendship.

3

Monastic friendship and Aelred of Rievaulx

'Shall I say – "God is Friendship"?'

Aelred, the twelfth-century Cistercian Abbot of Rievaulx, was able to draw on Scripture, on patristic tradition, and on Cicero, when making his exploration of 'spiritual friendship'. The Church, and particularly its monasteries, preserved the classical Latin learning in which its early scholars had been steeped, and from the ninth century onwards there was a fresh flowering of the literature of friendship in letters, poems and prayers in monastic and ecclesiastical circles. In wider society, feudal relationships 'encouraged the appearance of a form of *amicitia* which was merely a juridical bond. In many formularies, the numerous kinds of friends are differentiated according to the services each could be expected to perform.'[1] A whole spectrum of 'friendship', ranging from the political to the personal and spiritual, and sometimes combining all these, can be traced in the lives and correspondence of monks, nuns and ecclesiastical figures throughout the Middle Ages.[2]

Friendship in monastic tradition

Cassian and Germanus enjoyed 'spiritual brotherhood', but we should surely credit Paulinus of Nola (*c.*353–431) with the first literary appearance of 'spiritual friendship', *spiritalis amicitia*. He assured his 'brother in

Christ' Pammachius that their friendship was not *secularis*, 'of this world', but *spiritalis*, born of God and uniting them in the mysterious brotherhood of 'spirits' (*Ep*. 13.2). Much later, about the year 721, the Venerable Bede described St Cuthbert and Herebert the hermit of Derwentwater as united by the bond of '*spiritalis amicitia*'.[3] Aelred, who knew Bede's work, would positively encourage 'spiritual friendship' between monks.

Such friendship was, however, more normally seen as presenting difficulties. The first signs of dissonance between the ideals of Christian love and friendship had appeared with organized monasticism in the mid-fourth century. Cassian shows how friendship could exist between spiritual father and disciple, and generally among people of prayer. But less ideal friendships or emotional entanglements either with other religious or with those outside the monastic walls could threaten the monk's or nun's inner tranquillity and devotional orientation, and lessen equality of regard among the community. Cliques and jealousies could arise. The perils of outward sedition or inner distraction loomed large in the minds of monastic leaders and the predominant stance they took was to place communal harmony first and discourage particular relationships. Although the ethos of the community could be understood as a common friendship, it became rare to encourage personal friendships, grounded in and aimed towards Christian maturity, as enabling growth in love and so supporting the community. For many centuries monastic spirituality would provide the paradigm for lay holiness, so its apparent negativity towards friendship was significant well beyond the monastery walls.

One delightful desert story about two very different hermits, Arsenius and Moses, suggests the role also played by temperament. Abba Arsenius, formerly a Roman imperial courtier, sought solitude in the desert to be with God. A monk tried to visit him and was turned away, but was then welcomed warmly by Abba Moses. The baffled visitor requested another father to find out from God how it was that 'for your name's sake one flees from men, and the other, for your name's sake, welcomes them with open arms?' The answer came as a vision of two boats on a river. In one Arsenius sailed, alone with God's Spirit 'in perfect peace'. In the other sat Moses with a group of angels, all eating honey-cakes. 'The meaning', says McGuire, 'is brilliantly clear: Arsenius obtained peace through solitude, while Moses approached God through the good company of others. They became as angels to him, and their presence by no means threatened his soul.'[4] In the desert each finds his own way. A graphic illustration of introvert and extrovert spiritualities! Moses practised friendship openly, Arsenius through hidden prayer, which was humanly disconcerting.

Desert hermits often formed community groups, *coenobia*, around spiritual fathers or mothers. In AD 320 Pachomius (*c*.290–346) founded the first organized monastery at Tabennesi near the Nile in central Egypt. This founder had become a Christian through experiencing kindness from Christians while on his journeys as a young military conscript. In a Coptic work he says, 'Let us love men for then we shall be the friends of Jesus who is a friend to men.'[5] The essential aim of monastic life for Pachomius, however, was still to provide ascetic formation for future hermits. This demanded absolute freedom from ties of family or village, within a new community dedicated to promoting the spiritual growth of each member impartially and equally. To maintain inner and outer peace, with quieting of the passions, Pachomius also rules against particular friendship with, or among, younger monks. He nowhere affirms personal friendship, but teaches equal love of all.

Basil 'the Great' of Caesarea in Cappadocia, modern central Turkey, visited Syria and Egypt before founding the first large monasteries of Asia Minor. His discourses and Rules have guided Orthodox monasticism down the centuries. For him community, *koinōnia*, is the true human state and the monastery becomes a lifelong means for growth in love for God and for all, in an atmosphere of sharing according to Acts 4.32 and in anticipation of the heavenly life. Basil valued his own friendships, and wrote that brotherly love, *philadelphia*, among monks must have all the ardent depth of friendship, *philia* (*Shorter Rules* 242). From Basil's letters White concludes that the more classical idea of friendship among the few that had marked his youth 'developed into a vision of the Church, its members united by love founded on a common faith, in a relationship resembling a kind of extended, divinely endowed friendship' that afforded the peace necessary for living the Christian life and practising the love of God through contemplation.[6]

Basil did not proscribe true friendship. Yet certain phrases of his, or ascribed to him, came to be quoted against friendship. He sensibly stipulated that anyone given the task of distributing necessities in the monastery must treat all equally and be free of particular liking (*prospatheia*) or disliking (*Long Rules* q. 34). One brief 'ascetic discourse' ascribed to Basil does famously forbid 'particular friendships': all monks must be shown equal love, *agapē*, therefore contentions, cliques and 'partiality', *merikē diathesis* (Latinized as *singularis amor*, love of one person alone) must be banished from the monastery, because from 'particular friendships' (*merikēs philias*, *amicitia particulari*) and cliques arise suspicions and jealousies.[7] Physical attraction is also an issue. Young monks should flee from all intimacy with their peers, even on the pretext of spiritual love (*pneumatikē agapē*; *spiritualis dilectio*).[8] Conversation for pleasure with anyone, male or female, should be avoided: one should only speak as necessary, to obey the command of love (*Long Rules* q. 33).

As McGuire expresses it, 'Friendship and community had been seen in the aristotelian world as complementary; while in the monastic world of the early centuries they could be looked on as rivals.'[9] But the problems evidently lay, not in true friendship but in precisely that insecurity and immaturity that make the sharing of friendship impossible.

In the West the monastic tradition emerged in part from the milieu of philosophical communities like that of Augustine, also aspiring to the friendship-ideal of Acts 4.32. The 'Rule' associated with him is a bare protocol for living together in love, *caritas*, in a common life that could embrace 'like-minded pursuers of truth' united as friends in contemplation, together with many with whom philosophical exploration might be difficult and whom one might not humanly choose as friends.[10] As Henry Chadwick nicely puts it, 'He had intended his monastery as a battle-school for Christ's front-line soldiers, and many of his monks did go out to serve as bishops. But the Hippo house was also a hospital for some of the more striking misfits and casualties of life.'[11]

Western monasticism was finally shaped by Benedict (*c*.480–*c*.550) in whose Rule the monastery is a 'school of the Lord's service' (*Prol.*). Its master, the abbot, must love no monk more than another unless he finds someone advanced in good actions or obedience (*Rule* 2.16–17). Special friendship might therefore exist between virtuous monks and their abbot. 'The abbot set the tone of life, and if he were interested in monastic friendships, and thought they could be integrated into the discipline and daily life of the cloister, then Benedict's Rule allowed room for them.'[12] Benedict neither explicitly instructs monks to love one another equally, nor mentions particular affection, although he forbids anyone defending another for any reason (*Rule* 69). He repeats the by now usual provisions for good order and decorum, not least among younger monks. He advises monks to read Cassian, and Basil's Rule (*Rule* 73). Aelred, as a Cistercian, was an abbot in the Benedictine tradition.

Aelred's life

Aelred was born about 1110 in Hexham near Hadrian's wall, his father being a married priest.[13] He became a young courtier to David I of Scotland, son of St Margaret, growing up as friends with David's son Henry and stepsons Simon and Waldef. He learned to write good Latin, gained a lifelong interest in history, discovered Cicero's *De amicitia*, and came to love Augustine's *Confessions.*[14] Northern Britain had a strong tradition of monastic scholarship, due not least to the polymath Bede, and Aelred was to contribute to its renaissance. As in Ambrose's time, a new ascetic reform was sweeping through the Church. Waldef was the first to become a monk, and about 1134, having visited York on an errand to the archbishop, Aelred discovered the group of Cistercians recently sent by Bernard of Clairvaux to build their monastery of Rievaulx, in the wooded valley of the Rie near Helmsley Castle. He had found his heart's desire. He was accepted to join them.

Cistercians are reformed Benedictines. Founded at Cîteaux in 1098, their fervour and strict life of prayer, work, and study placed them at the forefront of the twelfth-century revival. They understood their life as a 'school of love', of *caritas*. Aelred's formation as a novice took him through the Cistercian scheme of meditation on five books of the Old Testament, designed to detach the monk from the world and lead him through moral purification to the mystical heights of the Song of Songs. 'Ecclesiastes to teach the vanity of worldly pleasures and ambitions, Proverbs and Ecclesiasticus to teach self-knowledge and the practice of virtue, Wisdom and the Song of Songs to lead the proficient towards a life of contemplation.'[15] Knowles remarks on the attractiveness, and the newness in contemporary monasticism, of 'the invitation to the mystical life which Bernard never ceased to make in his later years; the call . . . to seek that union with God which is the theme of his sermons on the Canticle.'[16] The language of the Song became the normal language of divine love for Cistercian writers. It is important in assessing Aelred's use of it to bear in mind its status as a mystical text and the extent to which its commentators allegorized its every word and phrase.[17]

Aelred's acute mind remained relatively untouched by the new scholastic theological methods. His insight was formed, as Bernard puts it, in the school of the Holy Spirit.[18] He had both the practical and mystical gifts of a spiritual director. The depth of his understanding of literary sources, his sympathy and ability to draw others into intellectual dialogue, have been called 'the quintessence of the Christian humanism of the twelfth century'.[19]

In 1142, just before becoming novice master, Aelred was sent on an embassy to Rome. En route he appears to have met Bernard at Clairvaux. Certainly Bernard now took an interest in him, commissioning him to write the *Speculum caritatis*, 'Mirror of Love', a picture of and apologia for the tough Cistercian life as a school of love. Aelred's career as a writer continued with several brief historical, exegetical and spiritual works, his many sermons and, most notably today, the dialogue on 'Spiritual Friendship'. Sadly his collection of over three hundred letters has not survived.

After a brief spell as novice master Aelred was sent as abbot in 1143 to a new monastery at Revesby in Lincolnshire. From 1147 he was Abbot of Rievaulx, head of the English Cistercians and a notable public figure. He died in 1167.

The 'Mirror of Love': Speculum caritatis

Aelred's dialogue on friendship builds on his teaching on love in the *Speculum*, which he knows his friends to have absorbed, where he had already begun to point to the role of spiritual friendship. We too then need to know something of the *Speculum*.[20]

The Cistercians regarded their strict asceticism as a sharing in Christ's suffering in order to learn love, *caritas*, the *raison d'être* of monastic life. Bernard commanded Aelred to write about the greatness and joy of *caritas*, compared with the oppression to which *cupiditas* leads. This 'mirror' is to reveal love's true nature as *caritas*, defend Cistercian asceticism as promoting it, and show how it is manifested in outward conduct. Aelred began to construct this work while he was novice master, sending instalments for comment to his close friend Hugh, prior of another house. Some passages reflect his instruction to novices, others are more devotional or polemical; one is a personal lament for his and Hugh's friend Simon (I.98–114).

Caritas sums up the law and prophets (I.49); it is God's eternal rest in which Father and Son repose in the mutual love of the Spirit, into which all rational souls long to enter (I.57–8; 62–79); it is the root and companion of all other virtues: of faith and hope, temperance, prudence, fortitude, and justice (I.88–94). Love (*amor*), Aelred tells us, is the heart's sense of taste and vision and its capacity to recognize and possess God (I.2). He expounds Augustine's theology of love, sensitively and with simple profundity. The happiness of rational creatures consists in adhering to God through the soul's three powers of memory, intellect, and will, that constitute the image of the Trinity. Adam's selfishness (*cupiditas*) corrupted this image and brought humanity into its present state of 'unlikeness' (I.9–12). Salvation, beginning with the new commandment and the inpouring of the Holy Spirit who is *caritas*, restores our likeness to God.[21]

'*Amor*' is both our innate power to love and its expression in action. As power, love is part of God's creation and good in itself. As action, it is good or evil according to the use we make of it (III.20). Used well, by a will that is assisted by grace and 'ordered' by justice, *amor* is *caritas*; otherwise, it will be *cupiditas* (I.27–47). Aelred analyses *cupiditas* under Augustine's triple heading from 1 Jn 2.16: 'the lust (*concupiscentia*) of the flesh and the lust of the eyes, and the ambition of the secular world'.[22] The aim of the monastic life is to re-order our love, replacing *cupiditas* with Christ's yoke of *caritas*.[23] *Caritas* is love free from all vice, and is to be shown to all (III.8). Perfect *caritas* becomes possible in eternal life, after the death of the body, when the image is perfectly restored and the soul, admitted to the full vision of God, will at last love God with all its strength and its neighbour as itself (I.14, 95). What is practically possible during our earthly life is '*caritas ordinata*', love so 'ordered' that we love 'God more than self, neighbour as self, God for his own sake, self and neighbour for God's sake' (I.97).

Love passes through three successive stages: first our 'choice' of whom to love (*electio*), then 'movement' (*motus*) and finally 'fulfilment' (*fructus*) (III.22). Monks have already chosen to love God and neighbour (III.27). The stage of 'movement' combines inner desire and outward action and springs from reason (*ratio*) and some kind of '*affectus*', a pleasant interior inclination, disposition or feeling (III.30–1). Problems arise here because reason is not always in charge as it should be, and there are many kinds of '*affectus*', inclination. Aelred lists six varieties.

'Spiritual inclination' may be inspired by the Holy Spirit or the devil, so discernment is required. 'Rational inclination' is admiration of virtue, 'irrational inclination' admiration of worldly vanities. 'Dutiful inclination' derives from obligations of service or gratitude; 'natural inclination' is felt for relatives. Finally, '*affectus carnalis*', physical attraction, is elicited by a person's pleasant appearance. It may be neutral or good, as when Pharaoh's daughter was attracted to the infant Moses; but if it is merely lust, it is evil (III.31–38). Reason discerns whether an inclination is due to divine inspiration or temptation (III.39), and reason has the power to motivate love of God and neighbour even in the absence of any spontaneous inclination (III.31–40).

Our 'neighbour' is either a friend, an enemy, or 'neither friend nor enemy'. A 'friend' is someone who treats us kindly, out of kinship or generosity (*gratia*). We love them for three reasons: from nature as human and as it were our kin, from duty because it is an obligation to love friends, and by commandment as our neighbour. 'Neutral' persons are loved from nature and by commandment; enemies solely by commandment (III.40). To attain perfect love in which reason and pleasure coincide, reason must direct which inclination is welcomed and developed and which rejected (III.48–68). Where love arises as spontaneous inclination and comes under reason's guidance, it becomes love 'in God'. Where no pleasant inclination is present, reason can nevertheless move us to love people, not 'because of themselves' but 'because of God'. So we love friends 'in God', enemies 'because of God' (III.62–3).

Ordered love finds rest and fulfilment in three interrelated spiritual 'sabbaths'.[24] Love of God, self, and neighbour are interdependent and cannot exist alone, and they come to perfection together (III.3–5).

> For Aelred the three loves (of self, of others and of God) are inseparable and interacting. This is a very interesting doctrine, and an original one. One cannot love oneself without loving God; one cannot love others if one does not love oneself, etc. And the process is not a kind of one-way traffic. One does not practice

> brotherly love in order to reach the love of God, and once arrived there, kick away the ladder. Aelred says specifically that we learn from the love of God how to love our brothers, and we can descend the steps and repose pleasantly in the love of our fellowmen.[25]

Aelred felt, deeply and intuitively, the dynamic interdependence of these three loves, in a way that was apparently unusual in the West: 'while of course there is clear distinction in this threefold love there is, wonderfully, a close connection within it so that each love is found in all, and all in each, nor can one be had without the other, and when one wavers all are lessened' (III.3). Which love begins this process? If, as Aelred says, the love of God is the soul of other loves and a 'certain part' of it must precede them (III.4), then grace must act first, drawing us to love God whose prior love for us makes all love possible.

The 'sabbath' of self-love is the rare sense of inner peace resulting from a good conscience and orderly thoughts, with thanksgiving (III.6). That of love of neighbour may be felt in inward sympathy for all one's brothers, and the sweet sense of union in heart and soul with them through the 'glue' of *caritas* (III.7). The third, the 'sabbath of sabbaths', is the love of God. The only full and unambiguous 'Sabbath of sabbaths', the year of Jubilee, is the perfect restoration of all things in the love of God. Its fullness is in the life to come, but here we have 'a certain foretaste' (III.2) when, purified by right love of self and neighbour, the soul breaks through the veil of flesh to the vision of Christ, to rest in God in the silent joy of contemplation, possessing God and possessed by Him (III.17–18).

Aelred divides all humanity into six kinds, to all of whom *caritas* must be shown (III.8). The top four are relatives, special friends, those bound to us by obligations of duty, and fellow Christians. The fifth are those outside the Church: Gentiles, Jews, heretics, and schismatics; the sixth are enemies (III.10). To love these two latter groups is to taste the fruition of love of neighbour, for when we love our enemies we are made sons of God, the likeness of divine goodness is restored in us, and we are freed from slavery to sin (cf. Mt. 6.12). Indeed, not only are we freed from being a slave, but we are even 'made a friend' (III.11, cf. Jn 15.15). Friendship with God is presumably foremost in Aelred's mind, but perhaps a secondary meaning can be read into his words, that of the gift of absolute universal friendship which, as he will shortly speculate, might be found in the saints.

These groups reappear in a delightful allegory of the human heart as a Noah's Ark bearing all humanity within itself. Enemies are wild beasts out on the open deck, where those outside the Church are accommodated in some kind of shelter. Inside the main rooms (*mansio*) are those who present no harm and are making progress, ranked more internally and on higher levels according as they are closer in kinship, or more kindly regarded in friendship or more firmly bound to us by acts of kindness. On the highest deck, like birds, are those close to God, capable of flying to heaven on wings of virtue; and among these are individuals joined to us in the joyful bond of 'spiritual friendship' (*spiritalis amicitia*), whom we welcome with the greatest intimacy. Finally, Christ alone, creator and restorer of this Ark, whose splendour fills it, who draws all that is in it into his love and who should be loved before all and in all, demands as his 'mansion' its highest, most interior place (III.103–6).

Love's fulfilment in friendship

When Aelred discusses the third stage of *caritas*, 'fruition', *fructus*, he looks forward with Augustine to the enjoyment of one another in eternal life, in pure unity of spirit, but he adds his own distinctive conviction that a foretaste of this joy can and should be experienced on earth. He defines 'enjoy' (*frui*) as 'to use with joy and delight' and cites Paul's statement that he hopes to 'enjoy' Philemon, as proof that fruition is possible in this life (III.108).[26]

In the present life we 'enjoy' only some of our fellow humans. We can 'use' some to test us and others to teach, console or sustain us; but we can only 'use' in spiritual delight, that is, 'enjoy', those to whom we are joined by pleasant inclination. *Caritas* can be shown to all in this life on the planes of choice and action, but when it comes to enjoyment there are 'few, if any' who, in this life, can show both rational and affective love to everyone (III.108). Aelred just leaves open the possibility of a saintly universal liking for humanity; and he himself later speaks of his affection for all the monks at Rievaulx (*Spir. am.* III.82). But, he continues, even in love for God many find that their experience of *caritas* on earth is limited to choosing and acting, the enjoyment being postponed until they arrive at the beatific vision of God in heaven. Perhaps, he suggests, the foretastes of that joy granted in contemplative prayer are better regarded as *usus* than *fructus*, as help for our infirmity rather than the full perfection of love (III.108).[27]

It is nevertheless precisely Aelred's determination to explore the fulfilment of love on earth that leads him to devote the final paragraphs of the *Speculum* to spiritual friendship.

> Furthermore, it is no small solace in this life to have someone whom you can unite to yourself with intimate affection and by an embrace of most holy love, in whom your spirit may rest, to whom your soul may pour itself out, to whose pleasant conversation you can flee as to a consoling song amid sorrows, into whose most kind embrace of friendship you can enter, secure among so many scandals of this age; by the great love of whose heart, if you unhesitatingly entrust him with your

innermost thoughts, and by whose spiritual kisses, as if by an application of medicine, you can rid yourself of the weariness of tumultuous cares; who weeps with you in troubles, rejoices with you in prosperity, searches with you in times of uncertainty; whom you lead by chains of *caritas* into the most secret place of your soul, so that even when absent in body he is still present in spirit, where you may converse alone one with another (*solus cum solo*) the more secretly the more sweetly, consult *solus cum solo*, and when the noise of earth is stilled you may repose, *solus cum solo*, in the sleep of peace, in the embrace of *caritas*, in the kiss of unity, the sweetness of the Holy Spirit flowing between you: indeed you so unite and attach yourself to him, and mingle soul with soul, that one is made from many. (III.109)

Thus we can enjoy those whom we love 'not only from reason, but also from pleasant inclination', and above all those to whom we are intimately united by the most joyful bond of 'spiritual friendship', *spiritalis amicitia* (III.110). Aelred expresses the conviction, for which he would have Cassian's authority, that Jesus himself legitimizes such friendship:

Lest this most holy kind of love (*caritas*) might seem to be worthy of disapproval, our Jesus himself, condescending to us in all things, patient and merciful to us through all things, transforming us in showing his love, especially granted to one, not to all, the reclining-place of his most sweet breast as a sign of love, so that the virgin's head might be supported on the flowers of a virgin's breast, and the secret perfumes of the heavenly marriage-couch might instil, the more intimately the more abundantly, the fragrance of spiritual ointments into virginal inclinations (*affectibus*). Hence, although all the disciples were indeed embraced by the most holy, loving master with the sweetness of the greatest *caritas*, yet to him he granted this distinguishing name that showed a more familiar affection, that he should be called the disciple whom Jesus loved. (III.110)[28]

These passages are replete with reminiscences of Ambrose's *De officiis* and the language of the Song of Songs.[29] As a Cistercian Aelred would naturally employ the Song's phraseology for love between Christ and his beloved disciple. From there it was an easy step to apply it also to the related inter-human love 'in God' that is spiritual friendship. Moreover, during this period the new movement of romantic love was adopting Cicero's friendship-language, which spiritual writers then promptly 'spiritualized'.[30]

Having established that the enjoyment of close friendship in this life is permissible and good, Aelred briefly considers its conduct. We must enjoy our friends 'in the Lord', in joyfulness of spirit, in wisdom, justice, and sanctification (1 Cor. 1.30). Wisdom excludes the pursuit of worldly vanities and falsehoods. Holiness excludes fleshly impurity, imparting the sweetness of chastity so that 'each one may know how to possess his vessel, that is, his own body, in sanctification and honour, not in the passion of desire' (III.112). Justice prevents adulation and flattery, grounding the friends' enjoyment of one another firmly on truth, enabling them to 'correct one another in the spirit of freedom, knowing that the wounds of a friend are better than the fraudulent kisses of an enemy' (III.111–112).[31] Spiritual friends should converse on Scripture and other morally serious topics, share their griefs, rejoice in future hope, and find mutual strength through confiding their deepest thoughts and sharing their longing for the blissful vision of Jesus. Even recreation times should be full of what is genuine, and devoid of mere levity, so that the standards of the friendship are honoured (III.112).

Spiritual Friendship: De spiritali amicitia

Aelred mulled over this topic as the years passed, asking himself what rules should govern friendship among monks? His dialogue on *Spiritual Friendship*, now his best known work, was completed late in life, not before the year 1160. Partly a transposition of Cicero, partly freshly conceived from Scripture and tradition, it sets friendship in the context of Aelred's Christian world-view, incorporating it into the spiritual life of those journeying towards God.[32] Here is 'the systematic treatise on Christian friendship which the Fathers . . . had failed to provide'.[33]

Aelred tells us about his sources. When he was a boy, he recalls in Augustinian style, nothing seemed nicer, better, or more confusing than 'to be loved and to love'. He had come across Cicero's book and was delighted to find a guide through the uncertainties of adolescent emotion and a 'formula' by which to recognize real friendship. After becoming a monk he was surprised to discover how much less attractive the book became, because it lacked the sweetness of the name of Jesus and the salt of Scripture; but its ideas still seemed good, and could perhaps be supported from Scripture. Besides, Aelred was now aware of 'many things' on friendship in the writings of the holy fathers. He too, then, decided to write on 'spiritual friendship and to draw up for myself rules for chaste and holy love'.[34] He will write systematically, first on friendship's nature and origin, then on its fruition and finally how and between whom it can be preserved to the end. He uses Cicero's own method, presenting his arguments in the form of a dialogue between himself and other monks, casting himself as the abbot and teacher.

He must surely have had a copy of *De amicitia* handy. If not, he must have memorized or noted it well, since Cicero's changes of subject are easily traceable in his parallel passages.[35] He seems to know Sallust's *Catilina*, and a sayings-collection attributed to Seneca.[36] Among the 'holy fathers', Ambrose, Augustine, Jerome and Gregory are all direct or indirect contributors. Aelred was well aware that he was continuing to expand Ambrose's work on Cicero: he names Ambrose and quotes him five times with at least five further allusions.[37] He falls in happily with Ambrose's optimism, sharing none of Augustine's weariness at the griefs of this world. Cassian's Sixteenth Conference is not directly evident, although Aelred surely knew it. He shares Cassian's concern for the control of anger, and had already echoed his argument that Christ's friendship with John legitimizes close monastic friendships.

Friendship's nature

The opening dialogue takes place early in Aelred's time as Abbot. It features Aelred and Ivo, probably the friend for whom he wrote a meditation on 'Jesus at the age of Twelve'. The scene is at Wardon in Bedfordshire, a daughter house of Rievaulx. Aelred greets Ivo, setting the context of Christian friendship: 'Here we are, you and I, and I hope a third, Christ, is in our midst' (I.1). As teacher and spiritual father he invites Ivo to 'open your heart . . . speak freely . . . and entrust to your friend all your cares and thoughts, that you may both learn and teach, give and receive, pour out and drink in' (I.1, 4). Ivo asks to be taught about 'spiritual friendship' (I.5). He assumes it should exist among monks and seeks to understand how it 'begins in Christ, is preserved according to the Spirit of Christ, and how its end and fruition are referred to Christ' (I.8).

Aelred suggests they adopt Cicero's formula to be their initial working definition: 'friendship is mutual harmony (*consensio*) in affairs human and divine, coupled with benevolence and charity (*caritas*)' (*De am.* 20; I.11).[38] What could '*caritas*' have meant to Cicero? Perhaps it signified a feeling or inclination (*affectus*) and *benevolentia* meant acting on it, while it is the *consensio* itself that is 'dear' (*cara*) to both friends.[39] Ivo concurs that this formula gives some notion of friendship – but it applies to all, even to pagans and bad Christians, and he thinks 'true friendship cannot exist among those who live without Christ' (I.16). So the effort at definition continues. 'Friend' (*amicus*) and 'friendship' (*amicitia*) derive from love, *amor*, an "affection" (*affectus*) of the rational soul whereby it seeks and eagerly strives after some object to possess it and enjoy it' (I.19). A friend is a 'guardian' of love and even of our soul, understanding it intimately, enduring and healing its faults (I.20).[40] Friendship is 'that virtue by which spirits are bound by ties of love and sweetness, and out of many are made one'. Even philosophers ranked friendship 'with the virtues which are eternal'. (I.21).[41] Scripture confirms that 'he that is a friend loves at all times' (Prov. 17.17) or as Jerome says, 'A friendship which can cease to be was never true friendship'.[42] 'Although he be accused unjustly, though he be injured, though he be cast in the flames, though he be crucified,' Aelred repeats, ' "he that is a friend loves at all times" ' (I.21–4).[43]

Ivo finds it unsurprising, given such high standards, if Cicero found '"scarcely three or four pairs of friends"' in history (I.25; *De am.* 15). Aelred reminds him the whole context has changed:

> Indeed, the Christian ought not to despair of acquiring any virtue, since daily the divine voice from the Gospel re-echoes: 'Ask, and you shall receive ...'. It is no wonder, then, that pursuers of true virtue were rare among the pagans since they did not know the Lord, the Dispenser of virtue. (I.27; Mt. 7.7; Jn 16.24)

Among the early Christians, persecution revealed 'thousands of pairs of friends' willing to die for one another, just as Christ foretold when he said: 'Greater love has no one than this ...' (Jn 15.13; I.28–30). The first Christians were also 'strong in the virtue of true friendship' when all who believed had one heart and mind, and no one said anything was his own but all things were in common (Acts 4.32). Here indeed is the most complete agreement in matters human and divine (I.28–9).

In that case, asks Ivo, is there no difference between *caritas* and friendship? (I.31). Aelred says there is a great difference in that 'the law of *caritas*' compels us to embrace with love both our friends and enemies, while friends are those bound to us by reciprocal trust, in whom we have no fear of confiding. Many more are therefore to be received into *caritas* than into friendship (I.32).

How does 'spiritual' friendship differ from that of worldly individuals who are united, most pleasantly as they believe, by agreement in mild forms of vice? (I.33). Aelred repeats the commonplace argument:

> he does not love his fellow-man who loves iniquity. 'For he that loves iniquity' does not love, but 'hates his own soul'. Truly, he who does not love his own soul will not be able to love the soul of another. (I.35; Ps. 10.6, Vulg.)

Nevertheless, their friendships still deserve the name because the friendly affection they feel bears some similarity to that felt by true friends (I.37) – the relatedness of things through closeness or partial similarity is one of Aelred's recurrent themes. It is therefore possible to define a range of 'friendships': carnal, worldly, and spiritual (I.38). This threefold scheme is an original one, taking up Augustine's division of love into *caritas* and *cupiditas* and the subdivision of the latter into 'carnal' and 'worldly' desires.[44]

'Carnal friendship' derives from an inclination led in all directions by the lust of the ears and eyes, bringing images of beautiful bodies and pleasurable objects into the mind. Friendship grounded in such things is a thoughtless agreement in pursuit of vice, momentarily enjoyable but completely unstable (I.39–41). Carnal friends, inappropriately applying the rule that friends should 'will and refuse the same things', involve one another in crime (I.40, 48).[45] Aelred has young Augustine's pear tree in mind. Such friendships are immature, superficial, but redeemable.[46] There are truly evil relationships but 'Of this type I refrain from speaking, since . . . it is not to be considered even worthy of the name of friendship' (II.59). 'Worldly friendship' is typified by the fair-weather friend (Sir. 6.8), it desires possessions and temporal advantage and is riddled with intrigue. Nevertheless, by agreeing in human matters such friends attain part of what constitutes true friendship (I.42–4). But true friendship itself is 'spiritual':

> For spiritual friendship, which we call true, should be desired, not for consideration of any worldly advantage or for any extrinsic cause, but from the dignity of its own nature and the feelings of the human heart, so that its fruition (*fructus*, fruit) and reward is nothing other than itself . . . true friendship advances by perfecting itself, and the fruit is derived from feeling the sweetness of that perfection. (I.45–6, cf. *De am.* 31)

Cicero's '*fructus*', 'fruit', links neatly in Aelred's mind with the 'fruit' of discipleship which consists in loving one another (Jn 15.16).

Spiritual friendship, then, is similarity in life, morals and interests among the good, a true '*consensio*' in things human and divine with goodwill and *caritas* (I.46). Cicero's definition therefore stands, if we take *caritas* to be the orientation of the will and love towards God so that all vice is excluded, and *benevolentia* as a loving feeling (*sensus amandi*) sweetly aroused interiorly (I.47). The two Ciceronian terms seem almost to have exchanged their meanings. Spiritual friends also 'will and refuse the same things' in the best sense, willing nothing unbecoming and rejecting nothing truly useful (I.48); and they exercise all the cardinal virtues: 'Surely, such friendship prudence directs, justice rules, fortitude guards, and temperance moderates' (I.49).

Friendship's origin

Friendship originates in the nature of God, who 'has willed . . . that peace encompass all his creatures and society unite them; and thus all creatures obtain from him, who is supremely and purely one (*unus*), some trace of that unity'. Even inanimate creatures such as trees and pebbles – the beautiful Rievaulx valley and its river immediately come to mind – each exist in 'a certain society with its own kind', animals enjoy companionable 'friendship' and the 'charity of friendship' prevents envy and dissension between the many orders of angels while love (*amor*) produces the same will and desire among them (I.53–6).

Genesis 1–2 tells of original friendship among humans; and Aelred insists in a remarkably un-Augustinian manner on equality between male and female:

> Finally, when God created man, in order to commend more highly the good of society, he said: 'It is not good for man to be alone: let us make him a helper like unto himself.' It was from no similar, nor even from the same, material that divine Might formed this help mate, but as a clearer inspiration to charity and friendship he produced the woman from the very substance of the man. How beautiful it is that the second human being was taken from the side (*de latere*) of the first, so that nature might teach that human beings are equal and, as it were, collateral (*quasi collaterales*), and that there is in human affairs neither a superior nor an inferior, a characteristic of true friendship. (I.57)[47]

Friendship is humankind's intended, natural human condition; but at the Fall *caritas* cooled and *cupiditas* crept in, elevating private above common good. Cupidity 'corrupted the splendor of friendship and charity through avarice and envy, introducing contentions and emulations, hates and suspicions' (I.58).

> From that time the good distinguished between charity (*caritas*) and friendship, observing that love (*dilectio*) ought to be extended even to the hostile and perverse, while no union of will and ideas can exist between the good and the wicked. And so friendship which, like charity, was first preserved among all by all, remained according to the natural law among the few good. They saw the sacred laws of faith and society violated by many and bound themselves together by a closer bond of love and friendship. In the midst of the evils which they saw and felt, they rested in the joy (*gratia*) of mutual charity. (I.59)

Reason, still present in fallen human nature, keeps alive the basic impulse towards friendship and society, thus even the wicked recognize their need for others to give them pleasure and praise. Friendship is a natural desire, experience strengthens it, and after the Fall law confirms and orders it (I.60–1; cf. 51).

'*Deus amicitia est*'

Aelred might have used various logical pathways to reach his much-quoted variant on 1 Jn 4.16: '*Deus amicitia est*' (I.69). The route he chose is not one that a modern reader would expect. His intention was to demonstrate the divine nature of the virtue of friendship, and he does this by showing its similarity to wisdom. Cicero had said that nothing better than friendship, except for wisdom, has been given us by the gods (*De am.* 20). Aelred says friendship is like the other excellences with which we are, at least in potentiality, endowed: 'friendship is natural, like virtue, wisdom, and the like, which should be sought after and preserved for their own sake as natural goods'. (I.61). Virtues can differ in greatness, for example 'widowhood is near to virginity, conjugal chastity to widowhood'; but friendship and wisdom are closely similar. Indeed, friendship is 'so close to or filled with wisdom that I could almost say friendship is nothing else but wisdom' (I.64–6). Aelred is actually switching his ground, from the human virtue of wisdom to Wisdom as divine attribute and ultimate source of wisdom.[48] Ivo is intrigued but needs convincing. Aelred reminds him that both friendship and wisdom are eternal, and cannot exist without *caritas*: 'Since then in friendship eternity blossoms, truth shines forth, and charity grows sweet, consider whether you ought to separate the name of wisdom from these three' (I.68). Ivo now enters into the excitement and wonders if he should say of friendship what John the friend of Jesus said of *caritas*: 'Shall I say . . . "God is friendship (*Deus amicitia est*)?" ' (I.69)

Aelred responds positively but with circumspection. Having elicited this exclamation from Ivo he reserves a degree of independence in his own persona. 'That would be unusual', he acknowledges, and it lacks scriptural authority. 'But still what is true of *caritas*, I surely do not hesitate to grant to friendship' because – as will become evident when he discusses friendship's fulfilment – 'whoever abides in friendship, abides in God, and God in them'. (I.70; cf.1 Jn 4.16).

Aelred might more simply have founded his case on the identity between the love of true friendship and *caritas*. Leclercq suggests that 'God is friendship' is true in that 'God has for each of us without exception a love that is singular, unique, particular. And we should be images of him in our friendships. If we are, we shall avoid the dangers of particularism.'[49] McEvoy comments that the 'true law of friendship' which Aelred discovered is that 'spiritual friendship is the highest created likeness of God's life: *Deus amicitia est*; that each friend is to be loved deeply and serenely in the Lord, and hence never lost in this life, nor even in death'. It is love in and with Christ, forming part of his commandment of love.[50]

Alternatively, it would be only a small step from friendship as the implanted reflection of the creator's Oneness, the binding force throughout creation, to the formulation *Deus amicitia est*. Had Aelred explored this avenue it should have led him to consider friendship within the Trinity; but his interpersonal analysis of the Trinity went only as far as Augustine's model of lover, beloved and their love could take him. He exults in the mutual love of Father and Son in the Holy Spirit who, proceeding from both, is the love between them (*Spec. car.* I.57–8). Commentators have nevertheless been keen to link this passage from the *Speculum* with 'God is Friendship'. Schilling says the impulse of friendship,

> is a trace of the unity in God, of the uncreated friendship . . . through which the Father rests in the Son and the Son in the Father, in that *caritas* and unity, consubstantial with both, which is the Holy Spirit (*Spec. car.* I.57–8). With some hesitation, – because the conservative Aelred cannot here rely directly on the authority of Holy Scripture, – but nevertheless consistently, he draws the conclusion: DEUS AMICITIA EST. (I.69)[51]

Making a similar connection, Hallier called the Trinitarian love an 'ineffable and living Friendship!' He assumes that for Aelred the impulse to friendship in human nature signifies a 'spiritual exchange between rational creatures, in the image of the continual and mysterious Trinitarian exchange'.[52] Aelred's spiritual friendship is mutual friendship *in* God which is also mutual friendship *with* God, a pattern that Hallier calls 'friendship-in-reference-to-God (*amitié-référence-à-Dieu*)' (p. 61). It is a union with Christ and a way towards God, in which Christ becomes the friends' common centre of attraction and union, their mediator and the 'place' of true friendship (p. 60). Hallier discerns this pattern in Aelred's opening words: 'Here we are, you and I, and I hope a third, Christ, is in our midst' (I.1), which he suggests allude to the kind of trinitarian conception of friendship that Richard of St-Victor was elaborating. Christ, present in every spiritual friendship, is the 'model, in his union with the Father, of the intimacy which must reign between friends.' (p. 61).

Richard of St-Victor (d. 1173), a contemporary of Aelred, went much further in exploring the mysterious interaction of all three Persons. Probably born in Scotland, he became Prior of the Augustinian Abbey of St-Victor in Paris and a scholastic contemplative. His *De Trinitate* seeks to demonstrate, from the nature of perfect love, why God should be three Persons. God has all perfection, therefore he has *caritas*, the greatest and most pleasing of all things. But 'no one is properly said to have charity on the basis of his own private love of himself . . . Therefore, where a plurality of persons is lacking, charity cannot exist' (III.ii).[53] Love requires at least two partners. God loves creation, but so as not to be 'disordered' God's ultimate and perfect love must have a divine object, worthy of itself (ii). It is inherent in love 'to wish to be loved much by the one whom you love much'; God's happiness therefore requires mutual love between the divine persons (iii). Supremely excellent mutual love, however, positively wishes that another, or others, should also experience the joy it knows through loving and being loved by its partner: 'Thus you see how the perfection of charity requires a Trinity of persons' (xi).

Richard does not use the word 'friendship' here but does characterize the truly loving person as a 'true friend' (xii, xiii).[54] He furnishes us with a theology of friendship in the deeply Christian sense that he shows how divine love transcends the classical dyadic model of friendship. He coins a neologism, 'love-together' *condilectio* (xix), to speak of this widened love. Aelred's understanding of the friendship that unites us with God and one another in eternal life could well be characterized by a similar neologism, 'friendship-together', *co-amicitia*. Aelred's mainly practical theology of friendship, and Richard's speculative theology of Trinitarian love, vitally complement one another.

Richard's speculations found little favour in the Middle Ages, although one later Paris scholastic, Henry of Ghent (d. 1293), took up his thesis as part of his discussion of human friendship as a virtue: friendship is perfected in the '*condilectio*' of love between at least three persons, and it can continue to exist as virtue in a good friend even when the relationship is destroyed by the badness of the other.[55] More recently Richard's 'elaboration of the themes of interpersonal relations and of human love as self-transcendence' have found a much more sympathetic audience.[56]

Friendship's greatness and fulfilment

Aelred resumes his dialogue after a break lasting many years. Ivo has died and the new conversation takes place at Rievaulx between Aelred and two monks, his irascible friend, secretary and biographer-to-be Walter Daniel, and Gratian. Aelred's original draft of *De spiritaliamicitia* had just been rediscovered, exciting Walter's interest (II.6).[57]

Walter enquires what practical advantage (*utilitas*) accrues from friendship? What is its final goal and fulfilment (*fructus*)? (II.8). Aelred responds that it bears fruit now as well as in eternity (II.9). It builds up all the virtues, confounds vice, moderates adversity, and enables the sharing of joys and inspirations. Without it, joy could scarcely exist on earth. But what security and happiness are found in a friend,

> someone to whom you dare speak on terms of equality as to another self; one to whom you need have no fear to confess your failings; one to whom you can unblushingly make known what progress you have made in the spiritual life; one to whom you can entrust all the secrets of your heart and before whom you can place all your plans! What, therefore, is more pleasant than so to unite to oneself the spirit of another and of two to form one, that no boasting is thereafter to be feared, no suspicion to be dreaded, no correction of one by the other to cause pain, no praise on the part of one to bring a charge of adulation from the other. (II.11)

Such friends are indeed 'the medicine of life', bearing 'one another's burdens' (II.13; Sir. 6.16, Gal. 6.2). Aelred adds further eulogies from Cicero (*De am.* 22–3). Then he makes his own distinctive claim:

> And, a thing even more excellent than all these considerations, friendship is a stage (*gradus*) bordering upon (*vicinus*) that perfection which consists in the love and

> knowledge of God, so that a man from being a friend of his fellow-man becomes the friend of God, according to the words of our Savior in the Gospel: 'I will not now call you servants, but my friends.' (II.14; Jn 15.15)

Even in an age when great interest was taken in analysing the stages of spiritual progress, Aelred was apparently unique in teaching that true friendship can be the highest stage leading to perfection (II.15), 'a stage toward the love and knowledge of God' (II.18), although as Dumont points out, 'This is quite in line with Cistercian spirituality, in which . . . the second degree, the love of others, opens the heart to the love of God'.[58]

Aelred's argument rests on the similarity between the experiences of spiritual and divine friendship, their being so close or neighbouring (*vicinus*) to one another that one easily leads to the other. This assumes the possibility of a real flowering of reciprocal love 'in the Lord' in the present life. Whereas in perfect charity we extend genuine, willing and holy love to many, even those who are burdensome and painful, it is the glory of friendship that trust, pleasure and joy are added to that same love (II.18–19). Friendship combines integrity and joy, pleasure and goodwill, inclination and action, all originating from, continued through, and coming to perfection in Christ (II.20).

> Therefore, not too steep or unnatural does the ascent appear from Christ, as the inspiration of the love by which we love our friend, to Christ giving himself to us as our Friend for us to love, so that charm may follow upon charm, sweetness upon sweetness and affection upon affection. And thus, friend cleaving to friend in the spirit of Christ, is made with Christ but one heart and one soul, and so mounting aloft through degrees of love to friendship with Christ, he is made one spirit with him in one kiss. Aspiring to this kiss the saintly soul cries out: 'Let him kiss me with the kiss of his mouth'. (II.20–1)

'Let him kiss me . . .' is the opening verse of the Song of Songs. Kisses induce a pleasant sense of union, commingling the breath on which life depends (II.22–3). Aelred elaborates a threefold explanation. 'The corporeal kiss is made by the impression of the lips; the spiritual kiss by the union of spirits; the intellectual kiss through the Spirit of God, by the infusion of grace.' (II.24)[59]

The bodily kiss, a natural good, is rightly given and received as a sign of reconciliation, at the Peace before Communion, between married persons, as a special greeting after a friend's long absence, or to greet a guest. But as 'every honorable person knows', its lustful use must be avoided (II.24). The 'spiritual kiss' unites friends by affection of heart, 'by a mingling of spirits, by the purification of all things in the Spirit of God', because of whom it already has a 'celestial savor' (II.26). It is not far from the 'intellectual' kiss except that Christ offers it by another's mouth, thus uniting friends 'so that it seems to them as if there were one spirit in many bodies. And they may say with the Prophet: "Behold how good and how pleasant it is for brethren to dwell together in unity"' (Ps. 132/3; II.26). The 'intellectual kiss' is the kiss of grace, the unmediated contemplative knowledge of God, for which the soul, realizing that Christ has been the origin of 'all this sweetness', now longs:

> So that now, after all earthly affections have been tempered, and all thoughts and desires which savor of the world have been quieted, the soul takes delight in the kiss of Christ alone and rests in his embrace, exulting and exclaiming: 'His left hand is under my head and his right hand shall embrace me' (Song 2.6). (II.27)

All this is rather startling to Gratian who remarks this is not how friendship is commonly understood. He had thought of it as identity of will, and mutual sharing and harmony, but no more. Walter enthuses that it was the very exaltation of friendship in the first dialogue that had inspired him to enquire more deeply. He wishes to know more about the ideal of friendship and how to put it into practice.

The ideal and limits of friendship

Christ himself, Aelred reminds them, set the bounds of friendship when he said, 'No one has greater love than this, to lay down one's life for one's friends' (Jn 15.13). Loyalty unto death is one criterion of true friendship. It is not, however, proof of it, since the wicked too may die for one another to serve an evil cause (II.33–6). Once again we find a discussion on friendship turning to the vexed question of integrity amid competing loyalties.

What obligations take precedence over a friend's demands? Aelred has none of Cicero's tolerance of peccadilloes. If friendship 'springs from an esteem for virtue' then its bounds are those normally binding on Christians, 'faith (*fides*) and uprightness (*honestas*)' (II.39). 'For it is not excuse for sin, that you sin for the sake of a friend' (II.38–40).[60] 'What, then,' Gratian asks, 'has friendship to do with us, who are not good?' (II.42). Like Cicero, Aelred assures him goodness can exist without absolute perfection: 'We call a man "good" who, according to the limits of our mortality, "living soberly and justly and godly in this world" (Tit. 2.12) is resolved neither to ask others to do wrong nor to do any wrong himself at others' request' (II.43).[61] But in response to the Ciceronian suggestion that one may do anything that pleases a friend provided one's country and neighbours do not suffer, Aelred considers it insane to protect the honour of others while besmirching one's own (II.44).

When Walter suggests we should have the same regard for our friend as for our self, Aelred responds that we should have a low regard for our self and a high regard for our friend. Cicero's motivation for holding our friend in higher esteem was that we frequently have less esteem for ourselves than we should (*De am.* 59); but Aelred seems to have humility in mind. It also reflects the new Christian context when Aelred dismisses the suggestion that friendship is simply the mutual return of services, not for Cicero's reason that it reduces friendship to a matter of accounting (*De am.* 58) but because duties and services must in any case be shared in common among those who are called to be 'of one heart and soul' (II.67).[62]

Walter brings up the difficulty that friendship is full of anxieties, fears and griefs (II.45). Should we not then avoid it altogether, or at least treat it as expendable, entailing no binding commitment? Aelred adopts Cicero's reply. ' "They seem", he says, "to take the sun out of the world who take friendship out of life, for we have nothing better from God, nothing more pleasant" ' (II.49). Like all commitment to virtue, it involves difficulty but is not to be shirked on that account, indeed it is less than human not to wish to love and be loved, to rejoice in others and entrust oneself to them (II.52).[63] Look at Paul's pastoral love, which as Aelred describes it has the shape of friendship: 'Paul must have been a fool, for he was unwilling to live without care and solicitude for others; but for the sake of charity which he believed to be the sovereign virtue, he was weak with the weak, on fire with the scandalized' (II.50; 2 Cor. 11.28). The implication is clear: if friendship is love's fulfilment, to avoid it is to reject love itself.

'Spiritual' friendships have their own bounds and expectations setting them apart from 'carnal' and 'worldly' friendships. 'Puerile' or immature friendship is normal in youth, but is carnal, a pleasant inclination as yet unmodified by reason, unable to discern what is licit and illicit and inclining to the latter (II.57). Some feeling of pleasant inclination usually precedes friendship, but 'ought never to be followed unless reason lead it, honor (*honestas*) temper it, and justice (*iustitia*) rule it' (II.57). If that is not the case the feeling will be unstable and poisonous to true friendship since 'the proper bounds of love, which extend from soul to soul' are liable to be transgressed: 'it rises from carnal desires and draws one to them, neglecting the spirit' (II.58). Right from the beginning, spiritual friendship must observe the bounds of purity of intent, discernment, rule by reason, and restraint by moderation. Then it will be rightly directed and emotionally satisfying (II.59).

'Worldly' friendship looks for advantage, thus excluding many worthy of love who, possessing nothing, can offer no temporal reward (II.60). Rewards certainly attend on spiritual friendship, but its motive lies in its own intrinsic value. 'For he has not yet learned what friendship is who wishes any reward other than itself' (II.61).[64] For Aelred and his friends its inherent reward lies in its closeness to the contemplative love of God:

'Such a reward friendship will certainly be for those cultivating it when, wholly translated to God, it immerses in the divine contemplation those whom it has united' (II.61).

Nothing less than the life of the body should be denied to a friend. We may die for them, but we may not put our soul in danger: we may not sin, not even for a friend (II.69).

The development of a spiritual friendship

The final dialogue, on the following day, outlines the actual development of a spiritual friendship, taking its model from Aelred's experience in the monastic setting and, of course, schematizing the process.

Such a friendship begins 'when he, whom reason urges should be loved because of the excellence of his virtue, steals into the soul of another by the mildness of his character and the charm of a praiseworthy life' (III.3). This spiritual love rests on the foundation of love of God, to which everything must be 'referred' and must conform (III.5). The formation of a friendship then passes through four stages or steps: choice (*electio*), testing (*probatio*), admission (*admissio*), and finally 'the greatest agreement (*summa consensio*) in things divine and human, with a certain *caritas* and goodwill' (III.8; cf. *De am.* 20).

Not all whom we love are worthy to be chosen as friends, that is, not all are likely to become:

> the companion of your soul, to whose spirit you join and attach yours, and so associate yourself that you wish to become one instead of two, since he is one to whom you entrust yourself as to another self, from whom you hide nothing, from whom you fear nothing. (III.6)[65]

The evil, avaricious, ambitious or slanderous cannot be chosen (III.59), but Aelred's discussion of 'choice' does evince a flexibility coming from his Christian understanding of forgiveness and repentance and specifically from his experience of monastic life with its emphasis on patience and its trust in grace to transform individuals. There is a range of lesser faults which although difficult, may be patiently borne and may even admit of cure through gentle remonstration. Hence, although 'the quarrelsome, the irascible, the fickle, the suspicious, and the loquacious' are not normally to be chosen, one may still choose them if they show a desire to 'regulate or restrain these passions' (III.55; 14–20). Aelred quotes Scripture on the disruptive effects of anger but shows from a current friendship in his own life, which Walter and Gratian have observed with interest and incredulity, that it is possible to bear with an irascible friend and encourage them to practise restraint (III.15–17).[66]

Scripture assures us that reconciliation is possible, even if a sword is drawn against us. There are however five vices which are likely to chase a friend away: 'upbraiding, reproach, pride, disclosing of secrets, or a treacherous wound' (III.22).[67] While slander and scorn are hard to bear, Aelred reflects that the effects of pride are most serious because it 'excludes the remedy of humility and admission of guilt by which alone the broken friendship could have been healed' (III.24). These faults are to be expunged in ourselves: 'if we chance to have failed in the law of friendship toward anyone, let us shun pride and seek to win back the favor of our friend by some humble service' (III.26).

The unfaithful and suspicious are by definition to be avoided, since 'a great fruit of friendship is the security whereby you entrust and commit yourself to a friend', as is the 'mutual peace and tranquillity of heart which the suspicious man never knows' (III.28–9 cf. *De am.* 62). Garrulity too offends against trust and gravitas (III.30).

Positively, we should choose someone with whom we harmonize. ' "Indeed, among dissimilar characters," as blessed Ambrose remarks, "friendship cannot exist; therefore, the grace of each ought to be mutually consonant." ' (III.30; Amb. *De off.* III.133). Each friend must take the spiritual life seriously and have a real commitment to grow in *caritas*. Friendship is most secure among those 'who suppress anger with patience, restrain levity by preserving gravity, drive out suspicions by the contemplation of love' (III.32).[68] Union is then possible: 'between perfect friends ... who have been wisely chosen and prudently tested and are united by a genuinely spiritual friendship, no disagreements can possibly arise' (III.49).

What if our choice turns out to be mistaken, or a friend's character changes for the worse so that harm threatens their partner or others? 'What sort of loyalty (*fides*) ought then to be preserved toward them and what sort of favor (*gratia*) ought to be shown them?' Aelred's first concern is for amendment of life; but should correction prove impossible then the friendship must, as Cicero advises, be disengaged gradually and as amicably as possible, or in the case of a gross fault severed immediately (III.39–41).[69]

Aelred comes nearest to characterizing Christian love as the love of friendship when he discusses how to behave after the dissolution of a relationship. Cicero said the wronged friend should honour the former friendship by refusing to do wrong in return.[70] For Aelred there is more: the love of a friend does not cease. 'Friendship, indeed, is eternal; hence: "He that is a friend loves at all times." ' (Prov. 17.17; III.44). Love must continue, even when wounded. A friend's conduct 'may compel the withdrawal of friendship (*amicitia*, in its complete sense of intimacy and trust), 'but never of love (*dilectio*)' (III.44). Complete friendship seems to consist in four elements: love, affection, security and enjoyment:

> Love (*dilectio*) implies the rendering of services with benevolence, affection, an inward pleasure that manifests itself exteriorly; security, a revelation of all counsels and confidences without fear and suspicion; enjoyment, a pleasing and friendly sharing of all events which occur, of all thoughts, whether harmful or useful, of everything taught or learned. (III.51)

If the last three are dissolved, love still remains. It is still the same love as when friendship was complete, so in this sense friendship itself does continue:

> a friendship is the more laudable, and gives the greater proof of being a virtue, in proportion as the friend who has been wronged preserves it undiminished, loving him by whom he is no longer loved, honoring him by whom he is scorned, blessing him by whom he is cursed, and doing good to him who plots evil against him. (III.49, cf. Mt. 5.44; Rom. 12.14–21)

If love remains, 'some traces *(vestigia)* of the former friendship always seem to remain' (III.52). Although his emphasis has lain so much on *amicitia* as the fruition of *caritas*, Aelred is surprisingly adamant that friendship in the sense of the love of a friend should persist even when there is no immediate expectation of reciprocity or fruition. This conviction derives entirely from his Christian understanding of divine love, love that is constant, universal and personal. He might have found a conceptual distinction between 'friendship' and 'friendship-love' of use here.

After choice comes testing. We tend not to think about it in a formal manner, but in reality life continually 'tests' friendship. Aelred aims to test for faithfulness, motivation, discernment and patience.

Faithfulness (*fides*) enables trust and so is friendship's 'nurse and guardian' (III.62); it will be proved in real adversity but can be tested in small matters. Whoever ' "is faithful in that which is little, will be faithful in that which is great" ' (Lk. 16.10; III.65). Motivation should come solely from the search for God and for the inherent good in friendship (III.61).[71] Christ's command to ' "love your neighbor as yourself" ' coheres with Cicero's statement that love for friends is like love for self. We are naturally dear to ourselves, and love for another means transferring that same free affection to them (III.69).[72] Just as Ambrose said, friendship is virtue and seeks no reward. Therefore, test to see whether your new friend seems to want you, or your possessions (III.71).[73]

Discernment (*discretio*) shows itself as sensitivity, understanding, acting in appropriate and positive ways with thoughtfulness and wisdom, and the ability to correct a friend helpfully. These qualities should be sought in our potential friend, together with the patience to receive rebukes without resentment and to suffer difficulties for a friend's sake. The opportunities for testing patience are endless! (III.61, 73).

With Cicero and Xenophon, Aelred regards the choice and testing of friends as essential. He differs from his philosophical forebears in adding: 'do not withdraw immediately from your proposed love or choice, as long as any hope of correction appears' (III.74). If testing goes well, goodwill and affection may gradually be given freer rein until we completely commit ourselves to our chosen friend.

Walter is now feeling daunted, and wonders whether life might be easier without friends of this sort. Aelred reminds him how closely happiness is linked to friendship. No matter how great our riches, our enjoyment of them is contingent on sharing them with someone we love. The more friends we have, the more our happiness must increase. Our vision of happiness is one of eternal mutual love. We await the time when God will spread abroad on all,

> so much friendship and charity, that thus each loves the other as he loves himself: and thus the happiness of each one individually is the happiness of all, and the universality of happiness is the possession of each individual . . . This is true and eternal friendship, which begins in this life and is perfected in the next, which here belongs to the few where few are good, but there belongs to all where all are good. (III.79–80)

Walking round the cloister at Rievaulx, Aelred has felt as if already in paradise: 'I found no one whom I did not love, and no one by whom, I felt sure, I was not loved', and overcome with the sense of oneness, 'I could say with the Prophet: "Behold, how good and how pleasant it is for brethren to dwell together in unity."' (Ps. 132/3.1; III.82). But again Aelred insists this does not mean every monk in the community has now been taken into his friendship. Friendship 'consists especially in the revelation of all our confidences and plans'. He quotes Ambrose's formula, '"that we do the will of our friend, that we disclose to our friend whatever confidences we have in our hearts, and that we be not ignorant of his confidences."' (III.83).[74] As an abbot, confidentiality would be vital for him. We love many 'before whom it would be imprudent to lay bare our souls and pour out our inner hearts! Men whose age or feeling or discretion is not sufficient to bear such revelations' (III.84).

Walter still demurs. 'This friendship is so sublime and perfect that I dare not aspire to it' (III.85). Isn't it sufficient for him and Gratian simply to enjoy one another's company and conversation – which is affectionate banter rather than profound sharing – enjoying each other's presence and so returning love for love? That is the friendship 'which your Augustine describes' (III.85–6).[75] Yes, says Aelred, but Augustine's youthful companionships were at best *amicitia puerilis*, carnal friendship rather than spiritual. That is acceptable as an adolescent beginning, but can and should lead to deeper friendship as grace and spiritual illumination increase, so that the friends 'mount to loftier heights from, as it were, a region close by (*vicino*), just as yesterday we said that the friendship of man could be easily translated into a friendship for God himself because of the similarity (*similitudo*) existing between both' (III.87).

When agreement (*consensio*) has been established, friendship flourishes in loyalty, openness and cheerfulness (III.88–9); the superiors make themselves equal to the inferior (III.90–7); and friends assist one another in every honourable way without waiting to be asked (III.97–102), giving correction lovingly (III.102–8).

As abbot, Aelred experienced the difficulties attendant on promoting his friends to office. He reflects on Jesus giving Peter the keys of his kingdom, while 'to John he revealed the secrets of his heart'. (III.117). Both cases demonstrate true friendship. We too, then, should both love, and be prepared to place burdens of office upon, our friends. In well-ordered friendship, reason takes precedence over feeling and appointments are made in accordance with the needs of the many, not just to please the friend (III.118).

He reminisces about two of his own friendships that had ended only with the other's death. The first friend is presumably Simon whom he lamented in the *Speculum* (*Spec. car.* I.98–114). The second was a much younger person whom he brought to Rievaulx from abroad before becoming abbot, eventually making him sub-prior and his complete confidant (III.119–27). This friendship had time to mature, and of it he writes:

> Was it not a foretaste of blessedness (*quaedam beatitudinis portio*) thus to love and thus to be loved, thus to help and thus to be helped; and in this way from the sweetness of fraternal charity to wing one's flight aloft to that more sublime splendor of divine love, and by the ladder of charity (*scala caritatis*) now to mount to the embrace of Christ himself; and again to descend to the love of neighbor, there pleasantly to rest? And so, in this friendship of ours, which we have introduced by way of example, if you see aught worthy of imitation, profit by it to advance your own perfection. (III.127)

Aelred recaps his whole argument. Friendship is founded on love. In order to love another as oneself it is first necessary to love oneself, 'allowing nothing which is unbecoming and refusing nothing which is profitable'. The same discipline is then applied to love of neighbour, which embraces many. Then we choose one whom we can 'admit in familiar fashion to the mysteries of friendship' in affection and openness (III.129). When they are fully tried and known 'you will experience that spiritual delight, namely, "how good and how pleasant it is for brethren to dwell together in unity" ' (III.131).[76] The advantages of sharing and bearing one another's burdens (III.132), are crowned by that of prayer 'which, coming from a friend, is the more efficacious in proportion as it is more lovingly sent to God' (III.133). Contemplative intercession for friends brings us, too, the touch of Christ's love:

> And thus a friend praying to Christ on behalf of his friend . . . directs his attention with love and longing to Christ; then it sometimes happens that quickly and imperceptibly the one love passes over into the other, and coming, as it were, into close contact with the sweetness of Christ himself, the friend begins to taste his sweetness and to experience his charm. Thus ascending from that holy love with which he embraces a friend to that with which he embraces Christ, he will joyfully partake in abundance of the spiritual fruit of friendship, awaiting the fullness of all things in the life to come. (III.133–4)

The life to come will be that universal friendship intended before the Fall: when all divisions of fear, enmity, and death are abolished, we enter into eternal rejoicing in the highest Good, and 'this friendship, to which here we admit but few, will be outpoured upon all and by all outpoured upon God, and God shall be all in all' (1 Cor. 15.28; III.134).

Aelred's teaching and significance

Writing on love flowered among twelfth-century Cistercians, springing fresh out of their experience as they gave themselves to the love of God in contemplative prayer. Aelred's reflections on friendship make a unique contribution, an experiential, practical theology of love whose originality lies in his belief that Christian life on earth should afford an experience of eternal union, not only with God in prayer but also between human beings. Christian spiritual life, including monastic life, should therefore ordinarily entail learning the wisdom of friendship. 'Spiritual friendship' also makes universal love concrete: in his doctrine of spiritual friendship, 'a true monastic discipline in his eyes, and an initiation into divine friendship', Aelred demonstrates a practical concern not to allow ourselves to be taken in by 'a love which in addressing itself to all, reaches no one'.[77] He wrote as an abbot and his teaching on the restoration of God's image and spiritual friendship 'cannot be understood unless it is studied in the setting of the monastic community and from the point of view of spiritual progress'.[78]

It can safely be said, nevertheless, that Christendom did not know how to react to a work that put the possibility of human friendship so squarely within the path of the advancing contemplative. Aelred's personal influence seems to have produced unique features in the style of monastic life at

Rievaulx and its dependent abbeys. 'Colloquies', gatherings for general conversation, were evidently taking place there in his time although the Rule made no provision for them, and a censure by the General Chapter at Cîteaux in 1152 on abbots who encourage them may have been directed at him. His interest in friendship and his provision of opportunities for it were probably seen as laxity. One reason why he was not widely followed must be that any abbot less skilled in human relations would find it easier to apply the Rule strictly than to pursue a more open policy. Close friendship was neither an expected nor intended feature of monastic life. No duties of friendship appeared in manuals of self-examination, suggesting that friendships somehow fell outside the realm of morality, or were non-existent or unreal.[79]

Aelred's affirmation ran counter to the theological trend that narrowed *caritas* to love directed to God while love of all else was secondary. A writer named Burridge who introduced Aelred to Benedictines in 1940 oddly suggested that he emphasized becoming 'detached from creatures' (p. 234), sought a perfection in which 'not an atom of love is longer spent on any other being than God' (p. 227), and sanctioned friendship only on the ground that friends assist us in our spiritual life (p. 243). These were common sentiments in monastic and even in wider spirituality prior to Vatican II but they are not those of Aelred, who like Maximus saw that the three loves of God, self and others must form an integral whole.

Aelred's optimism is grounded in theological hope. The image of God in us has not been entirely expunged and can in Christ be fully restored. Reason guides us to show *caritas* to all, and even if friendship in its full reciprocal sense is currently restricted to those whom we trust and to whom we feel attracted, still, in a world where renewal is possible, *caritas* must always in essence be potential friendship. The realization of that friendship goes hand in hand with the restoration of God's image in us: 'friendship is not, then, exclusive, but is limited by our present condition'.[80] Spiritual friendship merges with the experience of friendship with God when intercession for a friend passes into contemplation. Love and prayer for our enemies also 'makes us a friend' – of our enemies in potentiality and of God in actuality.

Martha, a special friend of Jesus, loved him through action and in one of his sermons Aelred urges us to follow her example in loving Christ now through service to those in need.[81] *Caritas* is then the broken and open arc of love with which we must reach out to all, including those, whether the immature, or enemies, or former friends, who cannot presently be invested with our full trust and confidence. It is already friendship-love in the sense of the steady practice of the willed and rational element of friendship. The source of this love is not in our will alone, but the 'love poured into our hearts through the Holy Spirit', conforming us to God's image and expressing through us God's love and delight in his creation. Hence saints may, even in this present life, be able to find all humanity attractive.

Aelred and sexuality

Any attempt to psychoanalyse a historical figure raises complex historical and cultural issues, but in recent years the question has been raised as to whether Aelred's accounts of his emotional attachments indicate a personality which in a later age might have recognized itself as homosexual. For a time during what became an intense debate, there seemed a danger that Aelred would suffer a new obscurity by being so thoroughly adopted by one section of the population as to become inaccessible to the rest.[82]

It is crucial to recognize that Aelred lived long before any kind of modern interest in the psychology and classification of sexuality. Perhaps no subject so well illustrates how near and yet how far he is from us. He could not have been a homosexual in the modern sense any more than, in a very real way, he could have been a heterosexual in the modern sense. The great dichotomy in Aelred's world was not between these categories, nor between those who had and had not established a comfortable identity within them, nor between holders of differing views on them, but between those whose orientation remained 'carnal' and those who had turned towards the 'spiritual'. Every variety of thought and activity of a physically sexual kind belonged to the realm of the carnal, and it is not in dispute that as a monk Aelred pursued an entirely traditional struggle against them.[83]

Supposing, however, that Aelred's orientation was homosexual and that this was a component in his desire to understand interpersonal love, would this imply that everything he says has relevance only for those who have the same orientation? He himself thought he was writing for all, and the answer must be that his human insight and breadth of theological vision are such that any limitation of this kind would be wholly inappropriate. As we have seen, in Aelred's understanding the original friendship was the marital friendship of the first man and woman. His conviction that solicitude for another can be integral to, not in competition with, union with Christ, and his theology of human relationship as a practical way of mutual sanctification fits marriage very well and applies to good friendships of every kind.[84] From the level of wise counsellor in personal relations – and all that he teaches is as relevant to relations between friends of different sexes as those of the same – to that of spiritual director and theologian, Aelred speaks to us all.

After Aelred

During his lifetime Aelred was well known in British political and ecclesiastical circles, but until recently he was never well known outside Britain. The Cistercians recognized him in 1250 as one of their own saints, and his shrine remained at Rievaulx until the Reformation, but he was never officially canonized. His advice to anchoresses and on imaginative meditative prayer exercised a quiet hidden influence through the Middle Ages and beyond. Hidden, because his writings were often quoted without attribution or attributed to Anselm, Bernard or even Augustine. Aelred's major works were first printed at Douai in 1616, J. H. Newman prompted his inclusion in *Lives of the English Saints* in 1845, and in the following century interest in him burgeoned.

The two books on love did not travel far. The *Speculum caritatis* hardly went outside England and the Low Countries. Clairvaux had only the *Compendium speculi caritatis*, the most notable of several abbreviations, which does reproduce in full the passage on friendship as fruition of love in this life.[85] Complete texts of the *De spiritali amicitia* had a similar distribution.[86] Five abbreviated versions appeared, one of which, the 'Book on Friendship' (*Liber de amicitia*) was attributed to Augustine and printed with his works in Paris in 1555. Meanwhile, about 1190, a sentimental plagiarism of Aelred's two works on love was compiled by Peter of Blois. This 'On Christian Friendship and the Love of God' (*De amicitia christiana et de dilectione Dei*) was printed under Peter's name in 1519. Its first part also became attributed to Cassiodorus, being printed in his works in 1577.[87]

The varied uses to which the *De spiritali amicitia* was put testify to its unique value as the hitherto missing Christian text on friendship. But it is notable that while Aelred achieved considerable success in setting personal relationships within a coherent theology and spirituality, his adaptors largely missed this fact, treating him almost entirely as a practical rather than theological writer. Each version does in some way incorporate Aelred's conviction that to love a friend in Christ is to be close to loving Christ himself, but his full theological scheme survives in none of them. No adaptation preserved the words '*Deus amicitia est*'. Possibly none regarded the logical steps Aelred used to reach it as worthy of repetition. Only one abbreviation, the *Dialogus*, includes Aelred's culminating vision of eternal life as restored universal friendship.

Aelred breathes an air of confidence, convinced of the significance of his subject and becoming increasingly sure in his handling of it. Yet no monastic writer after him until recent years wrote any sustained work on friendship and even on the rare occasions when they advocated its practice they did not do so in anything like the same way.[88] Only towards the mid-twentieth century did he become widely known, in a new milieu where his thinking could be welcomed and echoed.

Aelred's emphasis lay on the practice of the relationship of friendship. For Thomas Aquinas the central question becomes: what is the nature of *caritas*, Christian love?

4

Thomas Aquinas

'*Caritas* is friendship with God'

While the early Cistercians flourished in wild valleys, the cathedral schools and nascent universities of Europe saw the development of the new style of precisely argued philosophical theology which we know as scholasticism. Aelred is the practical theologian of friendship but its greatest theoretician, placing it at the heart of all Christian thought and life, is Thomas Aquinas (1225–1274), one of the most brilliant of scholastic theologians. Both were prayerful contemplatives, writing out of their lived experience of God's love in Christ.

Thomas's family held the castle at Roccasecca near Aquino, south of Rome. At the age of five he entered the nearby Benedictine school at Monte Cassino, but at university in Naples he joined the Dominicans, an order founded in 1220 to concentrate on the work of the intellect. Having studied in Paris and Cologne under Albert the Great, the order's most exciting scholar and theologian, he taught from 1252 to 1273 in Italy and in Paris, then the major university of Christendom, where he was twice professor. Tall, solidly built, with a large balding head, Thomas is described as a humble, joyful and attractive teacher with a widely retentive and creative mind. His output was vast, covering the whole range of theology in a united whole: biblical and philosophical, moral and spiritual.

Love in scholastic debate

In the thirteenth century the basic theological textbook was the '*Four Books of Opinions*' or '*Sentences*' compiled by **Peter Lombard** (*c.*1100–1159), a comprehensive collection of problems of faith with their solutions from patristic sources. While becoming a Master, a young theologian would lecture on the *Sentences*, developing his own ideas as he did so. Scholastic books invite us into a virtual lecture hall where we follow the steps of the disputation as a question is posed, arguments and counter-arguments are presented with support from Scripture, the Fathers, and occasionally philosophers; and the lecturer gives his magisterial response. In this milieu, Thomas contributed distinctively to an already well established debate on friendship and love.

Lombard mentions friendship in the context of Christ's laying down his life 'for friends and enemies, out of exceptional love'.[1] It should not, he adds, worry us that Christ said laying down one's life 'for one's friends' shows perfect love, because here 'he who lays down his life for friends, lays it down also for enemies, in order that they themselves too may become friends'.[2] In an age that showed great interest in honour and merit, Lombard agrees with Augustine that love for enemies is the most meritorious.[3] His definition of *caritas* is thoroughly Augustinian: 'the love (*dilectio*) with which God is loved on account of himself, and our neighbour on account of God or in God'.[4] Lombard also followed Augustine in identifying this love ('*amor*' or '*caritas*') with the Holy Spirit itself.[5] His successors would soon, however, distinguish love as a gift of grace, from the indwelling of the Spirit.

William of Auxerre, writing his *Summa aurea* in Paris about 1215, was among the first to record that faith, hope and love (*caritas*; 1 Cor. 13.13) were becoming recognized as the 'theological virtues', virtues solely in God's gift, which relate their recipient directly to God.[6] These supernatural virtues infused by grace came to be seen as 'superadded' to the four natural 'cardinal virtues' which we can attain by ascetic effort.

William also records another significant conceptual advance, the distinction between 'desiring-love', *amor concupiscentiae*, and 'friendship-love', *amor amicitiae*.[7] This analytical move at last enabled a clear distinction to be made between friendship-as-relationship, and friendship-love, facilitating the taking up of the love itself into philosophical and theological discussion. **Peter Abelard** (1070–1142) had recruited friendship as disinterested love through his extreme doctrine of *caritas* as love that refuses all thought of reward, which he derived from Ciceronian friendship both directly and through the prompting of **Héloïse**.[8] Thereafter, the tendency was to understand 'desiring-love' as interested, and 'friendship-love' as disinterested love. William defined '*concupiscentia*' as love for objects, such as wine, which we yearn to possess and enjoy, and '*amicitia*' as love for the persons for whom we desire good things and in whose joy we delight. He suggests that although we desire God we also love him with friendship, both by nature when we rejoice in his goodness in creation, and by grace.

Thomas's Franciscan contemporary **Bonaventure** made love triple, '*triplex*'. It is love of desire when we want something for ourselves, of friendship when we will good to someone else, and of 'delight' (*complacentia*) when we enjoy and rest in the presence of what we desire.[9] *Caritas* entails loving God with desiring-love, and our neighbour with friendship-love, wishing that they too may have the great joy of union with God. *Caritas* is thus a single act of love embracing both desiring-love directed to God and, within that all-pervading desire, friendship-love towards the other. Our final inherence in God will however embrace both desiring-love and friendship-love for God.[10]

Albert the Great, Thomas's flamboyant teacher, proposed six replies to Lombard's question 'what is *caritas*?'[11] Two are Augustinian, but the following three derive from Pseudo-Dionysius, the sixth-century Syrian mystical theologian whose scintillating thoughts were percolating more and more into Western minds. Albert quotes Dionysius' dictum that all love ('*amor*', from Dionysius' '*erōs*'), divine or created, is 'a certain unifying and commingling power', moving the superior to provide for those who have less, peer to communicate with peer, and the inferior to rise towards the better and superior (*Div. Nom.* 4.15). He continues, apparently from a commentary on Dionysius: 'love is the connection or bond by which all things are joined in unspeakable friendship and indissoluble union'; and 'love is the goal and quiet rest of the natural movement of all things that are in motion'. Paul provides Albert's final definition: 'the end of the commandment is *caritas* that comes from a pure heart, a good conscience, and sincere faith' (1 Tim. 1.5). All these definitions are, Albert asserts, correct, '*amor*' being included in '*caritas*'. He rejects the suggestion that 'virtues and the good things of life are to be loved with desiring-love, but God, self, our neighbour and our own body with friendship-love', deeming it false because we love God with enjoyment-love (*dilectio fructus*), and friendship-love is devoid of any desire for enjoyment; and besides it is inappropriate to say one loves one's own self with friendship-love, 'because friendship is a relation, requiring diversity between lover and beloved.'[12] Hence for Albert, at least during his Cologne years, *caritas* cannot be *amicitia*.

Albert remained a convinced adherent of the Abelardian view that friendship-love is radically disinterested love. His unfinished *Summa theologica* maintains there can be no true friendship-love in nature, because friendship must be oriented purely towards another but all natural love, even unfallen love when unaided by grace, is desiring-love, 'always curved towards itself', bending back what it loves to serve its own good.[13] '*Caritas* however raises the creature above itself, so that it reposes completely in the uncreated beloved who is God'. God needs nothing for himself; and by adhering in God we 'become one spirit with him' (1 Cor. 6.17).[14] Having no needs or insecurity, God freely wills good to the other. For Albert then, *caritas* is a sharing in the divine love – which turns out to be precisely the disinterested love he has defined as friendship-love. As Albert's student and then as his assistant, Thomas must have had many occasions to apply his own acute and much more systematic mind to the relationship between *caritas,* Christian love, and the love of friendship.

The question was posed urgently by the arrival in Cologne, about the year 1248, of the first complete Latin edition of Aristotle's *Nicomachean Ethics*.[15] It evidently arrived just after Albert had completed his commentary on Book III of the *Sentences*, since he did not use it in discussing Lombard's definition of *caritas*. Thomas was among the first scholastics to have that opportunity, and the only one to exploit it to the full. Meanwhile he attended Albert's lectures on the *Ethics* and was probably responsible for the notes that became Albert's *Commentary and Questions on the Ethics*. In this mainly philosophical work, *caritas* in the theological sense occurs only incidentally, thus the question: does separation in place dissolve friendship? elicits the reply 'Yes' if it is 'civic' friendship but 'No' if, as Jerome's *Prologue* to the Vulgate says, it is '*caritas*-friendship', the instantaneous, permanent, trans-spatial bond given in Christ.[16]

Albert's second, paraphrase commentary on the *Ethics* was written much later, around 1267–68. Here he enlivens Aristotle's *philia* with the Dionysian doctrine that love creates an 'ecstatic' union, the lover being 'taken out of themselves' to enter into the beloved. Thus understood, *philia* is no cool deliberate love based on accidental qualities, but 'friendship characterized by the passion of loving (*passione amationis*)' which 'transposes the heart and desire (*affectus*) of the lover into the beloved, so that each lover possesses no less in the other than in themselves'. This ecstasy is indeed a true 'agreement' (*consensio*) springing from *caritas*.[17] Albert discerns three levels of 'loving': simple loving (*amatio*) when there is a 'transposition of the heart' but the love remains blind and undirected; *dilectio* when reason guides love's passion; and *caritas* which, as love directed to a 'dear' (*carus*) or highly valued object, adds the motif of great worth. 'The beginning of the friendship we are examining here is a certain *amor*, but it proceeds in *dilectio*, and is perfected in *caritas*, which is why Cicero says ' "friendship is a certain agreement out of *caritas*." '[18] He adduces six reasons for including friendship in ethical discussion, one of which again links true friendship with *caritas*: 'Friendship tends, of its own nature, to the perfection of all good. Hence it is said, "Love (*dilectio*) is the fulfilling of the law" (Rom. 13.10), and again: "Have love (*caritas*) and do what you will".'[19] Albert still never quite defined *caritas* as *amicitia* but throughout his career, and despite his own convictions, he was dropping tantalizing hints that it might be possible to do so.

Thomas: *caritas* is friendship

Thomas was the only scholastic to define Christian love, *caritas*, fully and in every respect as friendship, *amicitia*. He developed this teaching steadily and consistently throughout his career, from his early commentary on the *Sentences* to his final *Summa theologica*. The availability of the *Nicomachean Ethics*, which compelled attention, made this development both possible and necessary. Thomas received his philosophical model of friendship from it, and quickly discerned a fundamental compatibility between Aristotle's *philia* and his own Christian understanding of love. Unlike Albert, Thomas mentions Cicero on friendship only once, and then merely to ascribe Sallust's *idem velle et nolle* (*Cat.* 20.4) wrongly to him (*ST* II–II 29.3). Thomas never cites Ambrose on this topic, and Aelred's work did not impinge on him at all.

In his mature work the key quotation with which Thomas opens his argument that *caritas* is *amicitia* is Jn 15.15; but his initial approach was made through Aristotle. In his *Commentary* or '*Scriptum*' on Lombard's *Sentences*, dating from his first lectureship in Paris in 1252–57, he outdoes his teacher by proposing seven definitions of *caritas*, culminating in his own new definition which embraces all the rest. (i) Augustine says *caritas* makes us desire to see and enjoy God, therefore it is *concupiscentia*; (ii) Dionysius says *dilectio* (*agapē*) is the same as *amor* (*erōs*); (iii) since it wills good, it is *benevolentia*; (iv) it creates unity, so is like *concordia* (1 Cor. 1.10); (v) it must be shown in action (1 Jn 3.18) hence it is well-doing (*beneficentia*); (vi) it is peace because it creates unity of spirit, which is the 'bond of peace' (Eph. 4.3); (vii) finally, it is friendship:

> It seems that *caritas* is the same as *amicitia*. Because, as the Philosopher says in *Ethics* IX, 'friendship is likened to superadundance of love'. But *caritas* has most superabundant love, which indeed is why it is called '*caritas*', inasmuch as it values the beloved at an inestimable price as though they were the dearest thing. Therefore *caritas* is the same as *amicitia*.[20]

By formally making *amicitia* a definition of *caritas*, Thomas broke new ground. It is remarkable, but fortunately not fatal to his argument, that at this crucial moment he depends on what appears to be a misquotation of Aristotle, one that he never repeats![21]

The substance of his proposal is that *caritas* and *amicitia* must be identical in that they both show the characteristics of love at its greatest. He immediately defends this innovation against five possible objections.[22] First, Aristotle says friendship is mutual love; but *caritas* extends to all, even to enemies. Thomas responds that just as when we love a human friend we love all who belong or pertain to them, even those among them who do not return love to us, so *caritas* causes us to love God principally and all people inasmuch as they belong to God. There is indeed a return of love, but that is between the principal partners in the friendship. Second, friendship is sharing of life and activity; but *caritas* is love towards God and the angels, whose 'conversation is not with men'. To this Thomas replies that inasmuch as human beings are 'made into the form of God' and perfected through *caritas*, they are raised so that their 'conversation is in heaven' with God and the angels. These first two responses would become permanent pillars of his position.

The third objection is that friendship is visible to observers, but *caritas* is supremely hidden in that one cannot be certain when grace is present. Thomas contends that friendship and *caritas* alike are recognized by signs that make the presence of love probable, rather than certain.

Fourth, according to Aristotle, friendship seeks above all to converse with and see the friend.[23] But according to Jerome in his *Prologue* to the Bible (*Ep*. 53, to Paulinus), '*caritas*-friendship (*amicitia caritatis*)' does not need this, being dependent only on unity in Christ. Thomas says true friendship does actually desire to see and delight in the friend, but not as an end in itself as in pleasure-friendship, and Jerome's point is simply that Christ and not pleasure constitutes the bond in *caritas*-friendship.

Fifth, friendship is shared only with the virtuous few; but *caritas* is love towards all, even the wicked. Thomas says friendship is principally directed to the virtuous but this does not prevent its extension, as above, to those who pertain to God our friend.

Thomas then pictures three cumulative levels of love: *amor*, *dilectio*, and *amicitia*, each of which includes the stages beneath it. *Amor* is felt in our 'senses', our lower passionate self. *Dilectio* introduces our will, our higher intellectual self. *Amor* includes *concupiscentia* which desires the beloved's presence. When rightly directed by *dilectio*, *amor* wills and pursues good, thus embracing goodwill and well-doing. Its effects are *concordia* and *pax*, and finally it reposes in the beloved. '*Amatio*' adds vehemence and intense feeling. *Amicitia* adds the mutual society of lover and beloved, who act from deliberate choice so that as Aristotle says, friendship is likened to 'habit', or virtue.[24] Friendship, therefore, embraces all definitions of love and manifests every possible aspect of it. *Caritas* must surely belong in the same perfect class:

> Friendship is the most perfect among the things pertaining to love, and it includes all the aforementioned; whence clearly *caritas* must be placed in this kind of genus, it being a certain friendship of human beings towards God, through which they love God and God loves them (*quaedam amicitia hominis ad Deum, per quam homo Deum diligit, et Deus hominem*) and thus a certain association of human beings with God is made, as in 1 Jn 1.7: 'If we walk in the light as he himself is in the light, we have fellowship (*societas*; *koinōnia*) with one another'.[25]

Thomas will consistently hold that friendship with God fulfils all the requirements of friendship as commonly defined. He usually omits the qualifying '*quaedam*', a 'certain' or 'kind of' friendship. The qualification here might indicate that this friendship with God has still to develop, and is not yet an unqualified friendship such as might be associated with unusual holiness. Or more probably it indicates that right from the beginning and including all who enter it, this is a supernatural friendship exceeding its earthly model. Thomas uses a comparable phrase, '*quaedam felicitas*', to indicate the happiness of eternal life which includes and exceeds all earthly happiness.[26]

The phrase 'friendship of humanity towards (*ad*) God' might suggest unidirectional love but Thomas immediately explains it as mutual. God who loved us first, as he writes later on in the *Summa theologica*, 'is our chief friend (*Deus maxime est amicus*)' (*ST* II–II 27.8). '*Caritas* signifies not only the love of God, but also a certain friendship with Him; which implies, besides love, the mutual return of love, together with a certain mutual communion . . . , "Those who abide in love abide in God, and God abides in them" (1 Jn 4.16) . . . "God is faithful; by him you were called into the fellowship (*societas*; *koinōnia*) of his Son" (1 Cor. 1.9)', and this 'fellowship' consists in a certain familiar conversation with God, begun here through grace, 'perfected in the future life, through glory' (*ST* I–II 65.5).[27]

God is not so far removed from creatures as to render friendship impossible. Rather, he is intimately present to and in all things, loving all creatures in that he wills their own natural good to them. He extends friendship in its fullest sense to rational creatures alone, to all 'antecedently (*antecedente*)' but 'finally (*consequente*)' only to the elect, willing for them the same good that he himself enjoys, 'the vision of himself, and the fruition with which he is blessed'.[28] This friendship becomes actual through the 'communication' of God's own life to us, and the shedding of *caritas* in our hearts by the Holy Spirit.[29]

Thomas proceeds confidently to use his new definition. In his *Summa contra Gentiles*, written 1259–64, he takes it as read that the love which is brought about by the Spirit between God and human beings, making us God's 'lovers' (*amatores*), is friendship. The Lord, he says, made his disciples friends when he revealed what he heard from the Father; and now the Holy Spirit makes us God's friends, revealing his secrets: 'eye has not seen, nor ear heard, nor has the human heart conceived, what God has prepared for those who love him, yet God has revealed these to us through the Spirit.' (1 Cor. 2.9, *SCG* 4.21 n. 4). As friendship, *caritas* demands that we share, and do good: 'How does God's love abide in anyone who has the world's goods and sees a brother or sister in need and yet refuses help?' (1 Jn 3.17). Through the Spirit, God showers us with gifts such as wisdom and knowledge (*SCG* 4.21 n. 5, cf. 1 Cor. 12.8–11). Friendship also implies forgiveness: if 'love covers all offences' (Prov. 10.12), and if we are made friends of God through the Holy Spirit, then God also remits our sins through the Spirit. Jesus said to his disciples 'receive the Holy Spirit. If you forgive the sins of any, they are forgiven' (Jn 20.22); and the reason why blasphemy against the Holy Spirit is unforgivable (Mt. 12.31) is that those who so blaspheme lack the very Spirit by which sins are removed (*SCG* 4.21 n. 8).

Friendship brings sharing of life and conversation (*conversari*), which, in divine friendship, occurs in contemplation. 'Our citizenship (*conversatio*) is in heaven' (Phil. 3.20). The Spirit, who makes us lovers of God, brings us into contemplation: 'all of us, with unveiled faces, seeing the glory of the Lord as though reflected in a mirror, are being transformed into the same image from one degree of glory to another; for this comes from the Lord, the Spirit.' (2 Cor. 3.18). (*SCG* 4.22 n. 2). We delight in our friend's presence, enjoying their words and deeds, seeking comfort in them: 'in sadness most of all, we flee to our friends for the sake of consolation'; and similarly through the Spirit we have 'joy and consolation from the Lord against all the adversities and assaults of this world' (*SCG*. 4.22 n. 3).

In friendship we consent to our friend's wishes, so if God's will is expressed through the Commandments, friendship with him entails putting these into practice: 'if you love me, you will keep my commandments' (Jn 14.15). The Spirit, making us love God, enables us to keep them as freeborn children and no longer as slaves or servants: 'all who are led by the Spirit of God are children of God' (*SCG* 4.22 n. 4–5; Rom. 8.14). Thomas uses 'child' and 'friend' of God synonymously.

On the human level Thomas praises marriage as exemplifying friendship to the highest degree (*SCG* 3.123 n. 6); and whatever his Aristotelian biological ideas, he later affirms the spiritual equality of men and women in that their souls (mind, *mens*) both alike bear God's image (*ST* I.93.6 ad 2).

Caritas in the Summa theologica

Thomas was capable of dictating three or four works simultaneously, and it was apparently within the short period 1271–2, while back in Paris as Regent-Master, that he produced his own commentary on the *Nicomachean Ethics*, a penetrating exposition of Aristotle's thought; a 'Disputed Question (*Quaestio disputata*)' discussing whether *caritas* is created in the soul or is the Holy Spirit itself; and the 'Second Part of the Second Part' of his *Summa theologica* (or *theologiae*; *ST*) containing his definitive treatment of *caritas*. This *Summa*, although unfinished, is Thomas's most comprehensive work, spanning the whole range of theology: the divine and human natures, the work of Christ, the sacraments, the virtues, and the gifts of the Spirit. In this same frenetic period he was also giving a lecture course on St John's Gospel.

In his *Summa* Thomas commences the discussion of *caritas* by immediately asking whether it is *amicitia*? He invites anyone who says it is not to consider Jn 15.15: 'I will not now call you servants . . . but my friends' (II–II 23.1 con). We can turn to the record of his lectures on John, made by his friend and secretary Reginald, to hear him expounding Jn 15.13–17, the scriptural heart of his teaching on love. He says that Christ's words, 'No one has greater love than this, to lay down one's life for one's friends' (Jn 15.13), reveal the measure of his own love for us, the love with which we also must love our neighbour; and he instructs us that love has to be shown in action. To die for friends signifies love at its maximum; and if anyone objects that dying for enemies is greater, since 'God proves his love for us in that while we still were sinners Christ died for us' (Rom. 5.8), the answer is that 'Christ did not lay down his life for us as enemies so that we should remain enemies, but so that he could make us friends'. We were not, when Christ died for us, his friends in the active sense (*amantes*) but in the sense of those whom he loved (*amati*).[30]

On the disciples' part, the sign that they are participants in this tremendous gift of friendship is that they keep Christ's commandments. A friend, as Gregory said, is 'like a guardian of the soul (*quasi animae custos*)'; so whoever keeps (*custodit*) the will of God can rightly be called his friend. God also acts, making us his 'lovers (*dilectores*)' and assisting those who love to obey him. Our obedience is 'not the cause of divine friendship, but the sign' which demonstrates God loves us and we him (15.3.i).

On Christ's part the sign of his participation in this friendship is twofold. Negatively, 'I do not call you servants any longer'. From being 'like slaves under the Law', we become 'like children' under grace (cf. Rom. 8.15). We can still also be called servants, but now we serve God through love, with 'filial' and not 'servile' fear (15.3.ii). Positively, Christ declares 'I have made known to you everything that I have heard from my Father.' The revelation of our heart's secrets signifies true friendship and unity because, since friends have 'one heart and mind', what we reveal still remains within our own heart. God reveals his secrets through imparting Wisdom: 'in every generation she passes into holy souls and makes them friends of God, and prophets'. (Wis. 7.27). Christ still has 'many things to say to you, but you cannot bear them now' (Jn 16.12), but he has revealed enough for us to commence our journey in faith, learning through love until at last we shall know as we are known, and Christ will 'tell you plainly of the Father' (Jn 16.25; 15.3.iii).

What causes this friendship? Many think, even in the case of divine friendship, that its cause lies in good works originating in themselves – but Christ excludes this: 'You did not choose me but I chose you'. Divine friendship comes about through God's gracious choice. It is not that we loved God, but that God loved us first (1 Jn 4.10). Christ chose us, with the purpose that we 'should go and bear fruit' (15.3.iv). It is above all our encounter with God's action, with grace, that will underpin Thomas's developed doctrine of *caritas*.

To return to the *Summa*. Having posed his question 'Whether charity is friendship?' and countered several stock objections with the words of Jn 15.15, Thomas then once again calls on Aristotle, according to whom friendship is mutual love combined with benevolence, founded on a sharing or 'communication':

> Accordingly, since there is a communication (*communicatio*) between man and God, inasmuch as He communicates His happiness to us, some kind of friendship must needs be based on this same communication, of which it is written (1 Cor. 1.9): *God is faithful: by Whom you are called unto the fellowship* (*societas*; *koinōnia*) *of His Son*. The love which is based on this communication, is charity: wherefore it is evident that charity is the friendship of man for God. (II–II 23.1)[31]

The word *koinōnia* was, as we have noted, used by Aristotle to denote the common sharing, whether in humanity, or in kinship, citizenship, or shared enterprise, that constitutes the ontological ground for natural friendship.[32] *Koinōnia* was later enriched with theological overtones in the New Testament. In Latin it becomes '*societas*' or '*communicatio*', and the latter rendering becomes Thomas's term for the sharing of divine life, imparted by God, that grounds the new supernatural friendship. First we are by nature attracted to God as our true end and happiness; then actual friendship with God follows, as God's gift.

We are on holy ground. About a century later the English anchoress Julian of Norwich asks how prayer is possible? God answers her, 'I am the ground of your beseeching. First, it is my will that you should have it, and then I make you to wish it, and then I make you to beseech it.'[33] If we beseech, she concludes, it is impossible we shall not receive the grace God wills to give us – not because of our beseeching, but because of his goodness. Julian and Thomas, with Paul, describe the same experiential mystery. God brings us into a new place, a shared life grounded in God, where God acts and we are somewhat aware of his acting. We are not sure how we got there, it is not something of which we could have conceived before. It is very joyful, but may well also in some way entail a participation in Christ's suffering.

Koinōnia features in the New Testament in such varied phrases as 'fellowship . . . in the breaking of bread' (Acts 2.42) or 'sharing in this ministry' (2 Cor. 8.4). The Latin word *communicatio* similarly denotes sharing, participation and fellowship, but it can also mean the act of communicating the ability to participate. Thomas employs its entire range of meaning: God imparts or communicates his 'beatitude', his joyful life, to us; and through this transforming gift we are enabled to share the divine life actively with him. *Caritas*, as Egenter suggests, summing up the conclusions of a vigorous scholarly debate, is in a sense its own foundation. Infused sanctifying grace lifts us towards God, the theological virtues transfigure our powers, *caritas* as transforming virtue becomes a habit of our will, and this sharing of divine life makes it possible to experience *caritas* as friendship with God.[34] Grace precedes *caritas*, according to most theologians; the two are not simply identical, but charity as active 'habit' is preceded by new birth.[35] We may meditate, with Coquart, on the consideration that some kind of conscious mutual divine-human love must normally exist before God raises it to the level of friendship; and that the sharing of life constitutes the essential bond of friendship between humanity and God, who are still far from equal even when likeness exists between them.[36]

Caritas *as virtue*

Until the thirteenth century, Western Christians were generally content to think of *caritas* simply as the indwelling of the Holy Spirit, uncreated *Caritas*. Thomas demurred, pointing out that the active principle in charity would then be God the Holy Spirit moving the soul directly, which would destroy free will. *Caritas* must rather be an inner habit or virtue 'superadded' to our natural powers and informing our will, 'inclining it to the act of love'.[37] But, moreover, since 'the Divine Essence Itself is charity' the love with which we love our neighbour is a participation in Divine love, and 'formally charity is the life of the soul, even as the soul is the life of the body'; 'by justifying the soul, it unites it to God'.[38] *Caritas* thus makes us 'deiform', restoring our likeness to God.

But Aristotle defines friendship not as a virtue but as founded on virtue. How then can *caritas* be both 'friendship' and 'a virtue'? Thomas argues that God makes us share his joyful life, a life that is natural only to God. As Aristotle points out, however, it is in friendship that we share another's life. Hence it is fitting, if we share divine life, that we have 'a certain friendship' with God, which is *caritas*. And, the *communicatio* of divine life exceeds the capacity of nature, which must be perfected for this by some 'superadded good', which is virtue, so 'it is fitting to call *caritas* a theological virtue, "poured into our hearts through the Holy Spirit which has been given to us"' (Rom. 5.5). Whereas Aristotle's virtue-friendship is consequent on similarity in virtue, friendship for God exceeds nature and cannot have such a basis, so it is fitting that we be raised to it by a special gift, 'and we call this gift a virtue'.[39]

In the *Summa* Thomas quotes Augustine: 'Charity is a virtue which, when our affections are perfectly ordered, unites us to God, for by it we love Him'.[40] Faith, hope, and love are virtues in that they are 'always the principle of a good act'. Every act is good 'which attains reason or God Himself' (II–II 4.5; 17.1). If *caritas* unites us to God it attains God, hence it is virtue (II–II 23.3). Thomas stays true to Aristotle in not calling natural friendship a virtue, and to Augustine in giving that accolade to *caritas*. Curiously he never pauses to make explicit the distinction between Aristotle's definition of friendship as relationship, and friendship defined as the virtue of friendship-love.

Natural knowledge of God can lead us to desire him as our highest Good insofar as we are able to participate in his goodness through its natural effects. We also naturally love God insofar as we have some similarity to him through our created nature. Unaided nature cannot, however, approach God in his life and beatitude, and therefore cannot attain to friendship which causes friends to share life together: 'therefore it is fitting that *caritas* should be superadded, through which we may have friendship with God, and love him, and desire to be made like him by participation in spiritual gifts, which is, through glory, made possible for his friends'.[41]

Aristotelian friendship and Pauline *caritas* both embrace all the virtues. Commandments imply the presence of virtues, and Paul says 'the end (*finis*, goal) of the commandment is *caritas*' (1 Tim. 1.5), hence all virtues are ordered towards *caritas*; which also resembles true friendship in that it excludes falsehoods, hidden agendas and sin.[42] Yet *caritas* is specific and distinct in being love for the divine goodness, hence it is not a complex of virtues but one virtue, deriving its unity from God as its object, 'one virtue by reason of the unity of the Divine goodness'. Although it apparently has two objects, God and humankind, these are not equal and competing: 'God is the principal object of charity, while our neighbor is loved out of charity for God's sake'. Whereas different kinds of temporal friendship are distinguished according to differing ends (useful, pleasant, and virtuous) or different 'communications' (kinship, or being fellow citizens or travellers), friendship with God has only one end, the divine Goodness, and one 'communication', of eternal happiness, and hence is one virtue without subdivisions.[43]

Caritas is preeminent among the theological virtues. Since their object is God, these are 'more excellent' than moral virtues (justice, courage, temperance and so on) or intellectual virtues (wisdom, knowledge, understanding) which 'consist in attaining human reason'. Faith enables knowledge of truth, hope equips us to receive happiness, but *caritas* rests directly in God and is the 'form, the mover and the root' of all the virtues, directing all their acts to God. Since our 'ultimate and principal good' is the enjoyment of God, no virtue is a true virtue unless directed to that end, that is, unless it is with charity.[44] Like friendship, indeed as friendship, *caritas* gathers all the exellences of our character to serve in harmony together.

Love's transformation of our will

As a theological virtue and gift of grace, *caritas* perfects natural love. We as humans have a natural love of God as our Final End, a love that is now disordered but, when perfected by *caritas*, will be re-oriented towards God and our fulfilment in God.[45]

> ... in the state of perfect nature man did not need the gift of grace added to his natural endowments, in order to love God above all things naturally, although he needed God's help to move him to it; but in the state of corrupt nature man needs, even for this, the help of grace to heal his nature. (I–II 109.3)

What is this human nature that needs healing? Using Aristotelian psychology, Thomas analyses the soul into a lower part associated with the senses and emotions (the '*sensitivus*' part) and a higher rational and intelligent part ('*intellectivus*'). Each part has a corresponding 'appetitive power' (*appetitus*) with which we desire things and plan to get them. The appetitive power that operates from our 'sensitive' nature is itself twofold: the 'concupiscible' desiring power, and the 'irascible' power, the latter comprising not only anger but also such propensities as fear and daring. These dual 'sensitive' powers are the seat of the passions, hence they are also the location of the moral virtues that control, direct and perfect them. Thus the virtue of courage guides our unruly 'irascible' capacity for fear or daring into positive and constructive channels.[46]

The appetitive power of our intellect is our will, which is capable of rational voluntary choice based on understanding and hence can be the seat of steady, freely chosen love (I 82.3–5). Love can arise from passion (as *amor*) and reason (as *dilectio*). It delights in the goods it possesses and seeks to possess more. It is aroused by whatever the lover believes, rightly or wrongly, to be their good (I–II 27.1). Evil can therefore be loved if it is seen as a 'good', that is as a means to pleasure or gain; and all love can contain elements of evil to the extent that the good it seeks may be something less than absolute good (I II 27.1 ad 1).

Since the divine good can only be recognized by the intellect, our will is the subject of *caritas* (II–II 24.1). Our rational nature is then further perfected in specific ways by wisdom, counsel, understanding and the other gifts of the Spirit (I–II.68.2). But our will is not only our intellective appetite: it is also our power to do good. Natural love in the will issues both in delight and in goodwill, and *caritas* is likewise characterized both by delight and goodwill (I 59.4 ad 2). Just as Aristotle described friendship as both teleological (desire for the good) and deontological (the will to do good) so in Thomas the combination of active well-doing, and the desire to rest in delight, that characterizes our will lies behind his definition of love as both unifying and benevolent.

Aristotle called love a 'passion' because he conceived of the appetite as 'passive' and acted upon by its object. The object forms in the appetite an 'aptitude' or capacity to feel delight or pleasure (*complacentia*) in itself, and awakens its desire so that the appetitive power moves towards the object and, possessing it, finds 'rest, which is joy' (I–II 26.2). This Aristotelian understanding affords one explanation of how love is, as Dionysius puts it, 'a unifying virtue' or power, '*virtus unitiva*' (*Div. Nom.* 4.15), since the passive transformation of our appetite into its beloved object brings about union:

> When the affect or appetite is wholly imbued with the form of the good which is its object, it takes pleasure in it, and adheres to it as if fixed in it, and then it is said to love it. Whence love is nothing but a certain transformation of the affect into the beloved object. And because everything that is made into the form of anything, is made one with it; for that reason through love the lover becomes one with the beloved, which is done through the form of the lover; and for that reason Aristotle says 'a friend is another self'; and 'anyone united to the Lord becomes one spirit with him'. (1 Cor. 6.17)[47]

Through delight, the lover stands in relation to the beloved object as though it were herself or part of herself.

All love, Thomas suggests, proceeds from some apprehension of unity between lover and beloved, thus with desiring-love we apprehend some object, such as food, as pertaining to our own well-being, while with friendship-love we will good to the other as if to ourselves, apprehending them as an 'other self'. A 'union' between persons, however, actually means 'togetherness', not merging into one. As Aristotle says, lovers desire to be 'one', but since that would destroy one or both of them they settle for living and conversing together, and being 'united together in other like things'.[48] Thomas distinguishes between 'real union' when lovers are enjoying the other's presence, and 'union of affection' which exists even when they are apart (I–II 28.1).

On how love causes 'mutual indwelling' (*mutua inhaesio*) Thomas quotes 1 Jn 4.16: 'those who abide in love abide in God, and God abides in them' (I–II 28.2). All love causes the lover to be 'in' the beloved. 'Indwelling' with respect to our cognitive power happens through knowledge and thought, the beloved 'dwelling' in the lover's mind and heart and the lover reciprocally seeking to enter the inmost depths of the beloved. Thus Paul held the Philippians 'in his heart' (Phil. 1.7), and the Holy Spirit as divine love 'searches everything, even the depths of God'. (1 Cor. 2.10). With respect to the appetitive power the beloved is 'in' the lover by dwelling within their affection through delight. In desiring-love the lover seeks to possess the beloved perfectly by penetrating into their most interior self. In friendship-love friends dwell 'in' one another in the sense of identifying with them as another self, regarding the good or evil that befalls them as happening to themselves, and treating their friend's will as their own; thus in friendship alone does fully mutual indwelling come about (I–II 28.2 ad 3).

In the thought of Dionysius, even 'God himself suffered ecstasy through love'; and since all love is a participated likeness of the Divine Love (*Div. Nom.* 4), then 'it seems that every love causes ecstasy': thus friendship-love causes a true ecstatic 'going out' from oneself when the friend is the object of our attention and action; but in desiring-love, although we do go out to find something we want, the movement finally returns to ourselves (I–II 28.3).

Thomas deals with the question whether it is correct to classify love as 'friendship-love' (*amor amicitiae*) and desiring-love (*amor concupiscentiae*) by demonstrating that these loves, rightly directed, are complementary and integral to one another. If to love is 'to will good to someone', love must move both towards the good that we will for our friend, and to the friend in their own person. Love for the person is friendship-love, while the love that seeks to acquire goods for them is desiring-love:

> that which is loved with the love of friendship is loved simply and for itself; whereas that which is loved with the love of concupiscence, is loved, not simply and for itself, but for something else . . . the love with which a thing is loved, that it may have some good, is love simply (*amor simpliciter*); while the love, with which a thing is loved, that it may be another's good, is relative love (*amor secundum quid*). (I–II.26.4)

Friendship comprehends both friendship-love directed to the person as an end in themselves, and desiring-love directed to the good things we wish for them as the means for their fulfilment. Friendship-love is directed to the person in themselves; desiring-love to the accidental goods that exist relative to them. These goods include happiness and virtues, including *caritas* itself, which can therefore rightly be 'loved' with *caritas* as desiring-love. '"He that loves his neighbor, must, in consequence, love love itself"';[49] and whoever loves, 'loves himself to love' (II–II 25.2).

Caritas therefore comprehends even love for irrational creatures, when they are loved as goods we desire for another.[50] That is how God loves them, with quasi-desiring love, ordering them to the needs of rational creatures.[51] Friendship-love for irrational creatures is impossible, however, because we cannot have benevolence towards creatures which have no capacity to possess and enjoy the proffered good. They do not share in the *communicatio* of rational life on which 'all friendship is based', nor are they endowed with the capacity to share the communication of eternal beatitude. Hence there can be neither natural friendship (save metaphorically) nor *caritas*-friendship with them.[52] For Thomas everything in material creation, except for our own bodies, has the status of a means, not an end.

Desiring-love is morally ambivalent in that the purpose for which we desire things may be good or evil, selfish or unselfish. In friendships of utility or pleasure, desiring-love is directed not so much to the other's good as to our own. Moreover, we easily dehumanize and instrumentalize persons, treating them not as ends but as means.[53] Friendship is truly present just to the degree that we truly wish our friends some good; but to the extent that we refer this good further to our own pleasure or use, the relationship 'loses the character of true friendship' (I-II 26.4 ad 3).

The distinction between the loves of friendship and desire affords Thomas a neat solution to the question whether similarity causes love or rivalry. Actual likeness causes friendship-love; but potential likeness, when one thing has in potentiality what another actually possesses, causes desiring-love and rivalry, which is what tends to happen in use- and pleasure-friendships. Moreover we delight so greatly in realizing our potential, that if anyone prevents our doing so we hate them (I–II 27.3).

Caritas is given 'by the infusion of the Holy Ghost, Who is the love of the Father and the Son, and the participation of Whom in us is created charity' (II–II 24.2). On our journey to God we approach him by the way of *caritas*, therefore *caritas* must be able to increase, which is achieved through our partaking more and more in it, since love is form and not quantity. Each successive loving action that we do 'disposes to an increase of charity', increasing our ability to act lovingly again. We must always be growing: Thomas quotes Bernard (attributing the saying to Gregory) that 'to stand still in the way to God is to go back'.[54]

The friendship of charity, imperfect here, will be perfect in heaven when our 'whole heart is always actually borne towards God'. Here we may reach relative perfection, seeking not to think or desire anything contrary to the divine will (II–II 24.8). The chief task of beginners, who are setting out on the traditional three stages of spiritual growth, is to avoid sin and any desires that oppose *caritas*; that of proficients is to increase in love; and the aim of the perfect, while still progressing, is union in love with God (II–II 24.9).

The potential for such growth in this life is unlimited. But equally, *caritas* can decrease. God can withdraw grace and will do so totally in the case of mortal sin. *Caritas* can be corrupted by lesser ('venial') sin or by our failure to act. As Aristotle says, failure to exercise a friendship can destroy it.[55] Repentance is always possible, but the theoretical possibility that we may so change that the activity of *caritas* could completely cease in us remains throughout our earthly pilgrimage. If we choose sin in preference to divine friendship, the 'habit' of charity is lost (II–II 24.11–12).

The four objects of caritas *as friendship-love*

Augustine, citing the 'ordering' of love in the Song of Songs (2.4), said that four things are to be loved: God, self, neighbour, and our own body.[56] Thomas applies Aristotelian metaphysics again, to suggest that God is loved with *caritas* as the 'principle' from which flows the 'communication' of divine life. We ourselves are direct participants in that communication, in which our bodies too participate by 'a kind of overflow'. We love our selves as 'one with us' in this joyful communion, and our neighbour as associated with us in it (II–II 25.12). These four are the objects of *caritas* as friendship-love. Thomas examines our 'friendship' with each one in turn.

Friendship with God

Loving God 'with our whole heart' (Deut. 6.5) means loving everything that pertains to God, with our whole self and without limit: the measure of this love is 'to love him without measure' as Bernard says, and 'the more we love God the better our love is'.[57] Although our wish to enjoy God pertains to desiring-love, in practice we love him more with friendship-love because the divine good is greater in itself than is the good which is our share in enjoying him – and hence we love God more than our selves (II–II 26.3). Thomas's metaphysic describes rather well how our love for God takes us beyond cupidity into the wider vista of love, into wonder and praise. Friendship can be a sheer rejoicing in the other as good, beyond what that goodness may bring to me. In friendship we love God for God's sake, praying and desiring that all things may be ordered to him and reflect his glory.

The 'communication' of natural good is the basis of natural love for God the source of all good. Even in nature, then, everything should love and work for God. Much more will this be true for the friendship of *caritas* grounded on the communication of grace, in which we love God as the source of the common good of all those who participate in beatitude (II–II 26.3). God as the source of happiness is to be loved before our neighbours, who participate with us in it. Our likeness to God also prompts us to love God first, because 'The likeness we have to God precedes and causes the likeness we have to our neighbor' (II–II 26.2 ad 2).

Friendship with God is experienced and developed through life and activity in conformity with God's will, and prayer and the sacraments lie at the heart of this relationship. Thomas studied and wrote prayerfully, celebrating Mass daily and understanding contemplative prayer as 'conversation' with God. In the section of the *Summa* completed shortly before his death he writes of the Eucharist as the effective sign and means of union, 'the sign of supreme *caritas*' which lifts our hope, 'from such familiar union of Christ with us' (III.75.1). We look forward to life in the bodily presence of Christ 'because it is the special feature of friendship to live together with friends ... Yet meanwhile in our pilgrimage He does not deprive us of His bodily presence; but unites us with Himself in this sacrament', promising that 'Those who eat my flesh and drink my blood abide in me, and I in them.' (Jn 6.56). This food of wayfarers, instead of being changed into our substance changes us into itself (III 73.3 ad 2). As we receive it, minor sins are forgiven and the fire of love renewed (III 79.4).

Friendship for our self and our own body

Loving your neighbour 'as yourself' implies that, after God, the second object of *caritas* is our own self. Thomas actually quotes Leviticus in its Vulgate translation, which reads 'love your friend (*amicus*) as yourself'.[58] We have friendship for our self as belonging to God our Friend; and if as Aristotle says, self-love *exemplifies* friendship, then it must itself *be* friendship.[59]

The 'I' that reflexively loves my 'self' is my will, which evidently has reflexive power since one can freely 'will oneself to will' (II–II.25.2). Rather than speculate further on the psychology of reflexivity Thomas simply rules that whereas mutual love (*redamatio*) is found in the friendship we have for others, it is not present in love for our self, whether for our soul or body (II–II 25.5 ad 3). Friendship for self does however take place within the relational dynamic of divine friendship. As Cates beautifully puts it, in love's complacency we 'rest in the reception of our God-related selves . . . we take our reception of the Other to be the inception of ourselves'.[60]

To show self-love's priority over neighbour-love, Thomas avers first that if self-love exemplifies other-love, we should love self more than neighbour because an exemplar exceeds a copy (II–II 26.4 con). Second, since love 'unites', and 'unity' is the metaphysical principle of 'union', a self as unity precedes its union with a friend (II–II.25.4). Third, my own direct participation in the divine good is a greater cause for love than the fact that another is associated with me in it (II–II.26.4).

Wrong self-love gratifies our lower 'sensible' nature (2 Tim. 3.1–2) but in *caritas* we love and seek to perfect our rational nature (II–II 25.4).[61] Loving self above neighbour means we may not, even when attempting to free a neighbour from sin, commit any sin that prevents our own participation in beatitude (II–II 26.4). Neighbour-love does however take precedence over love for our own body – which, participating in beatitude only by a kind of 'overflow', stands lower than both our soul and neighbour in the hierarchy of love (II–II 26.5). Hence we can and should risk physical, but never spiritual, injury for a friend (II–II 26.4 ad 2).

John Burnaby, commenting from the viewpoint of an Anglican classical scholar in the 1930s, rejected with profound shock this 'most flagrantly un-Christian thesis: "that a man should love himself in charity more than his neighbour" '. Behind Burnaby stands the then prevalent interpretation of Aristotelian friendship as being merely an extension of our naturally selfish, self-centred self-love.[62] This, he was convinced, had led Thomas astray. Moreover, Aristotelian metaphysics had further misled him into placing the 'unity' of the self above 'union' between persons. 'The true line of Thomas's thought points rather to union as the higher unity', but he had allowed 'the crude individualism of Aristotle to impair his own deeper intuition of the Agape which takes a man, even as it has taken God, "out of himself" '.[63]

Burnaby rightly detects the weakness, in the Christian context, of Thomas's position on 'unity'; and the insistence on protecting our individual moral integrity is unfortunately open to narrowly legalistic and egotistical interpretations. But the problem remains how to achieve the utmost possible love of neighbour while still loving God, and ourselves for God's sake? 'No one', so moral theology has maintained, 'can carry precisely the same kind of responsibility for another's as he does for his own soul.'[64] Thomas further contends that although a person 'goes out from' themselves to will and work for the friend's good, they still do 'not will the good of their friend more than their own good' (I–II 28.3 ad 3).

The resolution of the problem of self-love versus neighbour-love lies in showing how love does take us 'out of ourselves' when its focus embraces God or the common good. The common good approach is typified by the legal philosopher John Finnis who maintains that for Thomas the motivation for moral action is not the good for any individual in isolation, but the common good of all humanity. If the good for human beings is the 'integral fulfilment of all persons and communities', within which 'each of us should locate our own, our family's, and our state's fulfilment', then it is impossible, even on the natural level, for one individual to appropriate that good solely to themselves.[65] In the same way, friendship on the supernatural level is participation in the shared good of the *communicatio* of divine life, and all moral action, including whatever it may mean to preserve my moral integrity, must be consonant with that common sharing.[66]

Diana Fritz Cates resolves the problem by focusing love on God in such a way that our attentiveness to the human other takes place within the threefold dynamism of love of self, others and God. She extends Thomas's thought to show how, in the joyful contemplative resting or 'complacency' of self-love, we first receive our natural selves from our Creator, and then through grace we in a sense receive ' "higher" selves . . . to whom we assent with deepened knowledge and intensified passion as our own, renascent selves'. We begin to love with God's love, and compassion becomes possible.

> Resting in our received selves, we rest in the Conceiver (and Elevator) of selves, which allows us to rest, to some extent, in God's conception (and elevation) of selves other than our own . . . Resting in ourselves, then, we come to rest in God's knowing and loving of us. Resting in the knowing and loving of God for God's creatures, it becomes possible for us to know and love these creatures with a depth and intimacy akin to God's.[67]

We can rest in God's given presence and absorb 'something of the presence of others who too have their being and their good in that presence . . . Surprisingly, we see that all of this is accomplished by loving ourselves well.' Cates puts before us the same pattern as does Maximus, and Aelred in his three interconnected 'sabbaths'. Right self-love opens us to God and hence, in God's love, to others.

Thomas suggests that what all senses of 'self-love' have in common is that we love what we understand ourselves to be. Everyone naturally conceives of herself as soul and body, and 'loves' herself in wanting this composition to be preserved. Everyone primarily loves whatever she deems the most important aspect of her being, thus the bad misguidedly give pride of place to their 'sensible' physical nature while the good grant it to their rational mind, Paul's 'inner' nature (2 Cor. 4.16). The friendship of the good for their true inner self fulfils Aristotle's criteria of friendship:

a friend wishes her friend to exist and live, desires good for her, does good to her, takes pleasure in her company and agrees with her, rejoicing and sorrowing over the same things.[68] By contrast the hearts of the wicked are stocked with horrors, giving them no pleasure, and the gnawings of conscience prevent them from agreeing with themselves, so they merely love themselves in regard to their own corrupt 'outward' nature (II–II 25.7). In fact they do not truly love themselves at all, since 'whoever loves iniquity, hates their own soul'.[69]

The fourth and final object of the friendship of *caritas* is our body, which is singled out from the material world as a potentially resurrected body that will be capable of participating with us in eternal life. Already our body participates in grace 'by overflow', and is to be used in God's service. We ought to love it, desiring the removal from it of 'the evil effects of sin and the corruption of punishment'. When Paul referred to 'the body of this death' (Rom. 7.24) he meant, not bodily nature itself but the concupiscence and corruption that weigh down the soul, preventing it from seeing God (II–II 25.5 ad 1).

Friendship for our neighbour

If existence itself is a good, and to love anything is to will good to that thing, then obviously 'God loves everything that exists' (I 20.2). Friendship with God introduces us into God's universal friendship, in which we are commanded to love every person as our neighbour.[70]

But how can *caritas* be friendship if friendship requires return of love whereas *caritas* must be extended to enemies? Thomas's argument, as we know, is that we extend friendship to someone either on their own account, or on account of someone else. We can, he persuades us, so greatly love a friend that we also love their entire household and all their connections, whether the latter are friendly to us or not. Therefore to the extent that we love God, we shall also show love to our neighbour, just as we love a friend's children however unfriendly they may seem to us (II–II 25.8). Thus 'the friendship of charity extends even to our enemies, whom we love out of charity in relation to God, to Whom the friendship of charity is chiefly (*principaliter*) directed' (II–II 23.1 ad 2). Christian neighbour-love is taking shape as an open friendship-love, within the all-encompassing mutual friendship we have with God.

The same argument covers friendship for strangers, the wicked, and the many. For Aristotle perfect friendship with many was impossible. Now, the *caritas* with which we love God and our neighbour is the most perfect friendship, in which we love God for his own sake (*sui ipsius*) and all things because of him (*ratione eius*) and to the degree that they are ordered to him:

> We do not have perfect friendship for the many in the sense of having it for each and every one individually (*unumquemque*), but, to the degree that friendship is more perfect towards one person for their own sake, to that degree it can be extended to many on their account. And so *caritas*, because it is the most perfect friendship, extends to God and to all who can know God; and not only to familiar friends (*notos*) but also to enemies.[71]

As to love for sinners, here Thomas concentrates on our potential friendship with them on the basis of our shared human nature. The wicked are to be loved as made in the image of God, having the capacity for divine life, and '*caritas* does not require the actual presence of the communication of divine life, but it suffices that it be there in potential, because what exists in potential, does exist in a certain manner'.[72] Every human is our neighbour, and sinners are still human, therefore we should love sinners out of *caritas* (II–II 25.6). Their human nature, a created good, is distinguishable from their being a sinner, which is hated by God as an absence of goodness and hence as evidently not created by him (I.20.2 ad 4). We too then, must love sinners for God's sake with regard to their nature, but hate them in respect to sinfulness. As the proverbial summary of this doctrine has it, 'Hate the sin but love the sinner.' The requirement to love our enemies is satisfied when we will a sinner's conversion, thus willing their good and so loving them. 'We love sinners . . . not so as to will what they will . . . but so as to make them will what we will, and rejoice in what rejoices us' (II–II 25.6 ad 4).

Thomas, perhaps remembering his own family's violent objections to his youthful Dominican calling, interprets Lk. 14.26, 'whoever comes to me and does not hate father and mother . . .' as meaning one should 'hate' one's kin just in so far as their sinfulness makes them obstacles between oneself and God (II–II 26.2 con.).

Until now our authors have made nothing, at least in a direct manner, of Jesus' ironic title 'friend of sinners'. At last Thomas calls on it, to answer the objection that, although it is proper to friends to share life together, Paul instructs us to 'come out from among' sinners (2 Cor. 6.17). Yes, he admits, the weak should avoid the dangers involved in consorting with sinners; but it is laudable for the perfect to do so in order to convert them, 'for thus the Lord ate and drank with sinners, as Matthew says'.[73] Those who are sinners may, in the future, come to rejoice in the same things as ourselves. Even Aristotle urges that friendship should not be broken off as long as the friend is 'capable of being reformed'.[74] Although sinners do not return our love now, it remains true that they are born to do so, especially in the life to come. That shared life already exists in potential in the present, uniting those who are still strangers on earth. '*Caritas* never ends towards anyone in this life, however bad they may be, because in this life, within the economy of divine mercy, the possibility of the life of glory remains.'[75] But when this life ends, Thomas assumes, our destiny is sealed.

Similarly, love of enemies is directed to the person *qua* human, not *qua* enemy which would be to love the evil in them (II–II 25.8). Jesus said 'Love your enemies, do good to those who hate you' and Augustine comments, 'to do good to one's enemies is the height of perfection'.[76] Thomas concludes there are two levels of love for enemies, the 'ordinary' level which requires everyone to love and not to hate, and that of 'perfection' where we actively love our enemies.[77] Just as 'a special movement of love' for every person is, at least on the ordinary level, impossible and not required, it is not an ordinary requirement that we should have a special love for individual enemies. It is, however, necessary to pray for them, love them inwardly, and be disposed to love them individually in cases of emergency, for example by feeding them. Perfection however manifests itself in continual actual goodness towards its enemies:

> Outside cases of urgency, to show such like favors to an enemy belongs to the perfection of charity, whereby we not only beware, as in duty bound, of being overcome by evil, but also wish to overcome evil by good, which belongs to perfection: for then we not only beware of being drawn into hatred on account of the hurt done to us, but purpose to induce our enemy to love us on account of our kindliness. (II–II 25.9)

The more perfect our love for God, the more we are moved to love and beneficence to all, whether those close to us, or strangers and enemies (*Quaest. disp. de car.* a.8).

For Thomas, angels constitute a special kind of neighbour. We differ from them, yet share the same rational spiritual nature, capable of receiving the same 'communication' of divine life. Our 'conversation' with them, imperfect here, will be perfect in our heavenly 'homeland (*patria*)' where we shall become 'like the angels'.[78] We do not of course share with demons, we cannot wish the good of eternal life to spirits whom God has condemned eternally, 'since this would be in opposition to our charity towards God whereby we approve of His justice'. To the subtle suggestion that if demons are useful to us as tempters, they must be our friends, Thomas ripostes that this would make us friends not with demons but with God, who turns their evil intent to our profit (II–II.25.11 ad 3).

Priorities and intensities in friendship

Given that this finite existence places limits on our practice of friendship, who among our neighbours should have first claim on our love? Thomas sorts out our priorities in terms of natural and supernatural merit. We love our family with intensity and stability. In the natural order, the 'friendship of consanguinity' has priority. Other natural friendships such as that of citizenship vary in strength according to circumstance (II–II.26.8). We love those who are closer to us 'in more ways', for example as comrades as well as human beings (II–II 26.7). Alongside the natural order Thomas places a hierarchy of rightly ordered love in which each beloved object derives their value from their degree of closeness to God. We love everyone with *caritas*, albeit on a sort of sliding scale. In respect of benevolence we show equal *caritas* towards all in that we wish everyone the good of eternal happiness; but in respect of beneficence and depth of affection we are unable to love all equally. Rightly ordered love is felt more intensely in proportion to the nearness of the beloved, to ourselves but above all to God who is the 'principle' to whom love is ordered. Just as in Aelred's ark, a more intense love should be given to those who are closest to God (I–II 26.6):

> . . . for though the good which charity wishes to all, viz. everlasting happiness, is one in itself, yet it has various degrees (*gradus*) according to various shares of happiness, and it belongs to charity to wish God's justice to be maintained, in accordance with which better men have a fuller share of happiness. (II–II 26.7)

In part this is commonsense, but there is a good deal of the neo-Platonic side of Augustine in this hierarchical thinking, and perhaps it is above all in this area that we might want to debate with Thomas on grounds of the Gospel. He is much more immediately appealing when he moves to his next point, the merit inherent in love from the point of view of the one who is loving.

Love's intensity, he says, also depends on the lover's capabilities and how powerfully he or she is moved. Thomas lists four reasons why Aristotle may be right to suggest friendship lies more in loving than being loved. First, the beloved becomes our own creation; second, we see our own virtuous good in them; third, to love actively surpasses being loved; and finally, it is harder to give than to receive (II–II 26.12).

The theme of merit continues, but this time from the point of view of the active friend, the lover. Is it more perfect to love an enemy than a friend? In replying to this Thomas compares and balances the teleological (seeking what is good) and deontological (doing God's will) aspects of loving. In several ways loving an enemy would seem to be more meritorious than loving a friend. Matthew suggests love for a friend deserves no reward, while love for an enemy does.[79] Thomas suggests two thoughts. First, that love of friends is not meritorious if we love them in a merely human manner, as friends rather than enemies; but it is meritorious, if we love them for God's sake, not because they are our friends. Second, the greater the degree of *caritas* the more meritorious the action, and it is characteristic of the perfect children of God to love their enemies, whereas those whose love is still imperfect merely love their friends. The greater the effort, the greater the reward (1 Cor. 3.8), hence love of enemies must be more meritorious. Thomas balances these deontological points with the teleological one that 'it is better to love one's friend since it is better to love a better man, and the friend who loves . . . is better than the enemy who hates' (II–II 27.7).

Thomas concludes that love both for friends and enemies can be meritorious. From the teleological angle, a friend is a 'better' person and more conjoined to us, and hence 'more suitable matter for love'. But from the deontological angle the reason for loving with *caritas* is God, and 'it is possible to love a friend for another reason than God, whereas God is the only reason for loving one's enemy'. Hence to love an enemy is 'better'. Love for God is proved stronger and furnace-like if its heat reaches across distance to an enemy, but on the other hand, just as a fire best warms those closest to it 'charity loves with greater fervor those who are united to us than those who are far removed; and in this respect the love of friends, considered in itself, is more ardent and better than the love of one's enemy' (II–II 27.7). As an action directed to an object, love for a friend excels loving an enemy, but as a *habitus*, as virtue, love for an enemy requires greater effort of will and is perfect; and love that extends to enemies includes love of friends and not vice versa, so looked at in this way love of enemies excels love of friends.[80]

Finally Thomas asks whether it is more meritorious to love our neighbour than to love God? To love God brings the enjoyment of God, the most excellent reward. But love of neighbour for God's sake is more perfect, including both God and our neighbour in one act of love. 'The commandment we have from him is this: those who love God must love their brothers and sisters also'.[81]

Friendship and the Holy Trinity

If 'God is *caritas*' (1 Jn 4.8,16) and *caritas* is friendship, Thomas has in a way achieved Aelred's goal of saying 'God is friendship'. 'He is subsistent love; he is friendship (*Deus caritas est*): his very essence is to give himself to himself, to give God to God'.[82] Thomas takes us just that far, but like Augustine he never explored interpersonal friendship within the Trinity. His interest tended primarily, in traditional Western fashion, towards the unity of the divine essence rather than the mysterious dynamic of ecstatic love between the three Persons. He made no use of Richard of St-Victor. Paul Wadell, while entirely true to Thomas, evinces a modern interest in the Trinity when he writes: 'God's beatitude is the friendship love that is God, the perfect love relationship that is Trinity. Father, Son, and Spirit are one because that Spirit is friendship and that friendship, understood as God's life activity, is God's happiness.' The gift of the Spirit makes us partakers in this life: 'Our friendship with God begins when God diffuses in our hearts the happiness of God that is the friendship who is God.'[83]

Thomas's vision

The meaning of life according to Thomas, is that all of us are potential friends of God: 'in analogous fashion to Aristotle, the proper function of a human being is to be more than human, to have a friendship with God'.[84] We are so created that we find our happiness in God's friendship, and in that friendship we love our neighbour as our self.

Thomas brought together the particularism that characterized classical friendship, with the universalism of the Gospel love-command. In so doing he 'developed a rich notion of loving the other person, by filling that notion with content deriving from the Greek theory of noble, reciprocal friendship . . . that of benevolence, or willing the good of the other, and doing so for his own sake'.[85] Friendship-love is 'the moral determinant of the relationship to each and every other human being'.[86] It is so because that is the way God loves. This friendship-love is exercised openly towards all, without ceasing; with a view to, and in joyful hope of, a reciprocity that will be personal, universal and eternal.

Caritas as friendship with God touches eternity and the divine and is, in a far more committed and profound manner than natural general friendliness or philanthropy, an all-embracing love of humankind.[87] It cannot be exclusive. It must develop and become more and more actual in the life of each individual; but all who are touched by or taken into *caritas* are participants in this friendship from the beginning.

After Thomas

This adventurous and innovative theologian suddenly ceased work in December 1273, and died after an accident in March 1274. Gradually, he achieved wide recognition. By 1286 all Dominicans were required to promote his teaching, in 1323 he was canonized, and in the sixteenth century his *Summa Theologica* replaced Lombard's *Sentences* as the basic Catholic theological text. Dominican theologians were prominent at the Counter-Reformation Council of Trent and Pope Pius V declared Thomas a 'Doctor of the Church' in 1567.

The voice of Thomas on friendship, however, was scarcely heard. The decrees of the Council of Trent featured the statement that we are changed, by justification, from an enemy into a friend of God.[88] Henceforward 'friendship with God' was incorporated into moral theology as a technical term for the state of grace – but this did far less than justice to Thomas. Moral theology was becoming a matter of drawing up detailed manuals for the use of priests in their task of hearing confessions, and was consequently dominated by 'ordinary' legal obligations based on the Ten Commandments. The definition of *caritas* chosen by nearly all moral theologians was still that of Lombard: 'love of God for himself, and of neighbour for God and in God'.[89] The theological virtues of faith, hope and love were effectively banished into the now specialized realm of mystical theology, where 'friendship with God' was associated with the heights of contemplative life. The term trickled down into more popular literature as a synonym for piety and inward devotion.[90] Pinckaers makes clear why this disjunction between ethical and spiritual or mystical theology was deeply problematic:

> The preoccupation of Christian mysticism has always been love, its growth, and the different stages leading to its perfection, as well as its most concrete manifestations. Unfortunately, mysticism has been excluded from Christian ethics, as if it were intended only for the elite and as if morality could forgo this dimension without cutting itself off from the very strength and dynamism of charity.[91]

In 1879 Pope Leo XIII promoted Thomas as the preeminent Catholic theologian; but even after this he was valued for his philosophy and speculative theology while his doctrine of love was not studied in such a way as to make a dynamic impact: his moral teaching with its distinctive development of *caritas* was largely ignored. In 1960 Richard Egenter could still lament that Thomas's doctrine had still not 'achieved a livelier effectiveness' and that virtually no further theological exploration had been carried out on it.[92]

But a turning point was just then being reached. As the moral theologian Bernard Häring puts it, after a long period of individualistic 'defence morality' that viewed the world with wariness as likely to lead people into sin, Vatican II opened the way to a 'covenant morality' that saw the Church as 'a sacrament of creative liberty and fidelity, a "fellowship in the Holy Spirit"'.[93] Such a Church has a mission of love in the world. Häring himself uses the friendship motif sparingly, but in line with Thomas's intention: 'One cannot find one's own salvation, dignity, and final friendship with God without equal concern for the salvation of all.'[94] This climate of thinking, congenial to, and even already imbued with, an understanding of Christian love as friendship, came to characterize the wider ecumenical scene in the latter part of the twentieth century.

Much of the most original recent thinking in this area has come from theologians outside the Thomist tradition, but at the same time Catholic thinkers have been retrieving Thomas's scheme in its original wholeness, re-connecting his inner spirituality of friendship with God with the outward practice of friendship-love.

> If . . . a person is capable of true, unselfish love for God and neighbor – the love of friendship of which St Thomas speaks – then the desire for happiness can lead that person to be open to God and neighbor and become generous. Can we love others truly without wanting their happiness? In the same sense St Thomas, in defining charity as friendship, sees a sharing in God's beatitude as charity's foundation.[95]

Paul Wadell has shown how Thomas's ethical teaching on virtues and the gifts of the Spirit revolve around the central motif of friendship with God, and has cast this teaching in a popularly accessible form in his *Becoming Friends: worship, justice and the practice of Christian friendship*.[96] Diana Fritz Cates has drawn creatively on Thomas in her work on the 'virtue' of compassion, as a personal skill to be learnt in character-friendship and thence extended to 'those whom we would not ordinarily regard as friends'.[97] On a broader front John Finnis joins Thomas in grounding social justice in friendship and the common good. We are, it seems, open to receive what Thomas would wish to share with us about the all-embracing friendship with God that is intimate, transforming, and includes all our neighbours.

5

Catholics, Anglicans, Reformers and Philosophers

'Christian charity is friendship to all the world'

In the early years of the sixteenth century the Reformation parted Western Christendom into Catholic and Reformed streams, to be joined in the succeeding centuries by the new stream of rationalism and 'enlightenment' philosophy. We follow these divergent tributaries towards the ecumenical convergence of the twentieth century, picking up the story immediately after Thomas, when Western Christendom was not yet divided.

The Middle Ages after Thomas

During the late thirteenth century a movement of popular piety whose adherents thought of themselves as *Gottesfreunde*, 'Friends of God', spread through the towns and villages of the Rhineland, from the Low Countries up to Switzerland. Several women's communities formed within it and affiliated to the Dominican order. A relationship existed between this loose mainly lay network, and Dominican preachers such as John Tauler, in which Thomas's theology of friendship with God appears to have constituted a mutually congenial theme. The movement was mystical, encouraging a virtuous lifestyle and aiming at profound inner detachment from the world and union with God in silent contemplative prayer. Records are patchy and examples sparse, but in a Pentecost sermon Tauler says, for example, 'Every friend of God should likewise celebrate this wonderful feast every day and at every hour. We should always be receiving the Holy Spirit.'[1]

While loyal to the institutions of the Church, these 'friends of God' lived in an age of politico-ecclesiastical conflict and spiritual enthusiasm, with rival Popes, interdicts and inquisitions, whose tensions foreshadowed the divisions of the Reformation. Mechtild of Magdeburg (*c.*1207–82) attacked corrupt clergy as those who 'make war upon God and upon his chosen friends'.[2] The introduction to the *Theologia Germanica*, written within this movement about 1350, which together with Tauler's sermons inspired Luther, says God spoke 'this little book' through a wise 'friend' of his, a priest who teaches 'divine truth' and especially how to discern 'God's righteous friends and the unrighteous, false, disorderly spirits who harm the holy church.'[3] Enthusiastic 'friends' who took freedom to iconoclastic extremes had been its original target. Such polemic sits ill with Thomas's intention; but if there was any conscious lack of enthusiasm for promoting his teaching on friendship with God on the part of institutional authorities, its perceived subversive potential may well have been a contributing factor.

God's friendship for humanity was not a prominent theme in the fourteenth century, although the mystic Julian of Norwich in England does hail God as 'our friend' who has overpowered the devil, and Jesus as our 'highest sovereign friend' who wants us to keep close to him, however sinful we may be, and to follow his will and counsel.[4]

The friendship of Jesus figures significantly in the most popular text to emerge from the Rhineland, the hugely influential *Imitatio Christi* (*Imitation of Christ*), written about 1413 and attributed to the Augustinian canon Thomas à Kempis (1379–1471). The *Imitation* exemplifies the search of the *devotio moderna*, the 'new piety' that succeeded the 'Friends', for an affective relationship with Jesus through meditation on his life and particularly on his Passion. It urges us to denude ourselves completely of all earthly things in order to seek true friendship with Jesus alone: 'you must surrender all other love for his love' (2.7). A certain ambivalence remains, in that we may have human friends and love them for Christ's sake; but such friends are mortal and ephemeral so 'if Jesus is not your best friend, you will be exceedingly sad and lonely' (2.8).[5] The *Imitation* was continuously translated and read throughout Western Christendom, by Catholics and Protestants alike. It teaches a very individual inward devotion, a help and comfort and a way of holiness, but one that falls significantly short of friendship with God as envisioned by Thomas with its positive outward extension in friendship for all whom God has made.

Catholic spirituality after the Reformation

For the great Carmelite **Teresa of Avila** (1515–82) God is the one 'Whom no one has ever taken for a Friend without being rewarded; and mental prayer, in my view, is nothing but friendly intercourse, and frequent solitary converse, with Him Who we know loves us.'[6] Teresa must have heard echoes of Thomas's thought in her frequent conversations with 'learned persons', and not least with her young colleague John of the Cross. Like Aelred she encourages her readers to seek out spiritual friends:

> I would advise those who practise prayer, especially at first, to cultivate friendship and intercourse with others of similar interests. This is a most important thing, if only because we can help each other by our prayers, and it is all the more so because it may bring us many other benefits. Since people can find comfort in the conversation and human sympathy of ordinary friendships, even when these are not altogether good, I do not know why anyone who is beginning to love and serve God in earnest should not be allowed to discuss his joys and trials with others – and people who practise prayer have plenty of both. For, if the friendship which such a person desires to have with His Majesty is true friendship, he need not be afraid of becoming vainglorious: as soon as the first motion of vainglory attacks him, he will repel it, and, in doing so, gain merit. I believe that anyone who discusses the subject with this in mind will profit both himself and his hearers, and will be the wiser for it; and, without realizing he is doing so, will edify his friends.[7]

Teresa probably had laity particularly in mind, but in her vigorous reform and expansion of the Carmelite order she went against the norm by also promoting friendship as constitutive of, not inimical to, religious life. A mystic well aware of the possibilities of grace she was able, like Aelred, to integrate friendships into the advance to perfection:

> When a friendship has for its object the service of His Majesty, it at once becomes clear that the will is devoid of passion and indeed is helping to conquer other passions. Where a convent is large I should like to see many friendships of that type, but in this house, where there are not . . . more than thirteen nuns, all must be friends with each other, be fond of each other and help each other.'[8]

This positive exhortation is followed by a warning to avoid sentimental friendships which distract and cause factions. This warning seems, in the past, to have overridden the essentially positive nature of Teresa's advice. Francis de Sales and Fénelon echoed her encouragement of spiritual friendship, but only for laity.

At university in Salamanca, Teresa's protégé **John of the Cross** (1542–91) was thoroughly grounded in Thomist theology, giving depth when he speaks for example of 'the high state of union and friendship in which [God] had placed Moses', or of the Pharisee in the parable who vaingloriously sought God's friendship by boasting.[9] John's primary theme is bridal mysticism, but friendship language can feature within it: 'The soul, then, touched with love for Christ, her Spouse, and aspiring to win His favor and friendship . . .'; 'Giving one's breast to another signifies the giving of love and friendship to another and the revealing of secrets to him as to a friend.'[10] There may well be a reminiscence of Seneca, as well as of Christ crucified, in John's advice to a Carmelite nun: 'where there is no love put love, and you will draw out love'.[11] John's mystical path brought him into an extraordinary love that extended to those who mistreated him; and he shows how union with God at the summit of Mount Carmel issues in exultant delight in all creation.

One of John's teachers at Salamanca was Fray **Luis de León** (*c*.1527–91), biblical scholar, professor of Thomist theology, poet and the collector and publisher of Teresa's works. He, and his sense of humour, survived several years' incarceration by the Inquisition. His dialogue on the name 'Beloved', written in 1585 as part of his masterpiece *The Names of Christ*, is a passionate, lyrical, Christocentric exposition of friendship with God, the friendship for which Thomas had provided the systematic grounding. In every age, Luis writes, Christ will find 'a countless group of friends who love Him': Aristotle's strictures against 'having many friends' do not apply to Christ, who 'can love many people with great intensity and attention to each' and 'can and should have infinite friends and lovers', loving each one individually and forming an extraordinary friendship with and among them.[12] 'Christ inspires love among those who love Him, He connects and warms our souls, our minds' and 'fashions us into perfect friends of His' through the love 'poured into our hearts through the Holy Spirit', which 'turns men into gods' full of goodness and virtue, absorbing hurts and radiating love:[13]

> For our love toward Jesus is never selfish but rather in it and by it we embrace all other men and bring them into our bosom, with such pure affection that it can never be self-seeking or selfish, with so tender a bond that their hurts become ours, so full of care that we lose sleep over their fate, so unswerving that we will not stop caring unless we stop caring for Christ. It is rare for a friend to risk his life for the sake of friendship: and yet those who love Christ are willing to do so not only for people who are their friends but even for strangers, even for those who hate and persecute them.
>
> Our Beloved is so well loved by us that through Him we come to love all of mankind.[14]

After Luis, writers begin to show the effects of the new disjunction between mystical and moral theology. When **Francis de Sales** (1567–1622) wrote for nuns whose aim was the contemplative life, he could speak of friendship with God. Charity is 'the promised land' to which

God leads the soul. Charity is disinterested love for God and hence 'charity, in a word, is a friendship'. It is also friendship in being mutual:

> For by charity we love God for love of himself, in consideration of his most sovereign and lovable goodness: but this friendship is a true friendship, for it is reciprocal, God having eternally loved whoever has loved, is loving, or will love him temporally. It is mutually declared and recognized, in that God cannot be ignorant of the love we have for him since he himself gives it; nor can we be ignorant of the love he has for us, since he has made it so well known and we recognize that all the good we possess is due to his benevolence.[15]

Contemplatives are 'in constant communication' with God through his inspiration, his pull on the heart, his goodness and proofs of affection, sharing 'all his secrets with us, as with trusted friends'. God in the Eucharist is our true food; we are always free to approach him. Charity is a friendship of incomparable choice (*dilection*) by which we choose God, a 'supernatural friendship' produced by the love poured into our hearts by the Holy Spirit who, being the love between the Father and Son, is 'infinite friendship'.[16]

When writing on a more ascetic level for laity, however, in his classic *Introduction to the Devout Life*, Francis mentions only human friendship, warning against foolish attachments and encouraging virtuous ones. He is positive about the latter, showing the influence of Teresa to whose *Life* he had been introduced by the contemplative Madame Acarie in Paris in 1602.[17] 'Many', he writes, 'may tell you we should avoid all particular friendships because they occupy our heart, distract our mind and lead to jealousy, but such advice is mistaken.' In monasteries, he admits, each should support all in their shared aim of devotion so that special friends should be unnecessary. Laity who seek to live virtuously, however, do need the help of 'good and holy friendships' such as many great saints have enjoyed. Thomas was, he says, evidently referring to this kind of particular friendship when he called friendship a virtue.[18] That is a prim and narrow interpretation of Thomas; but Francis prefers the conventional line that charity as benevolence must extend to all, while friendship is a mutual communication that implies sharing the qualities of the other, and hence must extend only to the virtuous.

Francis de Sales balanced a deep 'abandonment to God' with a warm humanity. During his lifetime a far more austere strand of French spirituality emerged, which aimed to imitate Christ in the self-emptying (annihilation, *anéantissement*) of the Incarnation. Taken radically, this 'annihilation' of self is an Abelardian spirituality of 'pure' love of God for God's sake alone, even to the extent of refusing all thought of reward. Among its more moderate exponents was **François Fénelon** (1651–1715), whose priestly career began as an aristocratic spiritual guide at the court of Louis XIV. His loyalty to the prayerful but over-enthusiastic and difficult exponent of *anéantissement*, Madame Guyon, earned him banishment to become Archbishop of Cambrai. He was attracted by 'pure' love's most positive aspect, the call to love our friends without possessiveness:

> This renouncement consists of loving them only for God's sake, of using the comfort of their friendship seriously, according to our need, of being ready to lose them when God takes them away, and never trying to find in them our heart's true rest. This is the chastity of true Christian friendship which seeks only the sacred bridegroom in the mortal and earthly friend . . . this detachment from self and from all that you love, far from withering good friendships and hardening your heart, produces on the contrary, a friendship in God, not only pure and firm, but completely cordial, faithful, affectionate, full of a sweet relationship.'[19]

Fénelon had a Scottish friend, admirer and biographer, A. M. Ramsay, who quotes a letter of his to Louis, Duke of Burgundy, grandson of Louis XIV, whose tutor he had been:

> 'Divine Friendship', says he to this Prince, 'is not always accompanied by a sensible Fondness, but it is hearty, intimate, faithful, constant, and effectual. It has too its Tendernesses, and its Transports. A soul devoted to God would be no longer liable to the Dryness and Reservedness which the false Delicacies and humoursome Inequalities of Self-love are subject to. Love would make us bear every Thing, suffer every Thing, hope every Thing for our Friend. It would surmount all Uneasiness. From the Centre of the Heart it would shed itself abroad upon the senses. It would melt with Compassion from the Misfortunes of others, not considering its own as any Thing. It would console, it would wait, it would suit itself to every Circumstance; become little with the little, great with the great, weep with those that weep, rejoice with those that rejoice. It would become all Things to all Men, not by a constrained outside Appearance, and a dry ceremonious Complaisance, but from the Abundance of the Heart, in which Divine Love would be a living source to furnish it with all the sentiments and Dispositions of the most affectionate and substantial Kindness. Nothing is so dry, so hard, so cold, so close, as a Heart, which loves only it self. Nothing is so tender, so open, so sensible, so meek, so lovely and so loving as a Heart, which is possessed and animated by Divine Love.'[20]

This was friendship as Fénelon himself lived it, of a piece with what he described as 'perfect virtue' and the 'principle of Disinterestedness with regard to ourselves, and of Compassion for others, which is the true bond of society.'[21] Early in 1712 this Louis, by then heir to the French throne, had tragically died. Among those who sent condolences to Fénelon was the **Marquise de Lambert**, another admirer of his and herself the author of a number of short works on moral subjects including a 'Treatise on Friendship'. Madame Lambert's 'Treatise' is remarkable in advocating virtuous friendship between the sexes, which she had found to be rare but 'most charming'. Friendship is, for her, that virtuous relationship described by Cicero and Montaigne. She stands up for the education of women in subjects that elevate the mind and character, but since this is rarely allowed she doubts the possibility of virtuous friendship between women, due to their 'natural foibles'. Besides, 'their friendships are always formed from necessity, never from choice'.[22]

Like Teresa and Francis de Sales, Fénelon encourages spiritual friendship among the laity but warns nuns strictly against 'particular friendships', assuming them to be immature emotional crushes that undermine obedience, cause jealousies and intrigues and distract from prayer. 'Try', he urges, 'to cure yourself little by little . . . turn your affection to the supreme goodness . . . taste the pure pleasure of the charity which embraces the whole world . . . love her in God, and in God's way' and 'love God, his work, your community, and your salvation, more than the person in question.'[23] Advice like this, sensible but devoid of all positive encouragement to integrate true friendship with personal growth and holiness, continued to be the norm for both men and women in religious communities until well into the twentieth century.

It was, McGuire suggests, Vansteenberghe's article 'Amitié' (Friendship) in the *Dictionnaire de spiritualité* in 1937 that marked a turning point by taking seriously the corpus of positive Christian writing on this subject.[24] The first translation of Aelred into English appeared in London in 1942. The Benedictine scholar Jean Leclercq published his initial study of monastic friendship in mediaeval letters in 1945, amplified in 1957 in his book *The Love of Learning and the Desire for God.* New attitudes were rapidly forming. The flood gates opened with the Second Vatican Council in the early 1960s. By 1969 Thomas Merton could celebrate the change, writing that for Aelred Christian life involves 'the full flowering of freedom and consent in the perfection of friendship. Friendship with other human beings as an epiphany of friendship with God. In this, surely, he is quite modern.' Such friendship, Merton adds, is a matter of grace, not simply psychological fulfilment, it is not merely 'the flowering of our inborn needs: it is God's creation. An entirely new creation in Christ'. It does not therefore constitute 'an obstacle to some supposed "spiritual perfection" '; rather, 'friendship itself is Christian perfection.'[25]

Leclercq urges: 'That spiritual liberty – which involves much more than being master of oneself – which is found in friendship is not a monopoly of canonized saints. The ideal it presents must be part of the formation given to each religious.'[26] Friendship is 'a realization, a particular actualization' of the universal charity in which God wills to unite all human beings; and far from being exclusive, it is 'one way in which we are helped to give ourselves to other people, in the greatest possible number'.

'God has for each of us without exception a love that is singular, unique, particular. And we should be images of him in our friendships.'[27] A joyful challenge indeed, and one that expresses the call of the Gospel.

Anglican Divines and Reformed preachers

We return in time to the seventeenth century and to Anglican and Reformed circles. During the sixteenth century, as the high Renaissance brought renewed interest in classical culture while the Reformation focused Protestant minds on the letter of the biblical text, a new kind of mutual alienation sprang up between friendship, perceived as a classical concern, and Christian love as universal charity. The syntheses achieved by Aelred and Aquinas were forgotten, their achievements replaced by a new assumption that classical philosophy had everything, and the New Testament scarcely anything, to say on virtuous friendship. Montaigne, the first essayist, practised Catholicism but also considered himself an Epicurean. He relied exclusively on classical sources for his essay 'On Friendship', published in 1580 extolling the perfect relationship he enjoyed with his 'second self' Étienne de la Boétie. Francis Bacon, producing the prototype for many essays 'On Friendship' in English in 1612, also exercised himself in classical allusions with minimal reference to Scripture.

Christian thinkers faced with the reproach that their religion seems to ignore this virtue could either choose to agree, arguing for the superiority of universal charity over ancient friendship, or might feel and believe strongly that truth was being skewed and that friendship in some shape or form must be reclaimed for Christianity. The English sources reflect these tangled thoughts and the tensions arising from them.

Jeremy Taylor and Katherine Philips : 'Christian love is friendship'

Jeremy Taylor (1613–67) was one of the Anglican 'Divines' or theologians who in the seventeenth century created a learned and practical style of pastoral theology for the Church of England. Born and educated in Cambridge, he studied patristics in Oxford, served in a parish, became chaplain to Charles I and a spiritual guide to the royalist community throughout the Cromwellian period, and died in Ireland in 1667 as Bishop of Down and Connor. Twice imprisoned under Cromwell, he remained eirenic and gently persuasive in his approach both to Presbyterians and Roman Catholics. The words with which, following the convention of that time, he might close his letters: 'your very loving Friend and Servant in our Blessed Lord', ring true for him. Taylor used his gift for friendship both socially and as a pastor.

Holy Living and *Holy Dying*, the classics among his many works, were written in 1650–51 for the Carbery family to whom he was chaplain. Through them he came to know Mrs Katherine Philips (1631–64), a member of the first wave of English women writers.[28] She had an intense friendship circle involving both men and women, and friendship features among her poetic themes. She handles it with a sure touch, marrying an educated mind with felt experience:

Love, Nature's Plot, this great Creation's Soul,
The Being and the Harmony of things,
Doth still preserve and propagate the whole,
From whence Mans Happiness and Safety springs:
The earliest, whitest, blessedst Times did draw
From her alone their universal Law.

Friendship's an Abstract of this noble Flame,
'Tis Love refin'd and purg'd from all its dross,
The next to Angels Love, if not the Same,
As strong as passion is, though not so gross:
It antedates a glad eternity
And is an Heaven in Epitome

Nobler than Kindred or than Marriage-band,
Because more free; Wedlock-felicity
It Self doth onely by this union stand,
And turns to Friendship or to misery.
Force or Design Matches to pass may bring,
But Friendship doth from Love and Honour spring.

If Souls no Sexes have, for Men t'exclude
Women from Friendship's vast capacity,
Is a Design, injurious or rude,
Onely maintained by partial tyranny.
Love is allowed to us and Innocence,
And noblest Friendships do proceed from thence.[29]

Seldom had a woman's feelings been more poignantly expressed. William Penn, writing in 1693, echoes her view: 'Sexes make no difference; since in souls there is none. And they are the objects of friendship.'[30] Aelred and Aquinas also agreed on the spiritual equality of men and women, but in the realities of social life there was still some way to go before either women's friendships in themselves were taken seriously, or friendship between men and women was regarded as normal. Early in the nineteenth century the Reverend Sydney Smith, campaigner for women's education, wrote: 'Friendships should be formed with persons of all ages and with both sexes ... It is a great happiness to form a sincere friendship with a woman; but a friendship among persons of different sexes rarely or never takes place in this country.'[31] J. H. Newman thought of marriage not as originating in friendship but as a challenging exercise in forming it: 'persons who differ in tastes and general character, being obliged by circumstances to live together, and mutually to accommodate to each other their respective wishes and pursuits'.[32]

Katherine Philips, however, knew and sought affirmation for what she herself had experienced. She also had no hesitation in employing friendship as a metaphor for divine love:

> Oh! What a desp'rate load of sins had we,
> When God must plot for our Felicity?
> When God must beg us that he may forgive,
> And dye himself before Mankind could live?
> And what still are we, when our King in vain
> Begs his lost Rebels to be Friends again?
> As God with open Arms the World does woo,
> Learn thou like God to be enlarged too;
> As he begs thy consent to pardon thee,
> Learn to submit unto thy Enemy;
> As he stands ready thee to entertain,
> Be thou as forward to return again;
> As he was crucify'd for and by thee,
> Crucifie thou what caus'd his Agony.[33]

Katherine Philips wrote to ask Taylor 'How far dear and perfect friendship is authorized by the principles of Christianity?' He replied that she could have answered this question from her own reason and experience but, wishing to be 'open and communicative in my friendship to you', he responds to her with a 'Discourse of the Nature and Offices of Friendship', in effect an extended letter of spiritual guidance. He asks in a postscript that she share it with an eminent doctor friend of his. It was published in 1657, probably not long after it was written.[34]

A legitimate love

Looking first at Scripture, Taylor allows that, strangely enough, 'the word "friendship" in the sense we commonly mean by it, is not so much as named in the New Testament; and our religion takes no notice of it' (p. 71). 'Friendship with the world' is mentioned, as being 'enmity with God' (Js 4.4) and 'friend' is used in the general sense of 'all relations and societies and whatever is not enemy' – Taylor does not pick out Jn 15.15 at this point. But, he continues, the absence of the word is misleading because true friendship is indeed present, but under another name:

> by 'friendships' I suppose you mean, the greatest love and the greatest usefulness, and the most open communication, and the noblest sufferings, and the most exemplar faithfulness, and the severest truth, and the heartiest counsel, and the greatest union of minds, of which brave men and women are capable. But then I must tell you that christianity hath new christened it, and calls this 'charity.' (p. 72)

In consequence, friendship itself is now universal:

> The Christian knows no enemy he hath; that is, though persons may be injurious to him, and unworthy in themselves, yet he knows none whom he is not first bound to forgive, which is indeed to make them on his part to be no enemies, that is, to make that the word 'enemy' shall not be perfectly contrary to 'friend,' it shall not be a relative term and signify something on each hand, a relative and a correlative; and then he knows none whom he is not bound to love and pray for, to treat kindly and justly, liberally and obligingly. Christian charity is friendship to all the world; and when friendships were the noblest things in the world, charity was little, like the sun drawn in at a chink, or his beams drawn into the centre of a burning-glass; but christian charity is friendship, expanded like the face of the sun when it mounts above the eastern hills. (p. 72)

Taylor writes this with a spiritual authority tempered in the fire of recent civil war; but he recognizes he is saying something unusual. It came as a relief, he says, to notice that Cicero, at least as he reads him, thought the bond of *caritas* should naturally unite all but has been narrowed to embrace only a few, so 'when men contract friendships, they enclose the commons; and what nature intended should be every man's, we make proper to two or three' (p. 72).[35] Christ renews creation as God originally intended it:

> Friendship is like rivers, and the strand of seas, and the air, common to all the world; but tyrants, and evil customs, wars, and want of love, make them proper and peculiar. But when christianity came to renew our nature . . . then it was declared that our friendships were to be as universal as our conversation; that is, actual to all with whom we converse, and potentially extended unto those with whom we did not. For he who was to treat his enemies with forgiveness and prayers and love and beneficence, was indeed to have no enemies, and to have all friends.' (pp. 72–3)

Perfect friendship is therefore not only authorized by Christianity but 'warranted to extend to all mankind':

> and the more we love, the better we are, and the greater our friendships are, the dearer we are to God; let them be as dear, and let them be as perfect, and let them be as many as you can; there is no danger in it; only where the restraint begins, there begins our imperfection; it is not ill that you entertain brave friendships and worthy societies: it were well if you could love, and if you could benefit all mankind; for I conceive that is the sum of all friendship. (p. 73)

A good person is 'a friend to all the world', their friendship 'equal' towards all. Potentially our friendships are 'prepared for all mankind according as any one can receive them' although when they become actual within the accidents and circumstances of life, 'the universal friendship of which I speak, must be limited, because we are so'. But whenever 'we stand next to immensity and infinity, as in good wishes and prayers, and a readiness to benefit all mankind, in those our friendships must not be limited' (p. 74).

His biographer Hughes understood Taylor to be saying the love of friendship 'is really Christian charity' and 'there is nothing in Christianity against friendships; there is only a danger that they should become too exclusive'.[36] While this is true, Taylor says much more by working from the other direction, giving universal charity the nature of friendship-love and thus making the two identical. All our present loves, however, are limited by space and time and by human imperfection: 'all our graces here' are 'but tendencies to glory, so our friendships are imperfect too, and but the beginnings of a celestial friendship' in which we shall 'love every one as much as they can be loved' (p. 73). On earth our best will necessarily be imperfect, 'not only because friendship is charity, which cannot be perfect here, but because there is not in the world a perfect cause for friendship'. (p. 78)

Loving in practice

Like the sun's rays falling across the globe, warming the various nations unequally (the 'cold Russian', the 'scalded Indian') the geography of friendship shows unevenness. Its warmth extends to all through prayer, and through doing no harm, and desiring good for all and doing good wherever possible; but this warmth is not equally received, either because physical limitation allows us to meet only a few, or because we cannot give alms to all, or as a result of limited capacity in the other, since 'when men either are unnatural or irreligious, they will not be friends; when they are neither excellent nor useful, they are not worthy to be friends' (p. 74).

> I confess it is possible to be a friend to one that is ignorant, and pitiable, handsome and good for nothing, that eats well, and drinks deep, but he cannot be a friend to me; and I love him with a fondness or pity, but it cannot be a noble friendship. (p. 79)

Where both partners are capable of affection and delight, with 'great readiness to do good', there can be 'that special charity and endearment which philosophy calls "friendship", but our religion calls "love" or "charity" ' (p. 75). In Taylor's equation of the two loves, a character-friendship is a concrete instance of universal neighbour-love but has its own special glory: a friendship in which we love a brave and excellent person, 'is just so authorized by the principles of christianity, as it is warranted to love wisdom and virtue, goodness and beneficence, and all the impresses of God upon the spirits of brave men'. This in itself, Taylor suggests, proves special friendships to be legitimate for Christians. We grow through experiencing the kindness of good friends, which makes us too 'wiser' and 'better' (p. 82). As to practical help, a social convention was appearing at this time, and would make a strong appearance in Kant's Lecture on Friendship, which held that it was impolite to expect or seek actual help from friends. Taylor disagrees: there is nothing ignoble, when in need, about desiring the actual support of a friend. Christian love remains practical and uninhibited by the delicacies of polite society.

It is right, Taylor insists, that we recognize and are drawn to likeable characters, just as 'even our blessed Saviour himself loved S. John and Lazarus by a special love, which was signified by special treatments'. When the rich young man spoke well and wisely, 'it is affirmed, "Jesus loved him:" that is, He fancied the man.' (p. 80). Taylor envisages having a cheerful, wise and actively loving person as our best friend, as well as a range of other friends who are each gifted with some likeable 'excellency'.

The remarkable new feature in his otherwise familiar account of close relationships is the central place Taylor gives to marriage. Parents and children, or siblings, may or may not develop friendship; but the marriage bond is, in its very essence, friendship:

> marriage is the queen of friendships, in which there is a communication of all that can be communicated by friendship: and it being made sacred by vows and love, by bodies and souls, by interest and custom, by religion and by laws, by common counsels, and by common fortunes; it is the principal in the kind of friendship, and the measure of all the rest. (p. 90)

Taylor himself had married in 1639, and in *Holy Living* he already expressed the conviction that marriage is 'a conjunction of the whole life, and the noblest of friendships' (albeit with the proviso that in serious matters the husband must finally rule, being naturally wiser!).[37] One of the most attractive points of this, the first of our major writers to be married, is his recognition of marriage as a locus of friendship par excellence. Married partners, he advises, should share their friends. No one, however, must mean more to us than our spouse. Should that happen – divorce being unthinkable – Taylor likens the faithful partner to a soul separated from its body, longing for reunion in resurrection, still loving and praying 'till the other be perfected and made fit' (p. 90). If marriage is friendship's best model all friendships are in a sense marriages, partaking in the excellence exemplified in marriage while looking forward to perfection in heaven, 'the region of friendship' (p. 91).

The length to which friendship must go is well known: ' "Greater love than this hath no man, that he lay down his life for his friends" ' (p. 82). Taylor understands this to mean 'a man dies bravely when he gives his temporal life to save the soul of any single person in the christian world'. (p. 83). Christ's life was indeed given for 'every soul', but ours, so Taylor suggests, should be given only for someone at least as worthy as ourselves and preferably 'better for the public, or better for religion, and more useful to others than myself' (p. 83). Even if we are not called to go so far as to die, the true measure of friendship is to love our friends more generously than ourselves: making petitions on their behalf that we would hesitate to make for ourselves, praising them and seeking their advancement. Taylor discerns Christian virtue here: 'I so highly value this signification of friendship, because I so highly value humility. Humility and charity are the two greatest graces in the world; and these are the greatest ingredients which constitute friendship and express it' (p. 84).

Katherine Philips had asked in particular whether a friend may 'desire to enjoy his friend as well as his friendship'? (p. 93). She herself expressed her enjoyment in poetry, and Taylor sides with her: 'if I love a worthy person, I may please myself in his society' and provided that friends of different sex are 'prudent and free from suspicion and reproach', scandal-mongers may be despised: 'they must not fright us from our friendships, nor from her fairest entercourses' (p. 94). Alongside marriage, Taylor gives male-female friendship a quite new prominence: 'you may see how much I differ from the morosity of those cynics who would not admit your sex into the communities of a noble friendship' (pp. 94–5). Still, he speaks to us from the mid-seventeenth century: a woman, he says, has all the graces of friendship and 'can die for her friend as well as the bravest Roman knight'; yet 'a man is the best friend in trouble', being more experienced, capable of wielding a sword and handling finances, while 'a woman may be equal to him in the days of joy' (pp. 94–5).

Taylor closes with ten rules for friendship from classical and biblical sources. Negatively, he suggests we should not (i) require a friend to do wrong, nor do it if asked; (ii) choose a person we could ever come to hate; (iii) betray a friend or reveal their secrets (Sir. 22.22); (iv) accuse a friend nor believe an accuser, realizing all the same that humans are not angels and 'thou mayest need pardon as well as he'. Positively we should (v) give wise and loving counsel, freely, bearing no resentment if it is not followed; (vi) avoid acting as judge between friends who both want to win; (vii) never instil fear in a friend: 'perfect love casts out fear' (1 Jn 4.18) but tyranny destroys friendship; (viii) admonish kindly, praise justly, and not feel envy or slight when your friend is praised; (ix) esteem old friends like old wine; but also, 'if he be worthy, keep the new one till he become old' (p. 97); (x) 'treat thy friend nobly, love to be with him, do to him all the worthinesses of love ... bear with his infirmities till they approach towards being criminal; but never dissemble with him, never despise him, never leave him' (pp. 97–8). True friendship continues despite absence, even the absence of death, to which Christianity gives new meaning (p. 93). Human friendship is sustained by reciprocity in giving and forgiving, sharing and trust, and has 'something that is divine, because it is beneficent; but much, because it is eternal' (p. 98).

Katherine Philips was delighted with the 'Discourse', writing in verse to thank Taylor for having rescued friendship from derision and championed it as true happiness. 'Nations and Armies' she remarks with feeling, if they would but recognize this virtue, 'would lay down their Arms.' She congratulates Taylor on having raised a 'glorious Monument' to his own character.[38]

Critics of Taylor

Taylor quotes no Christian writers and tends to presume on his readers' knowledge of Scripture, citing it relatively little. He does call on Cicero, Martial, Theocritus, Theognis and unknown classical poets as well as reflecting Aristotle's threefold pattern and borrowing his ideas: for example, 'parents love their children because they love themselves' (p. 86). Hence although his thrust was to situate friendship in its theological context he left himself partially open to the complaint of the freethinker Anthony Ashley Cooper (1671–1713), that he drew 'all his notions as well as examples of private friendship from the heathen world, or from the times preceding Christianity'.[39] Ashley Cooper held friendship to be a classical virtue which, like patriotism, had been omitted from the Christian moral order and therefore, having no reward assigned to it, could be practised with disinterest by noble souls.

The modern critic Gilbert Meilaender approaches from the Lutheran perspective typified by Nygren, in which agape 'seeks not its own' and is 'nonpreferential and unconcerned with reciprocity'.[40] Philia however is a natural human love, preferential and reciprocal. Two very different loves, therefore, seem to him to lie behind Taylor's words: 'When friendships were the noblest things in the world, charity was little', and his attempt to equate them was surely doomed to failure because agape cannot be preferential. In this life, Meilaender suggests, human friendship exists in creative tension with agape. The parable of the Good Samaritan calls us to transcend our natural condition, trying 'to live even now as if the process by which the partial, preferential loves are transformed into nonpreferential neighbour-love were completed'; but the transformation will never be complete here on earth.[41]

Meilaender does see natural friendship as a school of love, in that mutuality is 'the hoped-for internal fruition of all love'.[42] Agape will ultimately be fulfilled in relationship, so the loves will at last coalesce. But he is rather sceptical about the effectiveness of grace in this life and considers Taylor simply mistaken in urging 'friendship to all the world' on limited and finite creatures.[43] He also refuses any notion of a 'love of friendship' existing beyond the bounds of actual reciprocal relationship, so he can accept neither Aquinas's view that charity is friendship even when directed to enemies, nor Aelred's that friendship can remain constant even when a friend falls away.[44] What was being described in both cases was simply a goodwill that is not presently being reciprocated, and therefore cannot be called 'friendship'.

In reply to Meilaender, Taylor is realistic about our finitude, but sees no reason in it for relinquishing the attitude of friendship that fundamentally colours the way we love 'all the world'.

Thomas Traherne and Richard Baxter: friendship with God

Taylor's 'Discourse' omits any mention of friendship with God, although the idea was not unfamiliar to him. He advised another female correspondent to pray briefly and frequently, but 'if love makes you speak, speak on, so shall your prayer be full of charity and devotion . . . love makes God to be our friend, and our approaches more united and acceptable'.[45] But for **Thomas Traherne** (1636–74), a mystical poet and one of Taylor's successors among the Anglican Divines, friendship with God is the dominant friendship-theme. As he opens his *Centuries of Meditations*, which lay unpublished until 1908, he praises the nobility of 'Divine Friendship' which is union with God through love. In his *Ethics* published in 1675 he writes: 'There is great talk of friendship. It is accounted the only pleasure in the world.' Its 'offices' or duties are universally praised, these being kindness, fidelity, communication of thoughts and secrets, 'an ardent willingness to impart lives and estate for the benefit of our friend', and the desire to serve and suffer for them, placing their needs before our own. The real secret of friendship, however, lies in its inward nature, in the agreement of souls and mutual ecstatic delight in each other's virtues and accomplishments; and its great paradigm is friendship with God:

> There are some slight aims and adumbrations of this friendship on earth, but the best and highest degree of it here beneath is but a rude and imperfect shadow. Only God is the sovereign friend. All adoration paid to any one beside is mere idolatry.

> Our hearts can be sacrificed to none but Him; because He alone is immutable in His goodness. We cannot infinitely honour and delight in any but Him: it is He alone that can infinitely honour and delight in us.[46]

To love God is infinite delight. 'There are two common motives of love among men; the one, the goodness and excellency of the person; the other, his particular kindness and love to us. And both of these are in the highest degree in God.'[47]

Human perfection consists in being united with God's will through love, which ushers us in to the community of love: 'He will accept of no love to Himself but what is accompanied with love to his friends and servants . . . All that He has done to secure their love to Himself, He has done to secure their love to us'. We can love God who infinitely desires our love, and love others, and so truly love our selves; or we can be 'eternally miserable'.[48] We have a free choice between the two; and yet whatever we choose and however unlovable we appear, God's love still embraces us through his 'transcendent' and 'supernatural' virtue of meekness. Meekness is the virtue springing from love, that meets wrongs and preserves love, 'it gives immutability to goodness, and makes our worth not to depend on other men's deservings, but our own resolution'. All natural love 'dies into distaste, when its object hath offended'. But meekness looks forward to restoration, and the 'future beauty and perfection of an object that is now deformed'. Grounded in 'hope and possibility' and yet guided by prudence, it aims at 'the restitution of amity between us and our adversary'. We know this virtue through Christ incarnate and crucified. It 'carries us above all the rules of nature, above all the principles of reason'. How God came to open his love to the evil as well as the good 'is an infinite wonder'.[49]

> Though now, since He hath first loved us who are so vile, nothing is more natural than that we should do as we are done unto – imitate Him, and love those whom our Creator loveth; with pity and benevolence at first, that we may hereafter do it with full complacency [delight].[50]

Traherne has focused piercingly on exactly how Christ's love transforms the limitations of natural friendship.

The Puritan Divine **Richard Baxter** (1615–91) tended, unlike Taylor, towards the more Reformed wing of Anglicanism, and finally found himself outside the Church of England; but he was of a deeply ecumenical spirit and, unusually, was well read in the scholastics. His hymn 'He wants not friends that hath thy love' expresses in verse what he expounds at length in a discourse on the words of Jesus 'I am not alone, for the Father is with me' (Jn 16.32), in which he wrestles with the relative reliability of earthly friendship and divine. Experience has taught him that good human friends are a blessing and it is delightful to look forward to loving them perfectly in heaven; but 'Man is frail, and the best too selfish and uncertain.'[51] God is 'our dearest everlasting Friend'.[52] He keeps us, heals us, forgives our sin. He can 'quiet my soul in the midst of trouble, and give me a well grounded everlasting peace and a joy which no man can take from me'; God's friendship makes even death easy and sweet.[53] The poor worry us; the rich spurn us; but God, like the father of the prodigal son, 'is never unready to entertain me . . . with Joy, with Musick'.[54] If 'God be my Father, and my Friend in Christ', then 'I have his Love and Preference who is All in All'.[55]

> Love God in his saints, and delightfully converse with Christ in them . . . but Remember thou Livest not upon them, or on their Love, but upon God, and therefore desire their company but for *His*: And if thou have *His*, be content if thou have not *theirs*.[56]

Baxter is Augustinian in his order of love. Human beings must never be treated as mere things to be discarded, but 'converse with man is only so far desirable as it tendeth to our *converse with God*: And therefore the *end* must be preferred before the *means*.'[57]

'Friendship to every individual man'?

After Taylor, the conflict of views over whether Christian love is or is not compatible with friendship continued to rumble on. In 1713 in his *Discourse of Freethinking* the deist Anthony Collins proclaimed Epicurus a greater moral teacher than Christ, because he taught noble friendship while Christ had not. To this, **Richard Bentley** (1662–1742), an Anglican classical scholar, retorted that Epicurus' friendship was decidedly *not* noble, and Christianity does indeed teach this virtue:

> In the Old Testament *friendship* is celebrated both by excellent precepts and eminent examples; but there was no occasion to do it in the New. That quality is so exalted and expanded there, that it loses its very name, and for *philia*, *friendship*, becomes *philadelphia* and *agape*, *brotherly love* and *charity*. Friendship in the pagan notion was *inter duos aut paucos, circumscribed within two persons or a few;* whence Aristotle's saying was applauded, *hōi philoi, ou philos*, *he that has friends has no friend:* but Christian friendship or charity, in the same degree of affection, is extended to the whole *household of faith,* and in true good-will and beneficence to all the race of mankind.[58]

Bentley immediately adds, 'Particular friendships, arising from familiarity and similitude of humours, studies, and interests' are not forbidden by the Gospel, but there was no need to command 'what nature herself, and human life, and mutual utility, sufficiently prompt us to'.

The nineteenth-century German scholar **Ernst Curtius** enjoyed Bentley's response, understanding him to mean that friendship is taken up into Christianity and fulfilled in universal love without losing its specific and personal nature. Curtius illustrates this through the imagery of sunlight: friendship, 'the distinctive soul of ancient life', was like the sun's rays heralding the dawn of Christianity:

> The single rays disappear when the sun has fully emerged from behind the mountains. But are they any less in existence, when they disappear into the fullness of light? They still exist as before, only stronger, more ardent, more enlivening! For when all human striving finds higher goals set, then to the same extent all spiritual unions are enriched and of fuller significance. Man can and should be more to man, than was ever the case in antiquity.[59]

Bishop Berkeley (1685–1753) had responded in similar vein to the deists' attack. Christianity, he affirms, aims 'to inspire its professors with the most noble and disinterested spirit of love, charity, and beneficence to all mankind, or, in other words, with a friendship to every individual man'.[60] The 'charitable person' is also the most joyful, because:

> He looks on mankind as his friends, and is therefore so far from being mortified, that he rejoices at their prosperity, and reckons it an addition to his own good fortune. As he wishes no harm to his neighbour, so he hath hopes of being relieved or assisted by them in any exigence. Every act of charity and beneficence carries its own reward with it – a sense of pleasing and of being acceptable to men, together with a secret joy flowing from the approbation of a good conscience.[61]

Despite such rejoinders, **Samuel Johnson** in 1778 still took it for granted that friendship and Christian love are mutually exclusive:

> All friendship is preferring the interest of a friend, to the neglect, or perhaps, against the interest of others; so that an old Greek said, 'He that has *friends* has *no friend*.' Now Christianity maintains universal benevolence, to consider all men as our brethren, which is contrary to the virtue of friendship, as described by the ancient philosophers.[62]

Mrs Knowles, a Quaker who was Johnson's partner in this conversation, was wholly unwilling to accept that dichotomy. She defends the Quaker custom of calling everyone 'friends', on the ground that we should 'do good to all men, but "especially to them who are of the household of faith"'. Johnson is not greatly impressed, since even the said household is rather large and love of all one's fellow Christians is hardly intimate friendship. Mrs Knowles returns to the attack. Against Johnson's assumption that Christianity ignores particular friendship she points out that Christ had, among the twelve apostles, '*one* whom he *loved*'. Johnson 'with eyes sparkling benignantly' congratulates her and – if Boswell is to be believed – admits that that was an application which had not occurred to him!

How did the Quakers acquire their name, '**Society of Friends**'? It appears simply to have happened rather than originating in deliberate choice. The phrase seems first to have appeared in an anti-Quaker tract of 1665. It was only adopted as their formal name around 1800, but their egalitarian spirit had caused them, from the earliest days of George Fox's journeys in the 1640s, to refuse titles and call one another 'Friend', addressing messages to their colleagues as 'the Friends' in such-and-such a place.[63] In 1680 William Penn even addressed a letter to 'the Friends of God' in Bristol.[64] They appear also to have felt able to address all people as 'Friend' on the basis of the freedom they owned, as persons trying to be obedient to God and valiant for truth, 'to walk cheerfully over the world, answering that of God in everyone'.[65] The writings of William Penn are aglow with this ethos, which continues to be fundamental to Quaker spirituality and their involvement in peacemaking and social justice.

'A lovely representation of religion'

The Anglican Divines helped initiate a perennial tradition of spiritual writing in English using the language and model of friendship. Its public face has shown itself in hymns, sermons and occasionally in more sustained treatments. Each writer has set out largely in ignorance of their forebears, inspired perhaps by a Scripture verse or a passage in one or two books, so this continually resurgent theme finds itself constantly treated afresh.

It seems the first work entitled *The Friendship of Christ* was a tract written in 1718, in simple, earnest verse, by an Edinburgh Presbyterian, **William Cheyn**. Although scarcely a poet, Cheyn strikes a sincere note, eulogizing God's love in Christ as that of the perfect friend. He draws a distinction between 'general' and 'special' friendship: 'Christ Gen'ral Friendship to all Men doth show . . . Whereas his Special Friendship doth appear, When Man he moves to turn from Sin to God.'[66] God's 'General Friendship' is shown through the blessings he showers even on the worst of us, while patiently awaiting our conversion. 'Charity' has for Cheyn the narrow and specific sense of giving practical help to the poor, and is the fruit of 'special friendship' with God.

The first book entitled *Friendship with God* was published in 1772 by the Presbyterian minister **Richard Jones** (1727–1800). Educated at the Dissenting Academy run by Philip Doddridge in Northampton, his ministry began in Cambridge and then at the historic Crosby Square in London's Bishopsgate, continuing from 1769 in Peckham.[67] In a farewell sermon at Crosby Square he pledged continuing friendship to his former congregation, and shortly afterwards he dedicated his book to a member of it.

One source that Jones mentions is Ramsay's *Life* of Fénelon; and he also quotes the judge, Sir Matthew Hale (1609–76), a friend of Baxter's: '"O keep God thy Friend, for most certain it is thou wilt have occasion for him again."'[68] The riches hidden in this theme seem to have taken him by surprise: 'I thought Friendship with God a lovely representation of religion, and have therefore carried it to an extent, beyond what I at first intended'.[69] If Abraham, a human being like us, he muses, was 'called the Friend of God' (Jas 2.23) we should raise our minds and form a more accurate notion of what we too 'are capable of being and enjoying'.[70] God 'made man for friendship with himself', and 'the restoration of that Friendship is the grand design of the gospel'.[71]

After a few classical allusions Jones launches into salvation history, presenting the relationship between God and humanity as a friendship created, broken, and restored. God's friendship to us is known through providence and the incarnation, and God invites us into reciprocal friendship: 'as the heaven does not confine God in his friendships, the earth should not confine us in ours'.[72] 'Delight in God is the temper and happiness of heaven . . . and in this valuable article heaven may be brought down to earth.'[73] By cultivating love, 'we are said to dwell in God, and to have God dwelling in us (1 John 4.16), an expression which imports friendship in the very highest degree'.[74] Our friendship to God is shown through prayer and 'cheerful service done to him, and for him'.[75] On the injunction to use our wealth to make friends with God and the heavenly inhabitants, Jones comments, 'If a mortal friend entrust me with a part of his substance, ought I not to use it agreeably to his will?' Much more with God, we are the 'almoners' of his bounty.[76] This little book, probably never widely known, is an attractive statement of the Gospel and a worthy first example of its genre. An expanded edition appeared in 1797 and a reprint in 1847, while a German translation, *Freundschaft mit Gott*, was published in Leipzig in 1810.

Mary Deverell was one of extremely few women to venture onto this ground prior to the twentieth century. Her 'Sermons' were not preached but were published in 1774 by the help of subscriptions from numerous well-connected admirers, clerical and lay, male and female. Her 'Sermon on Friendship' is an excellent theological essay. 'Friendship', she writes, 'is seated in the heart, and is equally estimable whether apparelled in a russet coat, or a royal robe' and 'The generous fervour of a steady friend, in whom are happily united the will and power of doing good, has such an emanation of the divinity in it, as must supremely exalt the character it animates.'[77] Jesus, a friend '"born for adversity"', sacrificed his life to friendship. The early Christians, holding everything in common, 'were all reduced to a level', which is 'the effect of true friendship at all times'.[78]

Of a number of published nineteenth-century sermons, the earliest and most widely read was preached on the feast of St John the Evangelist in 1831 on the text 'Beloved, let us love one another, for love is of God' (1 Jn 4.7), by **John Henry Newman** (1801–90), then at the height of his Anglican career in Oxford.[79] Possibly by then, and certainly a few years later, Newman was aware of Aelred.[80] What, he asks, was the meaning of Christ's choosing a special friend? It demonstrates his humanity and proves there is 'nothing inconsistent with the fulness of Christian love' in having special affection for a close friend.[81] Some have supposed Christian love to be 'so diffusive as not to admit of concentration upon individuals; so that we ought to love all men equally', while others assume that 'the love of many is something superior to the love of one or two' and neglect those nearest them while 'busy in the schemes of an expansive benevolence'.[82] Neither solution accords with 'our Saviour's pattern', which shows that 'the best preparation for loving the world at large, and loving it duly and wisely, is to cultivate an intimate friendship and affection towards those who are immediately about us'.[83] Love for friends is 'the only preparatory exercise for the love of all men . . . the love of mankind in general should be in the main the same habit as the love of our friends, only exercised towards different objects'. If the potential scope of love is daunting to us, God has mercifully arranged that 'we are to begin with loving our friends about us, and gradually to enlarge the circle of our affections, till it reaches all Christians, and then all men'.[84]

In practice, love for all means being well-disposed and ready to act as a friend to each person as occasion arises. Through practical love of friends we learn to see every person as an individual, so that all our benevolent actions, and treatment of colleagues, may be guided by intelligent sympathy and wise discernment.[85] Finally, love for friends and those near us is not only the source and discipline of Christian love, but also in some cases its perfection – and if friendship is 'not quite' a virtue in the same way in Christianity as in the classical world, still it often *tests* virtue, and a lasting friendship betokens the likely presence of grace.[86] Newman's final Anglican sermon, in 1843 on 'The Parting of Friends', is as much about love continuing as about the pain of separation.

Another nineteenth-century Oxford personality, **Benjamin Jowett** (1817–93) took up these ideas. Looking at various biblical, classical and Shakespearean friendships, he asks what difference Christianity makes?

Christian friendship 'in uniting us to a friend, at the same time unites us to Christ and God'. It is lived consciously in the presence of God, in his common service. It needs sustaining by prayer 'for human friendships constantly require to be purified, and raised from earth to heaven'.[87] Moreover, 'Christian friendship is not merely the religious aspect of the ideal of the ancients' but, as Christian love, it contains unique challenges:

> For it is not merely the friendship of equals, but of unequals; the love of the weak and those who can make no return, like the love of God towards the unthankful and the evil. Perhaps for this reason it is less personal and individual, and more diffused towards all men. It is not a friendship of one or two, but of many. Again, it proceeds from a different rule – 'Love your enemies.' It is founded upon that charity which 'beareth all things, believeth all things, hopeth all things, endureth all things.' Such a friendship we may be hardly able to reconcile with our own character, or with common prudence. Yet nothing short of this is the Christian ideal which is set before us in the Gospel. And here and there may be found a person who has been inspired to carry it out in practice.[88]

Jowett extolled Charles Dickens in a memorial sermon as someone who had attained this ideal. His human sympathy made him a friend to his readers and 'the friend of mankind, the philanthropist in the true sense, the friend of youth, the friend of the poor, the enemy of every sort of meanness and oppression'.[89] Jowett included women among friends, and preached on God as the ideal friend.[90] He believed 'the master of the house should be the friend, as well as the master, of all – of his servants, as of his children', and the clergyman 'the friend, physician, teacher . . . of everyone in the parish'.[91]

From a Baptist source, a regional gathering near Bristol in 1850 heard a sermon on 'Friendship with God' from **Charles Stanford** (1823–86), which became a much-reprinted pamphlet. He told his congregation that, as 'spirit' and hence akin to God, they fulfilled the 'natural' condition for such friendship. Although they might be poor and called 'low' class, they must 'never allow outward meanness to make you treat with harsh irreverence your inward grandeur'.[92] The necessary 'moral' condition for divine friendship is fulfilled in so far as they are justified and sanctified by Christ. In friendship we enjoy ease of access to God, and the sharing of divine 'secrets' in the form of inner spiritual strength and peace.

A warm evangelical sermon by **William Humberstone**, published as a pamphlet in 1875, celebrated Jesus as friend of sinners and the healer whose miracles, and above all his cross, evidence his love.[93] Several authors quarry the Bible, sometimes quite ingeniously, for further examples of friendship. To jump ahead a little, in 1919 **Hubert Edwards**, an Anglican clergyman concerned with the training of lay workers, found illustrations of hopefulness, unselfishness, teachability, prayerfulness, humility, hospitality and understanding in the love shown to Jesus by characters as diverse as Mary, John the Baptist and Zaccheus.[94] Back in 1853, the anonymous author **'Amicus'** ('Friend') presented the usual examples of biblical friendship: Abraham, David, the family at Bethany; but also a less usual list including Abigail, Elisha and Paul. He brings their relationships attractively alive. In answer to the perennial question whether divine or human friendship is best, he refuses to separate the two: the Bible, he affirms, knows nothing of the dogma of 'gloomy ascetics' that God alone should be our love, but teaches how we can ' "walk in the Spirit" through all the relationships of humanity'. Of course we all experience moments when the mutability or insufficiency of human friendship brings us to say with Job ' "Miserable comforters are ye all." ' At such times we should unhesitatingly turn to Jesus, and will find more than just comfort:

> When He is sought, He soothes the spirit, calms the trembling frame, and alters the ill-conceived, erroneous view we sometimes take of the intentions of friends, who perhaps have offended, slighted, or even injured us. He points to their infirmities, and reminds us that the strong should bear with the weak; that the servant of the Lord must not strive, but be gentle – must be meek and lowly, like Himself, not easily provoked, bearing all things, enduring all things; and thus He restoreth the soul to so incomparable a state of quiescence, that discord, then banished from the breast, leaves the relenting heart to throb again with generous love for those whom but now it was inclined to discard for ever. Forgiveness, be it remembered, forms a part of friendship; and he 'that hath friends must shew himself friendly'.[95]

The influential Scottish-South African devotional writer **Andrew Murray** (1828–1917) also explores the inter-relatedness of divine and human friendship. Rather in the manner of Aelred's three 'sabbaths' he portrays the structure of intercessory prayer in the 'Parable of the importunate friend'(Lk. 11.5–8) as a 'threefold cord that cannot be broken: the hungry friend needing the help, and the praying friend seeking the help, and the Mighty Friend, loving to give'. He adds, 'It is when we draw near to God as the friend of the poor and the perishing that we may count on his friendliness; the righteous man who is the friend of the poor is very specially the friend of God.'[96]

This same spirituality shines out from **Charlie Andrews** (1871–1940), missionary friend of Mahatma Gandhi, known in India as 'Deenabandhu', 'friend of the afflicted'. He frequently refers to Christ's friendship: 'I have been blessed with wonderful friendships. More than in any other way, my whole course has been directed by these. They have sprung out of, and been moulded by, the love which has been ever deepening in my heart for Christ, the Friend of friends';[97] 'He, the Friend of the friendless, will not allow us to neglect them [the poor] or to send them empty away'.[98]

The turn of the twentieth century saw a variety of approaches. **Anthony Thorold,** a former Bishop of Winchester, wrote a book-length 'essay' *On Friendship* exploring the nature and practice of personal Christian friendship as 'the development of the principle of the Incarnation'.[99] **Hugh Black**'s *Friendship* is a more substantial work by a well-known Edinburgh Presbyterian preacher and scholar who also served as Professor of Practical Theology at Union Seminary in New York. Philosophic friendship, he remarks, has been eclipsed by universal love and perhaps more recently by equal relationships in marriage and by personal relationships with God; but noble spiritual friendship is present in the Bible, and Black proceeds to write the most thorough treatment since Aelred of how to offer and receive friendship. He closes with a chapter on 'the Higher Friendship', the mystical relationship with God in Christ: 'We part with men to meet with God, that we may be able to meet men again on a higher platform.'[100] Picking up the same theme but in very different guise, *The Divine Friendship* by **Jesse Brett** who was chaplain to an Anglican nursing order, is a high Anglo-Catholic account of the spiritual life as mystical friendship with God, passing through dark nights and the way of the cross – but in the joy of Christ's companionship.[101] Very different again is **Robert Wells Veach**, a New York Bible teacher, whose turn-of-the-century vision of the friendship of Jesus as a force working through history was uncomfortably bound up with an uncritical belief in progress towards a 'Kingdom of God' characterized by commerce and democracy.[102]

Among these early twentieth-century writers the American scholar **Henry C. King** (1858–1934) acknowledges debts to the Quakers and Black, and while probably boasting no knowledge of Aquinas he emerges as his kindred spirit when he writes that, far from being ethically peripheral, friendship is 'the conception that unifies and simplifies for me the world and life, as does nothing else'.[103] He illustrates the contemporary intellectual shift towards a close interest in human personality and reverence for persons. Christian life, he states, is grounded on the belief that the most important, and the only eternal things are 'persons and personal relations . . . so that to be a true friend in every relation seems to be the sum of all'.[104] Since God is the source of our being and immanent in us, he is not separate and external to us as are earthly friends. 'But the personal relation to God is only the more close on this account, not the less real.'[105] We can know God as revealed in Christ, and from that point on the laws of the spiritual life are those of deepening relationship with others and God. King is practical as well as theoretical, he discusses the establishment of friendship, with others and with God in prayer; and seeks out the deeper qualities of a true friend in the Beatitudes and 1 Corinthians 13. Love promotes both character and happiness:

> The deepest laid stone in an enduring friendship must be this purpose to love truly, to be the friend one ought to be, to make the friendship of such a kind that it shall tend to bring out the absolute best in each, to make it easier for each to believe in truth, in God, in the spiritual world. Even so high is the test of friendship.

On God's part his love is such that 'He is seeking to bring out in us the image of his Son. He would not be a faithful friend else.' Only God knows our need and can hold us to it: 'the soul is made for God, and only he can fill it'.[106] King inherited the social optimism that saw the Kingdom of God evolving in universal human brotherhood, but saw it in terms of deepening communication and sharing, and the friends of God as serving that divine purpose.

Comparable to King in comprehensiveness but greatly differing in content is *The Friendship of Christ*, a series of talks on Catholic life and devotion given in Rome and New York by **Robert Hugh Benson** (1871–1914) and republished many times. The son of an Archbishop of Canterbury, Benson was ordained before migrating to Rome. An evangelical fervour combines with that of the convert as he invites us to know 'the maddening joy of the conscious companionship of Jesus Christ'.[107] He introduces 'countless avenues' along which Christ approaches us to seek our friendship: interiorly through hearing the Gospel and through prayerful spiritual growth; exteriorly in the Eucharist and in the Church and its saints; and as Christ crucified in the sinner who asks mercy, the beggar looking for alms, the stranger or the sufferer; as well as in all our less exotic everyday neighbours.

On a much lighter note, very tongue-in-cheek and secular, **Arnold Bennett**'s 'plea for the Feast of St Friend' expressed a genuine hunger for real relationship, proposing the replacement of family Christmasses with this new, chore-free feast![108] Serious treatments continued in such forms as sermons by **Mrs Bramwell Booth**, grand-daughter of the Salvation Army's founder, and **Maude Royden**, the first well-known female preacher in London.[109] The burden of **Leslie Weatherhead**'s *The Transforming Friendship*, with its homely and psychological slants, was that Christianity originated in a vivid personal encounter with Christ and remains the same today: it is 'the acceptance of the gift of the friendship of Jesus'.[110]

In Liverpool in 1929 the Student Christian Movement, then an ecumenical and missionary powerhouse, made friendship the theme of its quadrennial Conference: 'God means the world for friendship – friendship between nations, friendship between men, and above all friendship between man and God ... in this friendship is the meaning of the world and of your life.'[111] The Anglican theological teacher **Robert H. Moberly** echoed this in his Confirmation course in 1934, in which at last the Trinity makes a welcome reappearance:

> The life of the eternal God is not something cold and solitary. Mutual love, which is true friendship, is the very meaning of that life. Thus, if it be true that God stoops to offer us His friendship, He is simply inviting us to share His own eternal life.[112]

Just as Vansteenberghe's article in 1937 uncovered the extent of the tradition of theological writing on friendship for the first time, we finally encounter some awareness of the broad sweep of previous Christian reflection, of Aelred and Thomas Aquinas and Taylor, in the quite academic little book *The Friendship of Christ,* a 'devotional study' for the wartime Lent of 1945 by the Cambridge ecclesiastical historian **Charles Smyth.** Acerbic and cerebral, Smyth asks whether human friendship forms 'a parable, a similitude, or an extension' of divine friendship? Or is the latter merely an imaginary projection of the former? His own answer is to give priority to revelation: Christ's friendship teaches us what love is and that it is both like, and very unlike, its human analogy. While human friendship contracts our relationships, that of Christ 'involves us in obedience, and obedience involves us in loving one another'.[113]

C. S. Lewis by contrast, famously writing on 'Friendship' in *The Four Loves*, made no use of the tradition and attempted no theological development. This is a quite personal essay rooted in the kind of donnish companionship, redolent of pubs, pipe-smoke and walking holidays, that he himself enjoyed. Friendship, unlike romance or maternal caring, is a biologically unnecessary love, subversive within the crowd, a 'luminous, tranquil, rational world of relationships freely chosen', on the level of gods or angels.[114] His friends stand side by side, in a pair or at most a small group, all normally male, who have discovered they share some overwhelming mutual interest. Friendship, as Emerson has it, is to '"care about the same truth"'. Lewis arrives at the unusual conclusion that because it is already so 'spiritual', friendship is of little use as an analogy for divine-human relations. Familial metaphors are, he suggests, earthier and less easy to confuse with the reality they signify.[115]

Some years later Bishop **Stephen Neill** felt the neglect of this theme and chose to describe Jesus as 'the Friend through whom bad friends can become good friends'. Jesus not only binds his followers together but also, as 'friend of sinners', 'revealed new dimensions in friendship' that transcend the classical ideal. And the sinners, Neill ponders, 'do not seem to have found his presence disturbing or humiliating; yet they are aware that the friendly welcome he accords to them does not involve any condonation of their wrongdoing,' nor any evasion of their need for a radical change of heart.[116]

As an inheritor of this rich tradition, **James Houston**'s *The Transforming Friendship* is something of a *tour de force*, a beautifully deep and detailed study of the transformation of personality and relationships through prayer that draws us into the life of the Trinity. 'The Holy Spirit becomes our friend primarily to give us a deeper quality of relationship with God the Father and Son.'[117] This author, a Baptist scholar with wide ecumenical sympathies, draws on long experience as a teacher and spiritual counsellor and a depth of knowledge of the Bible and tradition, not least that of Christian mystical prayer. As Christ changes us, healing our past wounds, we are born again and enter a new world of relationships. 'No one can be the friend of Jesus without having many other friends.'[118] In an alienated world, a community grounded in such prayer must be a revolutionary force.

Continental philosophers and theologians

During the seventeenth and eighteenth centuries, the ages of 'reason' and 'enlightenment', the classical assumption that human beings naturally form communities and assist one another, and that justice relates to this universal tendency to friendship, was challenged by the opposite supposition that we are fundamentally self-interested, isolated and competitive individuals. The individual as subjective thinker or feeler took centre-stage. Moral philosophy became focused on defining individual rights and seeking a rationale for the overcoming of self-interest. Friendship faced relegation from the realm of ethics to that of sentiment and taste, culture and leisure. In this new milieu, Kant and Kierkegaard proposed very different understandings of friendship's role.

From Kant's 'love and respect' to Buber's 'I and Thou'

Immanuel Kant (1704–1804), although a theist, sought to base morality on reason alone. His *Fundamental Principles* [*Groundwork*] *of the Metaphysics of Morals* posits the existence of a rational moral law that is absolutely binding on all, and in relation to which we have duties that can be universally commanded. 'There is, therefore, only one categorical imperative, and it is this: *Act only on that maxim through which you can at the same time will that it should become a universal law*.'[119] He anchors this rule in a further postulate, that of the absolute intrinsic value of rational beings as ends in themselves. 'The practical imperative will thus be as follows: *So act as to treat humanity, whether in your own person or in that of any other, always at the same time as an end, and never merely as a means*.'[120] Later, in the *Doctrine of Virtue*, part of his *Metaphysic of Morals,* Kant describes ethical behaviour in less impersonal terms. It consists in the duties of 'love' (which is not aesthetic feeling, although that may come, but benevolence issuing in beneficence, gratitude, and sympathy) and 'respect' (in which we avoid placing our own dignity above that of the other, and allow them their own space). Perfect friendship is 'the union of two persons through equal and mutual love and respect', and we are worthy of happiness just to the extent that we adopt the universal 'duty of friendship', albeit as an ideal, it being impossible to fulfil it in practical friendship to every other individual. What is actually possible is to be a 'friend of man' in the moral sense, 'one who sympathizes emotionally with the welfare of all men (shares their delight in it) and will never disturb it without heartfelt regret'. Kant deliberately chooses the term 'friend', as connoting more than philanthropy, avoiding all idea of patronage, and implying equality among all 'as if all men are brothers under one universal father who wills the happiness of all'.[121] Friendship is a concrete instance of love which should progress to being universal: there do exist rare people 'of a kindly disposition . . . always prepared to look on the best side of things', who combine kindness with taste and understanding and 'whose capacity to form friendships with anyone might well earn them the title of everybody's friends'. To be such a 'friend of all . . . constitutes a high degree of perfection'.[122]

In the Danish philosophical theologian **Søren Kierkegaard** (1813–55) 'love of neighbour' takes on a Kantian flavour as love that is not contingent on feeling but commanded as absolute duty. His *Works of Love* published in 1847 is a vigorous polemic against the superficial Christianity, as he saw it, of the Danish Lutheran Church: its collusion with selfish, sentimental human love while ignoring Christ's call to a new, radically self-denying, divine love:

> Christianity has thrust erotic love and friendship from the throne, the love based on drives and inclination, preferential love, in order to place the spirit's love [*Kjerlighed*] in its place, love for the neighbor, a love that in earnestness and truth is more tender in inwardness than erotic love in the union and more faithful in sincerity than the most celebrated friendship in the alliance.[123]

Kierkegaard lumps erotic love and friendship together as passionate, preferential loves determined by their object. He eliminates any appeal to virtuous classical friendship by asserting that love of an 'other self' is nothing other than extended self-love, 'uniting the two in a new selfish self'. (p. 56) Friendship is exclusive, contains no moral task, happens merely by chance, and Christianity neither teaches nor praises it: the New Testament has not a single verse about 'friendship in the sense in which the poet celebrates it and paganism cultivated it' (p. 45); rather its entire message is love of neighbour which is sober, spiritual, self-renouncing, universal and eternal and constitutes 'the moral task which in turn is the origin of all tasks'.(p. 51) Every person is our neighbour, equal before God, to be loved unconditionally and exactly as they are. In 'erotic love and friendship', preference is the 'middle term', but 'in love for the neighbour God is the middle term. Love God above all else; then you also love the neighbour and in the neighbour every human being.' (p. 58).

Christians can have friends, and be married, but only by practising true love: the spirit's love, which is the absolute neighbour-love given to all. 'Love your friend honestly and devotedly, but let love for the neighbour be what you learn from each other in your friendship's confidential relationship with God!' (p. 62). 'Christianly, the entire distinction between the many different kinds of love is essentially abolished.' (p. 143). Christian love is a fundamental existential commitment to love every person, and since this is not within our natural power, 'It is God, the Creator, who must implant love in each human being, who himself is Love.' (p. 216).

> Christ's love for Peter was boundless in this way: in loving Peter he accomplished loving the person one sees. He did not say, 'Peter must first change and become another person before I can love him again.' No, he said exactly the opposite, he said, 'Peter is Peter, and I love him; love, if anything, will help him to become another man.' Therefore he did not break off the friendship in order perhaps to renew it again if Peter would have become another person; no, he preserved the friendship unchanged and in that way helped Peter to become another person. Do you think that Peter would have been won again without Christ's faithful friendship? (p. 172).

Kierkegaard's definitions distance him from sentimental friendship but his logic brings him in line with the tradition that sees God's love as that of a faithful friend; and indeed with Kant's ideal of universal friendship and Aquinas's friendship-love. He remains unwilling however, to call the sinner a 'friend' in the passive sense:

> You can . . . continue to love the beloved and the friend no matter how they treat you, but you cannot truly continue to call them the beloved and friend when they, sorry to say, have really changed. No change, however, can take the neighbour from you, because it is not the neighbour who holds you fast, but it is your love that holds the neighbour fast. (p. 65)

In life, Kierkegaard was less austerely individualistic than his writing would suggest; and even in his writing he is capable of celebrating reciprocity: 'Wonderful! There are a *You* and an *I*, and there is no *mine* and *yours*! For without a *you* and an *I*, there is no love, and with *mine* and *yours* there is no love' (p. 266). Human love, he believed, merely succeeds in creating a collective 'ours' which is 'augmented self-love' (p. 267); but within pure love of God the 'mine-yours' distinction is cancelled, replaced by a mysterious unity in possessing nothing, yet possessing all things (p. 268).

Kierkegaard's teaching on absolute neighbour-love was to lead in one direction towards Nygren's 'Agape':

> We human beings speak about finding the perfect person in order to love him, whereas Christianity speaks about being the perfect person who boundlessly loves the person he sees. We human beings want to look upward in order to look for the object of perfection . . . but in Christ perfection looked down to earth, and loved the person it saw. (pp. 173–4)

This is an existential ethic of subjective love poured forth from the transformed individual standing before God. As unconditional love, Kierkegaard's neighbour-love becomes Nygren's 'Agape'. Yet for Kierkegaard it focuses on the distinct person of the other, and when it is mutual it is inter-subjective, between ongoing independent existents, because for him there is no question of friends being welded into a single self. His thought therefore also leads in quite another direction, towards existentialism and personalism: 'Love to one's neighbour is love between two beings eternally and independently determined as spirit' (p. 56), it is between an 'I' and a 'You' (p. 266).

The 'I' and 'You' motif was picked up by **Martin Buber** (1878–1965) in his *I and Thou*, published in 1923. 'I–Thou' and 'I–It' are the 'two basic words' that relate us to others, to the world, and to God the 'eternal Thou'. In an 'I–it' relationship we treat the other as a thing, relating impersonally to them, or rather to their isolated qualities. In an 'I–Thou' relationship each person regards the other as a subject in all their depth and wholeness. The modern age had not only invented the isolated individual, but had thereby opened a path into a wholly new exploration of human inter-subjectivity. We shall pick up the thread of this new exploration in our next chapter.

The friend is a model of the neighbour: from Barth to Bonhoeffer

Several major twentieth-century German and Swiss theologians contribute to this discussion. 'Nature' and 'revelation' are worlds apart in the dialectical theology of **Karl Barth** (1886–1968). Nevertheless, he allowed that an analogical and pedagogical relationship exists between natural friendship and supernatural neighbour-love. By nature, human beings are determined towards freely chosen friendship. We are called 'to be friends of friends' and to discover ourselves in relationship to a Thou; and 'The concept of friendship is . . . the root of the concept of the *neighbor* which is so important in understanding the command of God' (188). When an adolescent discovers an *alter ego* in a friend, to whom no ties of kin or sexual attraction bind them, they are empowered to discover their family anew as friends. This new, free, spiritual relationship models that which we shall have to our neighbour. The command to love our neighbour comes to us as persons already capable of free relationship to the other through natural friendship, hence 'the friend is a model of the *neighbor*'.[124]

Barth's Swiss sparring-partner **Emil Brunner** (1889–1966) specified this link further. In Reformed thought, the moral life was divided into compartments concerned with the family, work, State and Church; but Brunner assigns friendship to the recreational realm, 'the community of play, and all free social life'.[125] No ethical significance attaches to this realm, yet in so far as we find 'pleasure in the moral being of the other', friendship constitutes a bridge to the ethical realm and as such it develops into 'a task or duty'. 'Friendship is only genuine where it is deliberately regarded not only as a gift but as an obligation.' Still, this does not quite lift natural friendship into the ethical realm of *agape*, love of neighbour:

> Real community, *Agape*, is foreshadowed, naturally, in friendship, and in the capacity for friendship; the fact that human beings naturally form friendships, whether they will or no, is an indication that they are destined for community, in the sense of responsible love. But friendship is not itself such community. For it is not based on the fact that I know that I am under an obligation to serve the other, but upon the fact that I take a delight in him. Friendship does not say: I love you because you are *there*, but it says merely: I love you because you are like this! Thus it is not unconditional but conditional, exclusive and not universal. A person who claims friendship with everyone has not begun to understand the meaning of friendship.[126]

Moreover friendship is human, and therefore, although it is God's refreshing gift to us it will always retain an element of selfishness: 'Friendship, too, needs to be reborn, and this new birth, even in the highest instance, will be only the beginning of a new life which is never perfect.'[127]

A suspicion that there may be more to friendship, and some questioning of the restrictive Reformed domains of ethical existence, seem to be stirring in the mind of **Dietrich Bonhoeffer** (1906–45). In a letter from prison just before his execution by the Nazis, he wonders about friendship as 'a subdivision of the concept of culture'. Culture, he writes, belongs to 'the free expanse of liberty' which encompasses the three recognized domains (family, state, work) of divine command and duty. Liberty, which is absolutely necessary for a complete life, perhaps belongs particularly to the 'fourth domain', the Church:

> It almost seems today, and is perhaps in fact the case, that the concept of the Church can alone make it possible once again to understand the free expanse of liberty, the field which includes art, culture, friendship and play. Perhaps, then, what Kierkegaard calls the 'aesthetic existence' [alongside the ethical and the religious], far from being excluded from the domain of the Church, should be given a new foundation within the Church ... Who, for example, in our time can still with an easy mind cultivate music or friendship, play games and enjoy himself? Certainly not the 'ethical' man, but only the Christian. It is precisely because friendship belongs to the domain of this liberty (the liberty of the 'Christian man') that one must confidently defend oneself against all the frowns of all 'ethical' existences, certainly without

> appealing to the *necessitas* of a divine commandment, but appealing nevertheless to the *necessitas* of liberty. I believe that within the domain of this liberty friendship is the rarest and most precious treasure. It is rare indeed, for where is it now to be found in this world of ours which is predominantly governed by the first three mandates? Friendship is not to be compared with the values of the mandates. In relation to them it is *sui generis*, yet it is as much in place among them as the cornflower in the wheatfield.[128]

It is in the experience of such struggles as that in which Bonhoeffer was caught up that the ethical significance of friendship makes itself starkly evident. For Moltmann friendship would become, not a wild flower but integral to ethical existence. Freedom and friendship create the new world. A way of thinking about love that places the relationality of friendship at its heart gathered pace through the later years of the twentieth century, and to its beginnings we now turn.

6

God's friendship, ancient and so new

Friendship, mirror and icon of the Trinity

At the oasis of Tamanrasset in the Sahara desert of southern Algeria there lived, at the dawn of the twentieth century, an unusual Christian hermit. Charles de Foucauld resembled the original desert hermits in that he had been a French cavalry officer, became a monk after a sudden conversion, and had lived and prayed in the Holy Land. He was unusual in that his vision issued in a contemplative life among people, imitating Jesus during his life in Nazareth, in what has often been called 'an apostolate of friendship'. 'If it is true that Jesus is our friend and he asks us to love others as he himself loves us, are we not obliged to love others in such a manner that we may become also in truth their friend?' 'One need only have a moment's contact, but that suffices to allow the existence of friendship to become evident.'[1]

Now, women and men who have chosen this way of life live all over the world in small communities among the poorest, learning friendship with one another in their own diversity and practising the apostolate of friendship in prayer, shared life and open, simple hospitality. In South Africa I came to know many unusual friends through these 'Little Sisters of Jesus'. Their network of friendship embraced the 'greatest' and the 'least' in an equal welcome. Somewhat like them is the Taizé Community in

France, founded in the 1940s to live a similar lifestyle, which draws members from many different Churches and nationalities into a living sign of ecumenical unity.

These are powerful paradigms for a life of Christian love as friendship. Some such way of friendship can be lived out in whatever circumstances or career a person may find themselves. It is a way to be leaven, a 'sign of contradiction', a sign of God's Kingdom and its justice and joy.

In what follows we trace developments over the decades from the 1930s to the present, a time of intense change, and of remarkable activity in the theology of love. During the 1930s the idea promoted by Anders Nygren's *Agape and Eros*, that Christian love is rightly described as absolute altruism, reigned supreme. It is not our intention to question whether a Christian should be capable of heroic altruism. Most certainly they should: altruism is contained within the spectrum of Christian love; but is it a wholly adequate description of what that love is? That question initiated the return of friendship, at first as a protest, then as increasingly central in its own right, while friendship itself evolves in the search to express more clearly the intention of Christ.

Friendship's reawakening

The case for Philia

It was perhaps the undying presence of friendship in Anglican devotion, combined with his classical knowledge, that led **John Burnaby** (1892–1978) to become the first academic since Aquinas to argue on a scholarly level for friendship as the quintessential model for Christian love. A humble and attractive lay classical scholar, Burnaby was later ordained and became Professor of Divinity at Cambridge.

In lectures on Augustine given in 1938, which became the book *Amor Dei* (*The Love of God*) he championed 'love of God' in the objective sense of love *for* God, which energizes Augustine and the entire Christian mystical tradition. He attacked Nygren's 'anti-mystical' tendency, his denial that we can rightly seek and desire God. But neither Augustine's nor Nygren's account of love seemed to him wholly satisfying, because Augustine conveys too little sense of love's reciprocity, and neither 'Eros' nor 'Agape' as Nygren depicts them affords an adequate account because neither contains within itself the ability to engender mutual relationship. 'But', Burnaby continues,

> ... there is a third element ... the neglect of which constitutes a serious, perhaps fatal defect in his whole construction. Eros and Agape are not the only Greek words for love. The Philia in which Aristotle discovered the richest endowment of human

> personality is strange neither to the Old Testament nor to the New. It differs both from Eros and from Agape in being a mutual relation, a bond which links two centres of consciousness in one.[2]

Philia is, in the Bible, not only a human relationship like that of David and Jonathan but also the love between God and human creatures in his covenant with Israel; and behind Christ's sacrifice on the cross lies 'the love wherewith the Father loved the Son before the foundation of the world, the unity into which all the friends of the Crucified are to be made perfect: *that they may be one, even as we are one*' (Jn 17.22). There is 'the Holy of Holies of the New Testament'. *Caritas* is not a one-way but a relational love, it is 'what it is in the mystery of the divine Being – the Holy Spirit of unity'.[3]

Burnaby investigates how various post-Augustinian writers, from Abelard to Bishop Butler, sought to deal with the inadequacy of his one-way account of *caritas*. Even as the 'love of friendship' (*amor amicitiae*) of the Middle Ages, *caritas* was too often interpreted only as a unidirectional disinterested love, missing its relational nature. To wish well, and even to act accordingly, is not enough to constitute Christian love. Burnaby does not mention Aelred, who was then little known and was in any case not a philosophical theologian. While criticizing certain points in Thomas, he is fundamentally in sympathy with Thomas's doctrine of *caritas* as friendship with God.[4]

Finally and briefly, Burnaby outlines his own account of Christian love. 'God has made men apt to find their completion in communion, because such communion is a likeness of the mutual love in which and through which Three Persons are One God', hence love 'can have no other purpose, as it can have no other source, but the mutual "inherence" of persons, life in one another.' Divine love is the offer of relationship: 'The love which endures, which offers itself to the unloving, is always the servant of its own high purpose – not to rest until the sundered fellowship is restored, till rejection is changed to response' (pp. 306–7).

> *If ye love them that love you, what reward have you?* [Mt. 5.46] It is indeed the *test* of a love which would be like God's, that it should be all-embracing; but we may be certain that Christ did not mean either that it is better to have enemies than friends, or that any outward act of beneficence can be a substitute for the inward disposition of heart which would make a friend out of the enemy. (pp. 307–8)

Mutuality, and even feelings of attraction, must therefore also be proper topics for Christian moral discourse. 'The reluctance to see Christian love in its purity except where it is not returned' owes much to Kant's belittling of the ethical significance of love that is not willed but depends on attraction; but it 'cannot justify itself by the Sermon on the Mount'. The religion of grace should surely not dismiss any love which comes as 'gift', either in the sphere of sex or as 'the basis of all natural friendship' (p. 308). Natural relationships, based on attraction and limited by parameters of 'preference', have commonly been contrasted with Christian love as 'universal philanthropy'. However, when Burnaby looks at the Good Samaritan what he sees is not so much universal philanthropy as a particular love governed by a special cause of preference, the condition of need itself; a love 'willing to meet need without respect of persons' (p. 308). It may therefore be that preferential love is not to be simply contrasted with universal Christian love.

A true preferential 'unity-in-duality', whether in marriage or of friends, should create persons who are mature, free from egoism – even from 'egoism à deux', and able to relate in love beyond the pair (p. 309). Friendships are the school for a wider love which in turn has friendship as its inner meaning and intent:

> Christian charity is not an *extension* of the love which has linked two persons together because of the good they were able to see in one another. The growth of charity does not take the form of a progressive removal of landmarks, an expanding circle of ever wider comprehensiveness. Charity grows intensively not extensively. It is the measure of an active conviction that unity in love is the greatest of all good things, expressing itself in the effort to overcome all hindrance to that unity. And therefore no one altogether incapable or ignorant of Philia, of love received as well as given, is in a way to have Agape. The love which has been enjoyed as a gift provides the motive for the love which is to give itself to others: the need which Agape goes out to meet is always in the end the need for love and for nothing else. (p. 310)

Friendship with God is immeasurably greater, like and yet very unlike that for a human friend, involving us totally in 'delight, desire, and devotion . . . the love of Him is more, though it is never less, than personal love'.

> No Christian philosophy can think of God as 'a person' among others, whom we may come to know and add to the number of our friends. The irreverence which we immediately perceive in such a thought consists in its implied pretence to equality between creature and Creator. We can only speak of friendship with God without danger, if we remember at every moment its *un*likeness as well as its likeness to all human friendship. (p. 311)

Burnaby pinpoints the source of embarrassment in the unreal 'friendship with God' that may be presented to us in *kitsch* piety: it proposes God as a cosy and tolerant companion, one among many whom we might care to collect as a friend, a congenial item to add when constructing a 'designer spirituality' for ourselves. That reduces God to the status of an existent among other existents, trivializing a relationship that if real, affects and transforms our whole being. 'Friendship with God' has at times been guarded exclusively for saints. A more modern danger is to reduce it to the casual and comfortable level, where the problem is sentimental unreality rather than 'irreverence'. If God, even as friend, is not awesome and challenging, we are not truly encountering God.

Remembering its uniqueness, the reality remains that we relate to God in mutual love. On our side we live this friendship both in the passivity of faith and the activity of obedience, knowing as Thomas did, that 'only God's grace makes it possible to our creaturely condition, only "in Christ" can we have boldness to enter the holy place' (p. 312).

> Friendship with God will rest upon the explicit recognition of His presence in the world . . . The friend of God will see Him everywhere – His face in nature's beauty and wonder, the working of the Spirit and the appeal of His love in men . . . Without this sense of the environing God, His infinite Otherness, the love of Him cannot keep its humility nor escape out of self-centredness to the service of His Kingdom. But it is no less needful to be aware of his presence within, to know that we ourselves are His temples, and that our own life is part of His self-disclosure. (p. 313)

With Augustine, Burnaby understands the ultimate Christian hope to be a union with God that will include the others – as he hopes, *all* the others – in 'the complete and final victory of love' (p. 317).

Psychology and grace

Burnaby's book established itself as a classic study of Augustine, at the same time suggesting to its readers a more relational account of love. A few years later, another English writer, the Jesuit, **Martin D'Arcy**, contributed to this debate from a psychological perspective. Introducing his own scheme which owes as much to the Roman poet Lucretius as to Jung, D'Arcy analysed the human soul or psychological nature into '*animus*' and '*anima*'.[5] Natural love, which he names 'Eros', springs from one or other of these aspects of the human self. The love of the *animus* is rational, controlling, self-seeking and possessive; that of the *anima* is irrational and self-sacrificing. He named his book *The Mind and Heart of Love*, associating mind with the *animus*, heart with the *anima*.

D'Arcy correlated the 'mind' of love with Nygren's 'Eros', the 'egocentric humanism' that seeks to understand, to possess, to augment the self. D'Arcy's Eros of the 'heart', ironically, correlates with Nygren's 'Agape' as seen 'from below', from the point of view of the soul encountering God's love coming 'down' and desiring to be possessed, in such a manner as to overwhelm reason and leave humanity to do nothing and God to do all. D'Arcy also took note of the fresh definitions of 'Eros' and 'Agape' recently proposed by the Swiss-French personalist Denis de Rougemont, whose 'Eros' is dark, pagan self-immolating passion, while 'Agape' is the personal, life-affirming mutual love revealed in Christ and exemplified in Christian marriage.[6] As love that sacrifices itself, de Rougemont's 'Eros' is the love of D'Arcy's *anima*. D'Arcy saw the fear and uncertainty of the human condition as resulting very largely from the unresolved conflict between the loves of mind and heart. He understood real love to come through the psychological integration of *animus* and *anima*, creating a person who is capable both of giving and receiving, of possessing without possessiveness and of being possessed in freedom. Such a person is capable of de Rougemont's 'Agape'; and D'Arcy understands Agape to be a mutual event between persons in whom 'mind' and 'heart' are reconciled. In a word, Agape is friendship, and for D'Arcy it was through the Christian revelation that this love came to be fully revealed in this world, bringing peace and joy:

> The perfection of love . . . is to be found in personal friendship, whether between a man and a woman, between man and man [woman and woman, as we would wish to add] or between man and God. When God revealed himself as love, the last fear was removed from man's heart. Neither God nor nature nor other human beings were enemies and a menace. They could all be looked at with interest and love, and in the case of persons love could be mutual.[7]

Buber's basic word 'I-It' is spoken by the *animus*, which treats the other as a mere object. 'I-Thou' is spoken by the integrated 'I' of Philia or Agape, which in addressing a 'Thou' is both confirmed in its own selfhood and drawn out into the presence of the other. As Buber says, ' "The primary word I-Thou can be spoken only with the whole being . . . I become through my relation to the Thou; as I become I, I say Thou." '[8] True love then, 'can never be understood save as a meeting of persons in a friendship', in which 'each becomes perfect in bowing to the other . . . egocentrism exists only when we love things; it disappears when we address another as Thou' (p. 156).

'Thou' can be another human being, or can be God. Nygren had objected that there can be no divine-human friendship because divine and human loves are unequal; friendship 'is excluded by the sovereignty of Divine love'.[9] D'Arcy insists on the counterbalancing mystery of our 'relative self-dependence and freewill', itself created by God's love. The perfection of our nature by grace mysteriously enables human participation, in a kind of equality, in the new 'supernatural friendship' with God without making the human person 'an automaton' (p. 106).

Human beings have by nature the possibility of a certain friendship with God, in that our mind encounters truth and our love desires goodness. God is truth and goodness, and an exchange of love is possible. Even outside Christianity 'we have to allow for many uncovenanted graces from God, who desires all to enjoy His friendship' (p. 108) although its full meaning can be comprehended only through our incorporation into Christ (p. 112).

In the perspective of existential anthropology the human being is a mystery of personhood: 'a person in being a person is *for* himself and *to* another; that is to say, he is both a living self-contained being and a living relation' (p. 105). In divine as in human relations, the 'law' of friendship is that 'we give what we are and we receive from the other' (p. 436). The human partner is 'energized' by grace and receives superabundant life, 'increasing instead of decreasing its personality' so that the soul joyfully knows that its own existence, 'even the beginning of its own acts and love', are God's gift and are making possible this new relation, in which Paul and the mystics rejoice, of 'friend with friend, beloved and lover'. (p. 440).

When Christ called the disciples 'friends' he set out the 'new law' of mutual love, which, although the appreciation of love as interpersonal has found new expression in the present day, has always been present at the heart of the Christian revelation (pp. 440, 432). Whenever Christianity awakens a 'new reverence for personality and the glory which it possesses' it awakens a new appreciation of friendship, which 'wanes and waxes according as the meaning and value of human personality is neglected or appreciated' (p. 153).

Over human history, D'Arcy suggests, three sorts or levels of friendship have appeared. First, the natural philia of the classical writers, 'a quiet ordered love ... which lacked the specific and supernatural character of Christian Agape and yet preserved a balance and discipline' (p. 57). Aristotle's teaching on it is rightly understood as a call to unselfish virtue (pp. 140–3). Next came friendship experienced by the ordinary Christian, who recognizes it as a 'foretaste or prophecy of a state of love in which all is well' (p. 436) but for whom, D'Arcy suggests, little change has actually occurred in practice because however much 'part of the struggle of our life consists in ... making ourselves free to love wherever the lovable is to be found' (p. 293), most of us remain bound by the conventions of an hierarchical 'order of respect' (p. 303) and the need to exercise judicious caution in our choice of associates (p. 436).

Beyond these, however, lies the grace to love with complete freedom and beyond ordinary capacity – but 'only the saints have the secret of giving love to all they meet and to unknown friends', a perfect love that 'can do without scaffolding and human conventions' (p. 302). Not all have this gift and therefore it cannot be assumed, as the slogan of 'equality and fraternity' perhaps does assume, that 'all at a word can live the highest form of love' (p. 303). Again D'Arcy quotes Buber:

> Love is responsibility of an I for a Thou. In this lies the likeness – impossible in any feeling whatsoever – of all who love, from the smallest to the greatest and from the blessedly protected man, whose life is rounded in that of a loved being, to him who is all his life nailed to the cross of the world and who ventures to bring himself to the dreadful point – to love *all men.*[10]

True love then is the love of friendship, of which the integrated, and much more the graced, person becomes capable. It is the same steady love from the moment of its first offer to its hoped-for completion in reciprocity, and it does not cease. **Ignace Lepp**, who became a Jesuit priest and depth psychologist after being an idealistic young French Communist, speaks of the maturity that continues to love even when a friend departs from a former cameraderie: 'Within Christianity the spirit of tolerance has made great progress in recent times. I know priests of unquestionable fidelity to the Church who remain on close terms of friendship with those who have left the Church's service. We may see this as a sign of psychological and emotional maturity.'[11]

Simone Weil: 'creative attention'

During these same years **Simone Weil** (1909–43), French philosophical writer, activist for the wartime Resistance, and mystic, developed an acute sense of the universal presence of God animating human love, indeed making all human love possible. For her, all our loves whether of neighbour, the beauty of the world, religious practices, or friends, are an implicit love for God. Extrapolating from her own experience, which she takes as universal, she suggests we love God blindly and impersonally until God grants us a direct encounter with himself. Thereafter, egocentrism is overcome and we become aware of love's supernatural nature, knowing that 'all points in the world are equally centres and that the true centre is outside this world'.[12]

Weil prepares the ground for friendship by speaking about love of neighbour, justice, and 'creative attention'. God's love, with which we love our neighbour, has the quality of 'creative attention'. In the Gospel, she passionately believes, love of neighbour is identical with justice, a 'supernatural virtue' which 'consists of behaving exactly as though there were equality when one is the stronger in an unequal relationship'. This 'most Christian of virtues' confers on the afflicted 'the quality of human beings, of which fate had deprived them', reproducing in some way 'the original generosity of the Creator with regard to them' (p. 100). Gratitude, the reciprocal love of the afflicted for their benefactor, has an equally divine origin: 'In true love it is not we who love the afflicted in God, it is God in us who loves them. When we are in affliction it is God in us who loves those who wish us well' (p. 107). Love, therefore, has an essentially reciprocal form.

On love and friendship, Weil says it superficially appears that friendship derives from our preferring someone because we seek some good in them or need them, whereas charity is available for all the afflicted. In reality, however, the two loves are profoundly related. Friendship desires good for the other; but since the 'central good for every man is the free disposal of himself', friendship is in its deep reality the transcendence of our need and of seeking our good, a miraculous supernatural transcendence which enables us to 'wish autonomy to be preserved' in our self and the other. Thus in friendship there is a 'supernatural union' between necessity and liberty (pp. 154, 156). There is neither domination nor a wish to please: 'the two friends have fully consented to be two and not one', they respect the distance that being two distinct creatures places between them. Friendship is thus very like neighbour-love. 'Through this supernatural miracle of respect for human autonomy, friendship is very like the pure forms of compassion and gratitude called forth by affliction.' (p. 157). There is a sense in which friends may be said to be 'one': we may desire direct union with God, and two friends who each have God within them may thus be 'one'. Weil's thought flows easily on into a striking depiction of friendship as both school and focal case of love:

> Friendship has something universal about it. It consists of loving a human being as we should like to be able to love each soul in particular and all those who go to make up the human race. As a geometrician looks at a particular figure in order to deduce the universal properties of the triangle, so he who knows how to love directs upon a particular human being a love which is universal. (p. 158)

When Christ added his 'third commandment', to 'love one another', he did so, Weil suggests, because the disciples were already bonded together, and bonds can slip into a dependency that easily transmutes into hatred and repulsion. 'We hate what we are dependent upon. We become disgusted with what depends on us.' Christ therefore commanded his disciples to 'transform these bonds into friendship', so that they should not slide into impure attachment or hatred (p. 159). Such friendship has a sacramental character: 'Where there are two or three gathered together in my name there am I in the midst of them'; and 'Pure friendship is an image of that original and perfect friendship which belongs to the Trinity and which is the very essence of God' (p. 160).

God is 'our perfect friend', granting us 'absolute liberty of consent' (p. 165). 'Every existing thing', she writes to her Dominican friend Fr Perrin, 'is equally upheld in its existence by God's creative love. The friends of God should love him to the point of merging their love with his with regard to all things here below' (p. 61).

Simone Weil was a suffering and wonderfully lucid soul who came to Christian faith from a non-practising Jewish background. She always maintained a distance between herself and the institution of the Church, but came to her first mystical encounter with Christ through meditation and chanted liturgical prayer at the Benedictine monastery of Solesmes. She makes 'love of religious practices' one of the modes of implicit love for God, describing it in arresting words: 'Attention animated by desire is the whole foundation of religious practices. That is why no system of morality can take their place' (p. 150).

In Weil's upholding of personal autonomy, in her refusal of domination and of the pressure to please others, we can surely find a link with her experience as a woman; but her philosophical roots tap into the Christian existentialism and personalism of her contemporary France. The personalism developed by Mounier, Marcel, Maritain and Nédoncelle sought to place the existence of free and creative persons, consisting of body and spirit, at the heart of all political, philosophical and theological agendas. It used a phenomenological approach, experiencing personhood from within, extending Buber's perspective on the inner meaning of relationships and probing the mystery of the 'availability' ('*disponibilité*') of one subject to another.

Intersubjective encounter and Thomas Aquinas

The influence of the new interest in persons has been all-pervasive. In philosophical theology it has been creatively interwoven with the thought of Thomas Aquinas. First, in 1946 the French Dominican **L.-B. Gillon** pointed to the contrast between the 'impersonal' object of Thomas's 'desiring-love', and the 'personal' subject who is loved with 'friendship-love'. An object is loved as a means, a subject as an end in themselves. In a subject, we recognize the personhood of the 'other'. In friendship-love, lover and beloved are both subjects, while the goods they desire for each other are objects. Desiring-love is 'imperfect' in that it is determined by accidental goods that are loved only in reference to some further end; friendship-love is 'perfect' in that it terminates and reposes in a substantial good that we love for itself.[13]

Developing these thoughts, the American Jesuit philosopher **Robert Johann** sought to understand love by synthesizing Thomas's thought 'as furnishing the metaphysical framework for a *philosophy* of intersubjectivity', with contemporary insights into the '*mystery* of intersubjectivity'.[14] For Johann, personality reflects God's own being and is of the highest order of reality, and hence our reflexive insight into our own consciousness pierces to the very mystery of being:

> The interiority of consciousness first reveals to us what it means really to exist. It presents being not as a flattened image or an impenetrable block seen only from the outside, but in all its inner warmth, depth and mystery. Through the direct, immediate and concrete consciousness of the self we first contact being as absolute, a value in and for itself, a deep center and source of initiative, an energy that poses itself and can, through a process of transcendentalization, be understood as founding the reality of all that is. This is the essence of being as *subject* or *subjectivity*.
>
> An object, on the other hand, is whatever cannot be, or at least is not, so grasped. It presents to us only its outer surface and conceals its deep existential uniqueness, offering us only matter for abstract analysis. (p. 5)

When we experience the other as 'subject' we encounter in them too 'a self in all the depths of his inner mystery' (p. 6). This occurs in friendship-love, dubbed 'direct love' by Johann, which treats the other as an end: it 'goes straight to a term willed in and for itself and rests there' (p. 10). The term of direct love is loved 'precisely as exercising its own act of existence. It is loved as ipseity, an *alter ipse* to the subject, and the subject acts and comports himself for the sake of the beloved even as he does for himself'; it is loved 'according to its proper and incommunicable reality, its subsistence'. The object of desiring-love or 'indirect love' by contrast is loved 'for what is communicable, for the perfection to be had from it' (p. 18). Both loves are however necessary. They should act together and are incapable of being understood in isolation.

In desiring-love I seek to appropriate the object so that it ceases to be exterior to myself. In friendship-love the other remains radically exterior. This is the contrast implied in Thomas's description of 'ecstasy', a going out from oneself, as an effect of love:

> in love of concupiscence, the lover is carried out of himself, in a certain sense; in so far, namely, as not being satisfied with enjoying the good that he has, he seeks to enjoy something outside himself. But since he seeks to have the extrinsic good for himself, he does not go out from himself simply, and this movement remains finally within him. On the other hand, in the love of friendship, a man's affection goes out from himself simply; because he wishes and does good to his friend, by caring and providing for him, for his sake. (*ST* I–II 28.3, quoted pp. 19–20)

Friends are distinct, and yet are one in sharing an essential likeness, according to Thomas's principle of 'similitude' or likeness 'based upon agreement or communication in form' (*ST* I 4.3). God as absolute Being is immanent in each being that exists; but at the same time each being is related to God as transcendent. God is separate from everything yet present in all things. This double relationship of creatures to God 'betokens at the same time *similitude* and *dependence*' (p. 29). All creatures are alike in that their 'unique subsistence' is 'rooted in, and constituted by, the creative presence of the one Absolute' (p. 30). What I love in myself or another person is 'a subsistent likeness of God', whose own absolute Being and unique Value, '*as participated*, is indistinguishable from that core of reality most proper to each creature, its own subsistence'.

> Since, therefore, what I love in being is the presence of the Absolute, I can love it in the other as well as in myself. And since as in myself it is myself, and in the other it is himself, so my own proper good, loved in myself, can be found by likeness in the other in that very trait that irreducibly distinguishes him from me, his proper subsistence. (p. 30)

Right self-love can now be defined afresh in terms of the value of every person – including myself. 'If a being is to find his own good in the proper and incommunicable subsistence of another, his own ipseity must first of all be a value to himself' (pp. 31–2). Only if I am conscious of myself and cherish myself, will I become able to encounter in the other 'the presence of a living and original intention, the profundity of personal consciousness' (p. 33). As Johann had remarked in an earlier essay, friendship thus has an intimate connection with personality and its development. 'For the self-giving that is characteristic of friendship implies, as a necessary condition, self-possession.'[15] To will good to the other as to myself, is to will the full unfolding in the other of 'that unique principle of action which he is in himself . . . the veritable subject with all his depth and mystery' (p. 34). Thus I love the other as a 'second self' and in so doing I am mysteriously one with them.

Personal growth is dual: towards individuation, with the full actualization of our potential nature, and towards the expression of our existence as an 'I' whose 'dynamic is towards a "Thou" ', towards God 'the transcendent Source of all personality' (p. 61). If we are not God, we have to look outside ourselves for another self, 'for only in the infinite being of God is there already a society of persons, of lovers and friends'.[16] Love's superabundance seeks friendship. It cannot stop short at benevolence but 'wishes always the *maximum of reciprocity*' (p. 37). The value that I love, in myself and in my friend, is 'the creative presence of God. My friend is a new revelation of that value; in him I am newly intimate to the plenitude of Being whose presence constitutes each of us in his proper subjectivity' (p. 62). God is both source and term of the love of friendship: 'the dynamism of direct love is in the creature a reflection and participation of

God's own love for Himself which is its foundation' (p. 62). My own selfhood matures through the giving and receiving of friendship-love. Johann quotes Nédoncelle's criticism of Nygren:

> There is a desire *(eros)* for generosity *(agape)*, a need to appropriate to oneself the spirit of renunciation, a longing to find one's soul in losing it. Why should *eros* be only a will for appropriation and utilization? It is desire for the best and hence it is destined not simply to use everything for itself but to understand that it must serve the spirit of generosity. The contrast proposed by Nygren is an error in psychology; he condemns *eros* outright when really the limits of *eros* are alone worthy of condemnation. Indeed, an *eros* that is sincere condemns its own limitations, since it discovers that its vocation is to convert itself to liberality.[17]

The desire to give oneself is fundamental to friendship-love, and never more so than in friendship for God. So long as I see myself as an absolute, and love merely my own nature, my love will be egoism and every other creature merely an object to meet my needs. But if I am oriented towards God I desire perfection for that further end, for God's sake. The purpose of our existence is that we, like God, should overflow with superabundant love. The simple fact is that whoever '*desires* the perfective must desire to *give* himself to Subsistent Perfection' (p. 69). The basic choice of the creature before God is 'not what good to acquire, but what orientation to assume ... Only by answering the gift of self with the gift of himself can he ever fully and consciously *be* what he is' (p. 71).

The irreplaceability of persons

This same unique value of the human person, the essential 'irreplaceability' of each individual, is the ground on which **Helen Oppenheimer,** an Anglican moral theologian, set out to elaborate afresh a Christian humanist moral philosophy on classical teleological lines. Secular humanism and Christianity can find common ground here. For Christians 'God is, so to say, the height of Personhood: He is the heart of value, and the existence and the value of every other person derives from Him'; but the experience of being among persons who are valuable, 'all ends in themselves if we are to be Kantians', is similar, if not at all levels of understanding the same, for Christians and unbelievers alike.[18] Burnaby's questioning of Nygren, Weil's 'creative attentiveness', and the developments in personalism, all inform her thought.

Given the irreplaceability of individuals, no doctrine of love is sufficient if it sees 'the neighbour' in merely vague and generalized terms. It is necessary to formulate a doctrine of love as directed to actual concrete persons, just as God's love for each human being is 'partial' in the sense that it singles out the particular and the concrete from the general mass of humanity and gives its contemplative 'attention' to the particular person who is at this moment in front of it. Friendship, Oppenheimer suggests, is the model for this love:

> If we can allow ourselves to take friendship alongside brotherhood as another promising model of Christian love, we shall be commending partiality; but partiality is not the same thing as exclusiveness. Exclusiveness is not properly a characteristic of friendship at all. There *are* exclusive loves, particularly the love of husband and wife; and some exclusive loves are good loves, even serving as pictures of the divine jealousy of God; but friendship at its best is essentially sharable. What it requires is not that we should 'forsake all other' but that we should seriously attend to what *this* person is like.
>
> Far from putting exclusiveness into friendship, what we need is to put friendship firmly into the exclusive loves. (p. 134)

A philosophy that upholds the value of each individual and champions their fulfilment in happiness, will not find an adequate doctrine of love in Nygren's 'Agape' which denies the legitimacy, indeed the very possibility, of a love that creates the person through mutual giving and receiving. Christian ethical discourse has ignored friendship as a topic that might have moral significance, because of the strong constraint to concentrate on the apparently harder challenge of a neighbour-love that is unconditional, unmotivated and brings no reward to the giver. While not wishing to lose sight of the degree of truth that challenge does contain, Oppenheimer suggests the pendulum has swung too far. There is another reality, the need of the loved person to be seen as a person, with liking and affection, and the need of the lover to find delight in appreciating the other.

Oppenheimer therefore calls for a re-examination of the relation between friendship and love of neighbour, 'not for the sake of justifying unregenerate human exclusiveness, but in the name of real relationship' (p. 133). The rejection of friendship as a moral theme, undertaken in the name of neighbour-love, inadvertently opens the way to 'the sort of "fellowship" which is no more than cameraderie or civility; the kind of "love of neighbour" which has no enjoyment in it' (p. 133), and the kind of 'charity' which 'people are apt to say that they "don't want"' (p. 124). 'There is a kind of Christian slide away from friendship which is supposed to be a progression in love, but which humanly speaking is apt to be a progression in shallowness' (p. 133).

Certain sayings of Jesus have been read as warnings against the practice of friendship *per se*, and as a command to put indiscriminate love in its place: 'For if you love those who love you, what reward have you?' (Mt. 5.46) and 'When you give a dinner or a banquet, do not invite your friends or your brothers' (Lk. 14.12). But 'friendship is under no more condemnation than brotherhood' (p. 133). Friendship is just as legitimate a relationship, on a par with that between siblings and between parent and child. It must be Christianized by being understood not as inherently exclusive but as a model of the love to be directed to all. As Barth suggests, 'The friend is a model of the *neighbour*'.[19] Luke, as well as John, shows that 'specific love for specific people is not remote from the imitation of Christ' (p. 137). The accusation that Jesus was 'a friend of tax collectors and sinners' suggests the love he showed was not Nygren's unmotivated 'Agape' but friendship, a genuine attentiveness that led to mutual appreciation and liking (pp. 137–8). Against Brunner's pigeonholing of friendship in the recreational domain, denying its ethical significance, Oppenheimer asserts that contemplative attention to others, and creative appreciation of them, is indeed of ethical significance (p. 133). Partial love is '*pro*' the other (p. 131), and God has a preferential love 'for' the poor, taking up their cause (p. 138).

While taking friendship's attentive partiality as her model for love, Oppenheimer prefers not to employ the phrase 'love of friendship' outside the situation of 'symmetrical' love: 'asymmetrical love, however good and genuine, is not called friendship' (p. 136). Whatever its name, however, she agrees it is the same love, so the way to acknowledge the special nature of the relationship of friends is not to emphasize the 'distinctiveness of friendship as a different *kind* of love' but to define friendship as the symmetrical relationship in which 'Friends attend to one another and do so on equal terms.' (p. 136). Oppenheimer also expresses concern, however, lest friendship's status as a model for Christian love might lead to an absolutizing of human personal relationships, making a cult of them as 'intrinsically holy and self-justifying' (p. 135). She does, therefore, distinguish between the model and the quality of love it illustrates: the practice of friendship is of ethical significance because aspects of it point to 'what love is meant to be' (p. 135). 'Friendship-love' thus implicitly receives a definition, as attentiveness to the person of the other.

With Oppenheimer we are manifestly moving away from classical assumptions about the necessary equality of friends, even including moral equality. ' "All men are equal" is too easily despised as a simple falsehood. "Each of us is irreplaceable" is both truer and more exhilarating' (p. 94). Between unique individuals, friendship is inherently prone to be 'asymmetrical' as to equality, while still capable of complete 'correlativity'. 'Unless we are Aristotelians, we attend to the particular characters of our friends, their value as individuals rather than their value as deserving. The relevant point is the attention and not the degree of moral esteem' (p. 142).

Can Christian appreciative love then embrace all people? Oppenheimer agrees with Brunner, 'A person who claims friendship with everyone has not begun to understand the meaning of friendship'.[20] But like Jeremy Taylor she interprets this as due, not to the exclusiveness inherent in preferential relationships but to our limited capacity as finite beings (pp. 135–6). Friendship is certainly a demanding model of Christian love, asking 'a lot more of us than the settled goodwill which is generally recommended as the sum of our Christian duty', but such a demand is justified by the Christian belief that 'there is something worth loving about any human creature' (p. 138).

As to loving enemies, most 'enemies' are in truth only rivals or opponents; but on the relatively rare occasions where evil is encountered, appreciative love cannot be offered because there can be no appreciation for what the person is at the present time. We can only decide not to hate, leave the person to God's love, and be open to forgive and form a positive relationship at some future time (pp. 128–30). Friendship, we can surely say with Thomas Aquinas, is present in our waiting, present in potential.

God too is Friend. 'If God is our Father and we are all brethren (Mt.23.8–9), may He not also be our Friend and make us friends with one another?' (p. 134). In this case love 'need not be symmetrical, but it ought to be correlative' (p. 112). Here again the point of comparison with the human model lies not in equality but in the 'attentive partiality' of this love (p. 137). It is in this contemplative sense, she implies, that we can claim to be 'friends with God' (p. 136).

Contemplative prayer is, in the words of John of the Cross, 'loving attention'. With Weil, Oppenheimer sees the likeness between friendship and the love we express in worship through attentive, contemplative (not necessarily silent!) delighting in God. Attentiveness to another provides 'our analogical path from the human to the divine'. In friendship 'we attend to what a person is really like and get into practice for attending to what God is really like' (pp. 145–6). The converse, we suggest, also holds true.

Liberation, solidarity and 'open friendship'

So far, the new insights into friendship we have seen emerging in the twentieth century have come through personalism. A related impetus to new thinking was to come through the experience of solidarity in liberation struggles. Cameraderie is not necessarily true friendship, but it can become so where persons are valued. The Peruvian founding-father of liberation theology **Gustavo Gutierrez** has shared his insight that solidarity with the poor cannot, for the Christian, be simply solidarity with a class: it is 'friendship', solidarity with actual people whom one knows and loves and with all who share their situation. Being a Christian, he adds, helps greatly in the development of this kind of human solidarity.[21]

It was out of an identical concern that **Jürgen Moltmann** in the 1970s heralded a new wave of liberation-oriented thought on friendship. He recounts how his own experiences of being drafted as a teenager in the Second World War, being taken prisoner and yet helped and forgiven by his captors, gave him a sympathy and solidarity with those in situations of oppression, and a deep intuition of God's involvement in suffering and hope.[22] Later he felt the necessity of developing a liberation theology for the oppressor that would help the powerful to connect with the situation of the oppressed. In brief but seminal passages, he invites us to know Christ as 'Friend' and to live out Christ's love as 'open friendship'.[23]

In his more popular account of 'open friendship' he introduces the topic through a children's poem, 'A Friend is Someone Who Likes You.'[24] 'Liking', he surmises, means simply being present in a friendly way, surrounding someone with an atmosphere of friendship. For the child in the poem, the world is friendly in this way. Trees, brooks and smiling passers-by, contribute to the 'open friendship that holds the world together'.[25] It is offered, we are invited to share in it. It is there in potential, inviting but making no demand. People can notice and welcome it – or reject and attempt to destroy it, replacing it with activities and objects of their own making, failing to be receptive and available in return. In the same way, sensitivity and availability allow us to receive and give human friendship. But the adult world is not noted for its sensitivity. The child who, if fortunate, had been aware of friendly surroundings moves into a progressively narrower and more regulated world containing enemies as well as friends, jealousies and disillusionment as well as trust. So he or she becomes a narrower person: 'we make friendships quickly in youth; with age it becomes more difficult, until we stop. We attach ourselves more infrequently, because we no longer open our hearts.'[26]

Social psychologists might debate this statement, but certainly no theologian who has the ever-widening society of the Kingdom in view has reason to accept any narrowing of friendship. Moltmann suggests that 'the radiance of childhood's friendly world remains in the grownup as a flicker of yearning, making one dissatisfied with one's unfriendly environment of jobs and functions, of roles and role-expectations'.[27] But it is eschatological hope for renewal, not nostalgia for a childhood Eden, that really fires him. In the childlike openness and simplicity of the Gospel, we are invited as adults to participate now in the messianic life of Christ.

Moltmann understands 'friend' as an essentially personal designation, conferring a status devoid of the functional expectations that attach to official titles and societal roles. Friendship is an offering of one's self in honesty, without pretence, seeing the other exactly as they are. He quotes Kant, that the love of friendship combines affection and respect.[28] It has a quality that makes it 'more than what we otherwise call love, eros or charity'. In this telling illustration from Brecht's *Calendar Stories*,

> Mr Keuner preferred City B to City A. In City A they loved me, but in City B they were friendly to me. In City A they made themselves useful to me, but in City B they needed me. In City A they invited me to the dinner table, but in City B they invited me into the kitchen.[29]

The special quality of friendship consists in needing the other just as they are, offering a welcome so natural, warm and informal, that it introduces the guest immediately into the heart of the home. In this immediate and un-self-conscious sharing of life there is no need to adopt postures of inferiority or superiority:

> There is no need to bow before a friend. We can look him in the eye. We neither look up to him nor look down on him. In friendship we experience ourselves for what we are, respected and accepted in our own freedom. Through friendship we respect and accept other people as people and as individual personalities.[30]

Friendship is the essential and enduring element in all loves. When 'the parent-child relation comes to an end, when the master-servant connection is abolished and when privileges based on sexual position are removed, then what is truly human emerges and remains; and that is friendship'.[31] The functions and offices of society represent a transient order, justified only so long as need for them exists, but the deep meaning of society is that people should 'live as friends with one another'. To be free means to grow in friendship with God and others, and unless that is their goal 'class and liberation struggles do not attain any human meaning, just as socialism without friendship degenerates into soulless bureaucracy':

> As friendship is the 'soul' of a free and just society, so, on the other hand, is a society without masters and servants the 'body' of friendship. No soul without a body, no body without a soul. Whoever does not hold them together will be blessed by neither friendship nor social justice.[32]

With openness comes trust and loyalty. 'We trust our friend and entrust ourselves to him.' Trust is not here made dependent on the other's conformity to an ideal, but on 'promise, loyalty to one another and openness'. The burden has shifted to the quality of the love, away from the worthiness of the beloved. Because Christianity offers a perspective of forgiveness and redemption unknown in classical debate, it becomes possible to claim that 'a friend remains a friend even in disaster, even in guilt'.[33]

Freedom and joy

Freedom is a strong mark of friendship: friendship 'arises out of freedom, consists in mutual freedom, and preserves this freedom'. In Germanic languages, Moltmann notes, these two words apparently share a common philological root. In Hegel's phrase friendship is 'the concrete concept of freedom'.[34] Paradoxically, human freedom consists in the service of God, but of a God who does not call us 'servants' but 'friends'. Freedom and relationship are inseparable: 'we are not by nature free, but become so only when someone likes us. Friends open up to one another free space for free life.'[35] Friendship is the means and end of true liberation: to be a friend is to liberate, and to be a true liberator is to be a friend.

The phrase 'concrete concept of freedom' also expresses the fact that friendship's reciprocal kindnesses do not rest on legal contract. We are no longer under law but help a friend freely, for friendship's sake. Here Moltmann draws creatively on the tendency we have seen in German theology to place friendship in the sphere of play or 'culture'. That does not, for him, render it unnecessary. We must recognize our real need for sheer giving and sharing, 'we need friends in order to communicate the joy of our own life and in order to enjoy our own happiness'.[36] Where we are sensitive to this need in others we can freely give them joy: 'sharing in another's joy without self-interest and without envy is a good turn that cannot be regarded highly enough'.[37] The *law* of reciprocation is invalid in friendship, but the *freedom* to reciprocate and give delight is fundamental to it.

Christ's love, and ours as his followers, is rooted in joy in God and others. Ultimately, therefore, the very basis of friendship is joy, it is born of the desire to share joy. Sympathy and the sharing of suffering follow, as the friendship is tested and proved.[38] Out of this joy comes the invitation to the messianic feast, and that is no superficial joy: 'to gaze on the risen one makes life a feast, but it is only the gaze on the one who was crucified and who descended into hell that makes "the whole of life" a feast' which does not end with death but is 'a "feast without end"'.[39] To root friendship in joy is to transform the common assumption that only persons who are in need, who are deprived of joy, can be touched by gestures of Christian 'charity'. Jesus' compassion always has the feast of the Kingdom in view; and he taught that those whose joy lies in things of true value are 'not far from the kingdom'. The invitation to the feast can be given, through the sharing of friendship, to those who are suffering and in despair – and such an invitation transcends mere 'charitable, and condescending help'.[40]

Christian faith allows Moltmann to affirm that 'friendship is ultimately stronger than enmity. Enduring friendship shall possess the world.' Ultimately only the cross and resurrection demonstrate the truth of this statement. Love is eternal, while Moltmann appeals to the command 'do not let the sun go down on your anger' (Eph. 4.26) to show how transient enmity should be in the face of God's reality.[41]

Christ the Friend

If Christ has made friendship of central importance to our Christian understanding of love, it is important we recognize him with the title of 'Friend'. The traditional titles 'prophet', 'priest' and 'king' describe his work and convey dignity and authority but place him at a distance from us. Certainly the Christological meanings of these titles are already different from purely worldly meanings. The 'prophet' is the 'derided man from Nazareth', poor and unpretentious; the 'priest' was crucified by those in power; the 'king' who rules in God's power does so from the cross. Thus understood, these titles harbour 'an unprecedented social-critical potential'.[42] But they still imply distance. They express the work and suffering of Jesus *for* us, but do not yet describe the new fellowship he brings *with* God and our neighbours. 'Friend' discloses the ultimate meaning of the traditional titles and describes the 'inner relationship between the divine and the human fellowship'; it describes this new existence *with* others, rather than simply *for* them.[43]

As prophet of the Kingdom, Christ becomes the friend of sinners; as priest he dies for his friends' salvation; as king he liberates us, making us friends of God and neighbour.[44] For Christ's followers, too, being 'with' rather than only 'for' others releases liberating power: both for those who are served, and for the server who can delight in life with them and yet, at times of need, sacrifice themselves 'for' them.[45]

In piety, 'Friend' may seem an unreal title for God, it 'borders always on kitsch'.[46] Such, however, is emphatically not the case in the New Testament. In Luke, Jesus is despised as 'a glutton and a drunkard, a friend of tax collectors and sinners!' Associating with the despised, he was perceived by the legalists as lawless and dishonourable; but in truth he was adhering to the law of grace, 'the righteousness of the kingdom of God':[47]

> The inner reason for Jesus' friendship with 'tax-collectors and sinners' was to be found in the joy of the messianic feast which he celebrated with them. It was not sympathy, it was overflowing joy in the kingdom of God, a joy that sought to share and to welcome, that drew him to people who were outcasts in the eyes of the law.[48]

His denouncers intended to compromise him but ironically they voiced 'a profound truth from Jesus' own point of view':

> Jesus becomes the friend of the sinful and the sick. By forgiving them their sins he gives them respect as people and becomes their friend . . . As a friend, Jesus offers the unlovable the friendship of God. As the Son of man he shows them their true and real humanity, through which they are liberated from their unrighteousness.[49]

In Jn 15.15 Jesus calls his disciples into 'the new life of friendship'. He acknowledges friendship as 'the highest form of love', which 'leads to actually risking one's life to protect a friend'. Christ's faithful death makes his disciples his friends for ever and 'they remain in the circle of his friendship when they keep his commandments and become friends of one another'.[50] The invitation to joy is the same for both disciples and sinners, and Jesus gives his friendship unconditionally but, as Moltmann implies, our keeping his commandments is the condition for our actual life and growth in that friendship. Open friendship binds Christians together making them a sign of newness, and is the love with which they must love the world. In the friendship of Jesus we experience God as Friend in his innermost nature. Equality is not an issue. 'If God is experienced as a friend, then men become the friends of God.'[51]

'Open' friendship with Christ answers the concern expressed by Charles Smyth, that to call Jesus 'friend' might lead to an individualistic Christocentrism: 'Friendship concentrates our affection: love distributes it. Each individual disciple as a friend of Christ is as it were a terminal of His affection. But Christ as the object of man's friendship must point beyond Himself to the Father on the one hand and to the brethren on the other.' Smyth consequently thought 'love' a safer word than 'friendship' for the relationship of disciples towards Christ.[52] For Smyth, friendship was inherently individualistic, whereas for Moltmann it is inclusive. But it is important to bear this warning in mind if friendship with Christ is not to slide towards exclusivity.

Aristotle's friendship could unite only those who are equal, excluding the others. The Church falls into the same trap when a social evening means socializing with 'people who are alike, who feel, think, and talk the same way', when people who happen to be different in age and sex split into different groups.[53] That is the unredeemed friendship of this world, hurtful to those outside and boring to those inside. Jesus breaks through this closed circle of friendship, reaching out alike to God, the disciples, and the tax-collectors and sinners.

As an antidote to exclusivity and narrowness, Moltmann emphasizes the 'public' exercise of friendship. Modern friendship risks existing only in the private area of life so that its values cease to operate in the public area. To live in Jesus' friendship is to widen our understanding to include the 'public protection and public respect' of others.[54] Intimacy is not thereby excluded. The messianic feast is both ' "the marriage of the soul with God" ' and ' "the festival of the earth" '.[55] To have the messianic feast as our primary point of reference implies the development of 'a total concept of friendship . . . which includes the soul and the body, the people who are like ourselves and the people who are different'.[56] That is the ideal for the Church, to be worked out in its life at many levels.

Freedom in prayer

Prayer is the primary context in which we experience friendship with God. The parable of the importunate friend (Lk. 11.5–8) shows God's response to a friend's confident request. Similarly in John, 'friendship leads to certainty in prayer: "so that whatever you ask the Father in my name, he may give it to you" ' (Jn 15.16). In prayer both partners are free: 'Thanks to this friendship there is room in the almighty liberty of God for the created liberty of man' and the human person is drawn into the loving activity of God: 'In this friendship there is the opportunity for man to have an effect upon and with God's sole effectiveness'.[57] Unlike the servant, who assumes God is obliged to respond in a certain way, or the child, who has not yet learned to respect God's freedom, the friend 'prays out of freedom and trusts to the friendship of the free God'.[58]

In effect Moltmann is describing the mature prayer of the contemplative, for whom all that happens can be received and known as blessing. Here, as in the tradition, the mature Christian is the 'friend of God'. But he wants the term to have a wider embrace. In tradition, he suggests, an exclusive strand reserves the title for ascetics, martyrs and those, like Moses, who pray in an exalted way; but 'at the same time, a broad, inclusive formulation has always been there too; that is, that through Christ's friendship, *all* Christians have become friends of God'.[59]

In summary, 'the new man, the true man, the free man is the friend'.[60] 'Open and total friendship that goes out to meet the other is the spirit of the kingdom.'[61] As all our authors have said, 'Love is the friendship of man with God and all his creatures.'[62]

Feminist voices: a community of equals, of justice-seeking friends

Feminist theologians are far from being monochrome. They have varied in background and belief, some more orthodox, some less; some married, some single, some lesbian, some celibate. An outpouring of feminist theological writing on friendship began in the early 1980s, deriving from two concerns: to identify non-gendered, inclusive metaphors and models; and to articulate the experience of women and make their voice heard. Feminist theology reads Scripture anew. On the whole it has been able to make little use of tradition. Its distinctive source has been praxis in the form of the lived experience of women.

When Jürgen Moltmann proposed the title 'Friend' for Christ in the mid-1970s he aimed to show how 'open friendship', not distance and domination, animates Christ's roles as prophet, priest, and king. He wrote in German, in which 'friend' is gendered, taking masculine and feminine forms. As the translations quoted above with all their 'men' reveal, a sensitivity to inclusive language had hardly yet begun to take hold in the English-speaking world at that time, but it would immediately strike an English-speaker that 'friend' has additional potential as an inclusive, non-gendered model. Already in 1975 Elisabeth Schüssler Fiorenza was wondering why Mary Daly had not adopted 'friend/friendship' to speak of a new humanity, rather than resorting to 'sisterhood of men'![63] **Sallie McFague** began the exploration of 'Friend' as a non-authoritarian, non-familial, and non-gender-related metaphor for God, briefly in 1983 in *Metaphorical Theology*, following up in 1987 in *Models of God*. It seemed to her a helpful model in a time when friendship has come to have a high profile in our consciousness: 'all kinds of people are working together for common causes, [and] friendship expresses that ideal of relationship among peoples of all ages, both sexes, and whatever color or religion'.[64]

McFague took the by now well-established view that friendship is not just easy empathy between the like-minded, but a love that thrives on differences and extends to strangers. 'Jesus, in his identification with the sufferings of others throughout his life and especially at his death, is a parable of God's friendship with us at the most profound level.'[65] In Jesus, God 'suffers for us and, by so doing, invites us into a fellowship of suffering, with God and for others'.[66] Within such an 'egalitarian' and 'immanental' friendship God's authority becomes that of 'the companion whom we wish to please and who attracts our cooperation', which may be more powerful for us than 'the model of God as father or king who commands us to be obedient children or servants'.[67]

'Salvation' may be easier to understand if it means God acting mutually with us to heal, to free, and to bring about new life for ourselves and humanity.[68] The elements of worship: confession, thanksgiving, intimacy, mystery, are intrinsic to friendship and much more to friendship with God, with whom to be friends 'is to be friends with ultimate mystery'.[69]

Returning to this theme in 1987 McFague sought to express her core Christian faith in God who is on the side of life and its fulfilment, in words suitable to an age that knows anxiety about ecological or nuclear disaster. She experimented with a Trinitarian pattern, associating Agape with God as mother, Eros with God as lover, Philia with God as friend, and imagining the universe as 'God's body'. God is then sacramentally present to us through the world, and relates to it and suffers in it as parent, lover and friend. We become participants in that divine caring for creation.

McFague threw anchors out towards both classical and newer ideas of friendship. She accepted the dictum of C. S. Lewis that friendship is the least 'necessary' of loves. Mary Hunt was to criticize this intensely, riposting that among the poor and marginalized friendship is essential to survival. Positively, however, with Moltmann, McFague takes friendship's 'unnecessary' nature to mean it is of all loves most free. Her baseline definition of friendship is traditional: 'a bonding of two by free choice in a reciprocal relationship'.[70] This is expanded and extended by introducing three contemporary insights: that the basis of friendship is freedom, it implies inclusiveness, and it presupposes a mature adult capacity to interrelate and to bear responsibilities.

A bonding by free choice rests on trust and, as Lewis suggests, a shared commitment to some vision or project. We can as it were join with God in the mutual project of the world's well-being. Evidently this is a common project involving many like-minded but diverse people. The love of friendship is 'trust, commitment, common vision, inclusiveness', diversity, delight, attraction.[71] This 'solidarity view of friendship'[72] speaks of God the sustainer, God with us, Emmanuel, who rejoices and suffers with the world, creating a joyful inclusive fellowship, the shared meal of friends at which the stranger is welcome. Our participation in this love affects our existence in two ways: by countering our fear of others, and by promoting our care for them and the cosmos. The Church becomes 'a community of friends united by a common vision of fulfillment for all'.[73] 'The model of God as friend says that we are not our own, but also that we are not on our own: as friends of the Friend of the world, we do not belong to ourselves nor are we left to ourselves.'[74]

The 'solidarity friendship' experienced in liberation struggles and common action for peace and justice significantly modifies classical ideas. More adventurous feminist thought was to follow. **Elisabeth Schüssler Fiorenza**'s *In Memory of Her*, written in 1983 has provided the chief lens through which this movement has viewed its biblical roots. Her reconstruction of earliest Christianity portrays it as a radically alternative community of equals in the midst of patriarchal society. She calls on women in the present to reclaim 'our baptismal call to the discipleship of equals'.[75] God is seen through the aspect of divine 'Wisdom' (the feminine word 'Sophia') who 'in every generation commissions prophets – women and men – and makes them friends and children of God'.[76] Jesus' God is this gracious 'Sophia–God' and as God incarnate he is 'Jesus–Sophia'.[77]

The Gospel is 'the communal proclamation of the life-giving power of Spirit–Sophia and of God's vision of an alternative community and world'.[78] Liberation struggles pass through a caucusing stage where the oppressed can mutually discover themselves. That stage, as well as a vision for a changed Church in the future, is suggested by Schüssler Fiorenza's conclusion that women who hear this call become the '*ekklēsia* of women', committed to the overcoming of dualisms and the liberation, not only of women, but all peoples.[79]

While Schüssler Fiorenza evoked the 'topos' or the ethos of friendship rather than using its language, **Susan Nelson Dunfee** brought 'friendship' to the fore. She responds to the challenge posed by radical feminist voices that have denounced and dismissed Christianity as irretrievably 'patriarchal'. Can Christianity, she asks, empower women to experience their own liberation? Dunfee is theologically creative, starting from women's experience but taking Jn 15.15 equally seriously and drawing on tradition in the shape of a number of modern theologians. She investigates whether the motifs of 'service' and 'altruism', frequently applied to the situation of women, are adequate to bring out the full Christian experience? They are, she determines, liable to result in bondage and loss of selfhood for those on whom altruistic service is imposed. Women in particular have suffered from such imposition. Yet altruism is implicitly dipolar, it assumes the existence not only of the other but of a self that is capable of love, and Christian liberation to full selfhood rightly has a dual focus: 'the importance of being a self' together with 'the understanding that true selfhood is expressed in a life of vulnerability lived in concern for others as well as the self'.[80]

Dunfee has in essence raised the perennial question of right self-love, but in a new and particular form: what constitutes right self-love for women? In patriarchy the answer is, the cultivation of the submissive virtues. In feminism, the cultivation of freedom and responsibility. From a close and penetrating exegesis of Jn 15.15, Dunfee concludes that 'Jesus's intent is in fact to call people to be a community of friends who are not to be slaves to one another but who are freed to respond to one another's needs "in their own voices."'[81] The intent of Jesus proves to be in reality closer to the feminist liberation view than to that of patriarchy. The response of historic Christianity to Jesus may have been deeply inadequate, but his new commandment still stands: to be friends to others, to engage our freedom for them and spark their own freedom. 'Jesus ... makes people his friends, engendering a new authority, a new spontaneity in them, calling them into selfhood.' (p. 154)

Service and altruism alone will not bring the loving self into existence. Alone, they can disempower both server and served. Something more is needed. Dunfee cites Moltmann that the truly liberating and empowering relationship is found in being 'with' rather than just 'for' others.[82] That is friendship, which liberates those whom it serves and empowers them to become free and autonomous agents, speaking with their own voices. Friendship characterizes Christian love. Christianity is therefore better described as 'freedom and authority grounded in friendship with Jesus', than as 'service and altruism'.[83] This freedom is contextual, it is offered and exists within Jesus as the vine, within the community and mission of Jesus. Christianity does invite to freedom and joy, and should not be arbitrarily discarded as 'patriarchal'. 'God also, then is known as vulnerable and caring and personally involved with each one.'[84]

The intuition that Jesus teaches more than 'service' had been passionately expressed sixty years earlier. In 1929 when friendship with God and neighbour was the leitmotif for a large Student Christian Movement conference on God's purpose in the world, several speakers linked friendship with service but the personalist philosopher John Macmurray looked deeper:

> The world-revolution of the Christians came when Jesus discovered the true centre of human life. 'Not servants but friends' is a proclamation of the revolution. The key-word of the Christian gospel is not service but friendship ...
>
> 'But surely', you will say, 'we are called as Christians to serve Christ and to serve the world.' No! we are called to be the friends of Christ and the friends of men. That is not at all the same thing.[85]

Christ's revolution, he proclaims, is 'Copernican'. 'Make service your centre, with its laws and duties and self-sacrifices, and life is a bondage. Make friendship the centre and life is freedom.' We overcome the fear of giving ourselves freely as friends, and the Kingdom becomes present reality. Fear, Macmurray perceptively thought, is love's greatest opponent. God's friendship is not a live issue in his philosophy. Without denying divine transcendence he focused on immanence. He spoke of 'the friendship of Christ' being 'realised in our friendships with one another'.[86] Macmurray was deeply influenced by Buber, feeling he thought as one with him. Like some of his feminist successors he abandoned active membership of his Church because it failed to live up to his ideals, although he considered himself Christian and eventually became a Quaker.

'Tenderness' and 'Eros'

Feminists also emphasize love's mutuality and relationality, within which lesbian feminists in particular, although by no means in isolation, have highlighted the motifs of 'tenderness' and 'passion' or 'Eros'. Among these voices, that of **Carter Heyward** has called for an encounter with Jesus as the 'messianic friend' who humanly incarnates God's active presence in the world and who invites us to do the same, in mutually fulfilling relationships. She dispensed with high Christology, seeking 'to "follow him" by participation in a mutual messianism that was neither begun nor completed in the life of Jesus . . .'.[87]

Mary Hunt's stance was more radical by several degrees. In her eloquently polemical *Fierce Tenderness* she accepted friendship as 'a useful paradigm of right relation for the whole of creation . . . the model of healthy relating and the goal of human community'; but of historical texts emanating from males she says, 'unfortunately these sources only distract since they are rooted in patriarchal worldviews that systematically pass over the particular experiences of women';[88] they construct 'a false generic of human experience based on males' and can at best be only generally helpful.[89] Buber, she allows, began moving in the right direction, but for new discoveries that are useful for all she looks to female experience.

The insights Hunt wants to contribute stem in part from her sharing in liberation theology in Argentina, but most pressingly from American feminism and specifically from a lesbian experience of relationships. The 'Copernican revolution' she sees as under way is a move from 'an individual ethic based on limited experiences to a collective ethic that grows organically out of the many relational experiences that good people choose to live in right relation'.[90] These would include, but not as previously prioritize, heterosexual marriage. Hunt largely blames an historical emphasis on marriage and family for the theological neglect of 'friendship' seen as the more central and universal relationship. Our own study would suggest, however, that friendship's historical problems sprang essentially from other causes.

What is 'fierce tenderness'? It is 'fierce' in the quality of its attention to persons, 'tender' with a friend's 'quality of care and nurture'.[91] It is an existential stance, embodied and political, embracing relationships to 'the divine', others, and the earth; it emerges from women's experience but is meant for all. In it people 'intend one another's well-being and . . . that their love relationship is part of a justice-seeking community'.[92] It combines love that unites and generates; awareness of our embodiment; power to choose; and 'spirituality' defined as 'the religious impulse toward meaning and value' expressed concretely in 'making choices about the quality of life for oneself and for one's community'.[93] Its themes of 'attention', 'generativity' and 'community', 'all converge on justice'.[94] Theology, Hunt urges, should enable 'a political vision of fierce tenderness in action'.[95]

Hunt's 'fierce tenderness' has close affinities with 'the erotic' as defined by the black American lesbian poet Audre Lorde, whose 'Eros' is 'the personification of love in all its aspects – born of Chaos, and personifying creative power and harmony'. 'The erotic is a resource within each of us that lies in a deeply female and spiritual plane, firmly rooted in the power of our unexpressed or unrecognized feeling.' As the lifeforce that impels towards 'excellence' in every area of being, 'the erotic' is only artificially restricted to the realm of sex. It is known in deep sharing of feeling and joy, in becoming 'responsible to ourselves in the deepest sense', and making connection with others 'with our similarities and our differences'.[96] Thus understood, 'the erotic' became a basic feminist motif.

Hunt wrote as a disaffected Catholic, rejecting all developments since the ideal time of the early 'Jesus-movement' as envisioned by Schüssler Fiorenza. For Hunt the Church should be that 'discipleship of equals', 'justice-seeking friends who unite in unlikely coalitions', who 'do theology in order to right injustice'.[97] Its connection to Jesus is tenuous, however. Hunt rejects the cross and resurrection as male motifs, seeming in the process to deny the possibility and reality of suffering, and any creative redemption of it. Friendship with God in any traditional sense is out of the frame. Hunt's concept of 'the divine' proves to be a friendly polytheistic designer pantheon, perhaps not quite so remote but otherwise strangely reminiscent of that of Epicurus.[98]

In contrast to Hunt's dismissal of history, **Diana Fritz Cates** reveals Aristotle's character-friendship as itself having 'passional dimensions': his friends long for each other's actual company, delighting in life together. If the 'erotic' is 'a fullness and intensity of physical as well as emotional feeling as persons in relation, then', Cates affirms, 'we will surely want to recognize that the best of character-friendships have an erotic dimension'. Aristotle had no intention of eliminating these aspects, rather they are implied by his statement that goodwill is not yet friendship unless it has 'intensity or desire'.[99]

All this will raise the obvious questions. Is not the whole construct of 'femininity' as precarious as that of 'masculinity'? Are not men capable of tenderness, women of being cool and cerebral? Do not all humans, given power, employ it in all too similar ways, either of cruelty or love? But Hunt does eloquently draw attention to aspects of human relating that have been more obvious to women, and which make friendship more profound, dynamic, and inclusive.

An English writer, **Elizabeth Stuart**, followed in Hunt's footsteps. Her own thought was at first strongly coloured by a neo-Freudian conviction that all friendships are grounded in sexual desire. Lorde's 'Eros' seemed to have become re-sexualized.[100] A broader view, in which the

Jesuit, Ignace Lepp would side with Lorde, would understand affective energy not as sublimated sexuality but as 'absolutely undifferentiated in itself' and capable of nourishing 'erotic love . . . filial, paternal and fraternal love, the love of science, of art, of philosophy, friendship, and even the mystical love of God'.[101]

Stuart hammered the point that lesbian and gay people identify their relationships as 'friendship', and friendship, therefore, as more fundamental and universal, should replace marriage (unrelentingly assumed to represent a structure of domination) as the relationship of primary concern to the Church. This extreme *cri de coeur* was set within a more orthodox Christian framework than that of Hunt, but reliant on some dubious assessments of historical texts.

In a later modification of Stuart's thought, the thread of inclusiveness represented by friendship has been joined by the concept of 'queer theology'. 'Queer theory', she tells us, at first referred to the postulated fluidity of sexual identities among non-heterosexuals. Now, as she presents it, it takes all sexual and gender identities to have been socially constructed, and 'questions the very notion of sexual identity' right across the board.[102] 'Queer theology', therefore, has in view the person as a unique individual, not as identified by sexuality or gender. It blurs or demotes sexuality. Stuart suggests that a foundational strand in Christian anthropology and spirituality does the same: 'There is no longer male and female; for you are all one in Christ Jesus' (Gal. 3.28). In the spiritual and eschatological perspective, gender and sexuality are neither eternal nor the be-all and end-all of human life. 'Queer' theology may therefore, she proposes, claim a link with the Christian ascetical tradition, sharing a common view of the self as transcending gender. Baptism confers a new identity not by 'construction' but by 'gift'. In that new creation all other identities are relativized and the Christian 'looks to a life beyond gender which can be anticipated in this life'.[103] Stuart proposes that 'queer theology' might provide a meeting-place where more conservative thought might make connections with gay and lesbian theology.

Again, questions immediately pose themselves: is this gnosticism, denying the reality of material creation? Or a way forward in an age of rapidly evolving, changing, relativizing and competing perceptions as to what constitutes human nature? At the very least, dialogue on such issues should itself have the character of encounter in friendship.

Rediscovering friendship with God

In contrast to Hunt and Stuart, **Elisabeth Moltmann-Wendel** stands within historical tradition, welcoming feminist insights as 'an important step forward from old patterns' but warning lest they be enshrined as a new absolute.[104] The English title of her book *Rediscovering Friendship* is less precise and powerful than its German original, literally: *Wake up, my woman-friend. The return of friendship with God.* God as friend is, she suggests, a healing and reconciling image:

> Anyone who is tired of the discussion about using the metaphors of father or mother for God, who misses a personal element in the images drawn from nature and the figure of Wisdom, can rediscover in friendship with God something of the breadth, closeness, goodness and companionship which people today so urgently need.[105]

Masculine imagery for God had, she suggested some years previously, obscured 'women's experiences of Jesus . . . Jesus as a friend who shares their life and is ever near them, a friend who offers them warmth and tenderness in their loneliness and powerlessness'. Breaking the mould of patriarchy, women who have recovered this experience of the friendship of Jesus must lead the way as the Churches become 'a new community of women and men'.[106]

Jesus is known as our ultimate Friend in the Eucharist and is necessarily the centre of this new community. With him the sharing of a meal became 'a banquet of unusual friends, men and women, and these unusual friendships become a basic religious and social pattern of the Jesus movement'.[107] Moltmann-Wendel introduces recent work on the idea of self-giving and sacrifice by German feminist theologians to suggest Jesus is the friend who gives himself, not as sacrifice 'for sin' but in conscious self-surrender 'for friends', that is, for the community he joyfully but scandalously formed at his table. That behaviour led to his death. 'So he did not die for our sins but for those men and women who had been his friends, for friendship as a passionate human relationship and liberation.'[108] Consequently we should, she suggests, see sin in terms of sickness to be healed and separation to be reconciled, which is how the Gospels predominantly portray it. The Eucharist is then above all a celebration of Christ's friendship, of his healing and liberating activity through a life of 'total loving self-surrender to the Father and us'.[109]

Where sin and guilt are seen primarily as sickness and division, forgiveness becomes a ministry of healing. The objective reality revealed by Christ's death 'for friends' is God's eternal friendship, from which no one is excluded and into which all are invited through the attractive, reconciling power of Christ's love. Jesus was not an impractical idealist but, as Martin Luther King pointed out, a practical realist. 'Love even for enemies is the key to the solution of the problems of our world . . . The degree to which we are able to forgive determines the degree to which we are able to love our enemies . . . love is the only force capable of transforming an enemy into a friend.'[110] 'Without forgiveness', as Desmond Tutu graphically puts it, 'there really is no future.'[111] Moltmann-Wendel expresses amazement that no 'christology of friendship' has emerged, as against the christology of sacrifice.[112] We might respond that no 'christology of friendship' would be likely to emerge until friendship itself was widely recognized as transfigured by Jesus' actions. Might we now be nearing that stage?

Friendship as we now conceive it, she continues, combines 'intimacy, trust and closeness' with 'detachment, respect for the otherness of the other, the mystery of his or her strangeness'.[113] Women specify friendship further by describing how it can awake through embodied experiences of touching and hearing; in celebrations and in everyday life; through their discovery of themselves as persons; through respect for creation, 'in the magic of mutuality', and in tenderness.[114]

Moltmann-Wendel traces 'tenderness' to a theological initiative, not by women but by men in the late 1960s which called for embodied love expressed in touch; communication through bodily senses; overcoming dualism, knowing our body as a place of healing and salvation; concern for humanity and justice; the sacralization of matter, and ecological concern. Heinrich Böll who began this 'cultural shift' in 1969 called for a theology of Mary Magdalene. Moltmann-Wendel considerably extends his suggestion. Even without the help of the apocryphal texts she mentions, it is very possible to rediscover Mary Magdalene, loyal and compassionate, healed by Jesus and strikingly modern in her singleness and independence, as the model friend of Jesus. Alongside Mary his mother she forms an intriguing alternative model for the Church.[115]

'Tenderness' was, as Moltmann-Wendel puts it, replaced in the 1980s by the new feminist definition of 'Eros'. As Audre Lorde's deep life-energy, potential, joy, 'Eros becomes the revolutionary banner in a world in which women now seize the power to define Eros and liberate it from its narrow sexual connotations so that it becomes a primal power of passionate self-knowledge, relationship to others and the world.' Both 'tenderness' and 'Eros' are, in Moltmann-Wendel's view, 'spontaneous, irrational attacks by love on a world in which love is dead'.[116] And an 'Eros', she suggests, that puts us passionately and positively in touch with the world and others, delighting in them, is not opposed to but contained in New Testament Agape. 'Tenderness and Eros are possibilities of approaching oneself, others and the world afresh. It is a way on which we are hurt, but it is a way against hardening and being torn apart and an attempt at healing and friendship.'[117] Friendship so understood can embrace God, others, my body, and the Earth.

God the Holy Trinity as Persons-in-Mutual-Relation

The Trinitarian thought of the Catholic theologian **Elizabeth Johnson** incorporates many of these new insights. In her contemplation of the mystery of the Trinity, Johnson also reflects the recent move in the West to recover the relational understanding that has always been more marked in Eastern Orthodox than in Western theology. She explores the mystery of the triune God through the motif of divine Wisdom (Sophia), in terms of Mother–Sophia, Jesus–Sophia and Spirit–Sophia.

Johnson joins Moltmann in suspecting that the 'concentration on singleness in God', including the Orthodox view of the Father as origin within the Trinity, that has marked classical theism has provided legitimacy to monarchical or patriarchal thought-patterns in the Church and world. Relationality challenges these patterns, and the freedom, commonality, mutuality and open hospitality of friendship give clues to understanding relationality. Within the mystery of the Trinity, the relationality which alone distinguishes the Persons in their being has 'a powerful affinity with women's ownership of relationality as a way of being in the world'.[118] Augustine bypassed friendship as a model for Trinitarian relations because to him 'friend' denoted sameness; but in Johnson's view, strong bonds of love are 'creative of personhood' and 'friend' can convey distinctiveness. If 'friendship with God and genuine human autonomy grow in direct and not inverse proportion, how much more intensely is it not the case that Holy Wisdom's own inner befriending is constitutive of "personal" distinctiveness. In love unity and differentiation are correlates rather than opposites of each other.'[119] Friendship also implies no hierarchy of ultimate origin within the Trinity, but points to the equal perichoresis and mutual coinherence of the three Persons.

As Spirit–Sophia who 'passes into holy souls and makes them friends of God and prophets' (Wis. 7.27), God 'herself' is our 'friend'. In God's friendship modelled by women's experience of a solidarity in love that is gift, and is challenging yet supportive, 'human beings can know themselves to be never alone with their personal and globe-encircling anxieties but supported and energized by gracious compassion and powerful sympathy, similarly directed'.[120]

Jesus, divine friendship incarnate, welcomes all in open hospitality and calls us friends. God as creative Mother loves the universe and each individual 'with a friendship brimming with desire for the well-being of the whole of her creation'.[121] God's friendship 'engages us in partnership to renew the earth and establish justice', creating in us 'an attitude of profound friendship toward all others, even those most unlike ourselves'.[122] Genuine friends, who may be drawn from the entire diversity of humanity, 'dwell within each other, in each other's hearts and minds and lives, with an affection that engenders broad scope for individuality to develop'.[123] So friendship, structured 'not according to the model of domination-submission but of genuine partnership in the freedom of difference' becomes a metaphor for God's indwelling in us and ours in God.[124]

Ecumenical contacts with the Orthodox churches have led directly to a rapprochement between eastern and western thought about God. The Orthodox theologian **John Zizioulas** has significantly contributed to this convergence. In an influential work, *Being and Communion*, he brought together the Christian insight into God's nature as three Persons in one indivisible Unity, with a modern appreciation of personhood. He extended the Greek word '*hypostasis*' ('*persona*' in Latin) which, as he shows, was already invested by patristic theologians with the ontological sense of unique personal being, to embrace something of the full modern western meaning of 'person'. He finds Being itself in the relationship of love that is 'communion', *koinōnia*. 'The expression "God is love" (1 John 4.16) signifies that God "subsists" as Trinity' and that 'Love as God's mode of existence ... constitutes his being.'[125] Communion is therefore also our own authentic mode of being. Humanity's 'fall' consists in a 'rupture between being and communion', and salvation restores us to communion.[126] Our 'divinization' means becoming a participant in the personal existence of God, entering into eternal existence as person, as 'a unique, unrepeatable and free "hypostasis," as loving and being loved'.[127]

An icon that depicts a saint or a theological mystery can be likened to a window, transparent to the reality beyond. Zizioulas opens a window into the ultimate mystery of love, and **Paul O'Callaghan**, another Orthodox writer, builds on his thought by suggesting that Christian friendship can itself be viewed as ' "iconic" ', a precursor of eternal love that allows us a glimpse into divine and human reality. The unity of friends in Christ who is the 'New Adam', is 'a manifestation of an even deeper spiritual unity of humanity in the person of the God-man.'[128] Such friendship also 'mirrors the life of the Trinity', prefiguring the fulfilment of universal love in the Kingdom of God; it is mystical and sacramental, not an end in itself but continually beckoning beyond itself, not a human idol, but like an icon 'transparent to the eternal and the divine.'[129] Human friendship is not itself divine, but it enshrines and points us to the truly divine.

Finally, the theology of creation seeks to understand the relationship between God who is 'mutual, equal, and ecstatic friendship' and this ancient and evolving, 'radically relational and interdependent' universe.[130] The Australian Roman Catholic theologian **Denis Edwards** suggests, taking up an idea from Hans Urs von Balthasar, that we may view our universe as 'a play within a play', unfolding ' "within" the trinitarian relations of mutual love.'[131]

> In this life of God, the one who is Matrix and Source, Mother and Father, eternally gives self away in love in the act of begetting the one who is Wisdom and Word, and this springing forth of divine life eternally transcends itself ecstatically in the one who is Holy Spirit. . . . Creation, including the evolution of life, occurs within the 'space' of this divine life.[132]

God is the ultimate communion of Persons in friendship. In God 'we live and move and have our being' (Acts 17.28). Relationships therefore, with God, with other human beings and the rest of creation, will be primary in our worldview and practice. We are made for friendship.

7

Conclusion: living friendship

During a march against unemployment in the English Midlands, a group of Anglican nuns walked beside one of the unemployed. He turned to them and said, 'I can't get over you sisters walking with us. The Church has done things *for* us but has never done things *with* us.' He was not quoting any theologian! 'That remark', wrote Sister Maureen Henderson, 'made a deep impression on me.' Formerly a missionary nurse in Tanzania she was embarking, in the early 1980s, on years of developing inter-faith relationships and common work on social issues with Muslims, Sikhs, Jews, Hindus and others in the English Midlands and in London. 'True friendship enlarges horizons and draws others into its orbit . . . My relationship with God grew and matured alongside my deepening relationships with friends from other faith traditions.' Simple means are enough: 'Our friendship centred very much around hospitality; it was in our eating and talking together that we celebrated our joy and gratitude for life and creation and shared our concerns about all that marred these gifts of God.'[1] Sister Maureen has continued her apostolate of friendship as a solitary, a Christian hermit-in-everyday-life, in a parish in Surrey, facilitating workshops to explore Christian spirituality in a multifaith world.

The practical theologian John Swinton tells the story of Dana, a young mother dying of AIDS. Members of the church to which she and her husband belonged were constant in visiting, helping, sharing grief and laughter. Friendship was just as vital a source of healing and support as any professional help.[2] Swinton writes, too, about people living with mental illness, and the hope and affirmation that lay people in local congregations can provide simply through friendship, despite the real difficulties. Friends focus on the person, not the illness. Practical 'messianic friendship' is '*radical* in that it transcends the relational boundaries that are constructed by contemporary tendencies to associate with others on the basis of likeness, utility, or social exchange'.[3] Its primary dynamic is towards those whom one would not, conventionally, seek out as friends. Therefore, it does not just happen: 'the type of friendships that resemble those of Jesus do not arise naturally from normal social encounters. Rather, forms of friendship that seek to move beyond natural social attraction to embrace those who are often considered "strangers" need to be nurtured.'[4] As a chaplain and 'friendship facilitator' for people coming out of hospital into the community, Swinton found that to overcome resistance, stereotyping, and fear on the congregations' part, both appropriate education and the experience of genuine encounter with their new friends are fundamentally important. His suggestions clearly also raise questions about the meaning of traditional pastoral injunctions to ministers not to make friendships with parishioners.

Sister Maureen helps the unsure to seek how to be Christian in deep interfaith encounters. As a pastor, John Swinton has assisted people to discover how to make unusual friendships, to be channels of the friendship-love of Christ. Examples and opportunities like these abound in virtually every situation, whether local or regional or international. Christians have the essential counter-cultural calling to be friends on earth, to offer love which may be in the truest sense sacrificial, to build community, to be peacemakers and healers, to seek and promote compassion and justice, to walk with the oppressed and help their voice to be heard, to celebrate with all. It is God who gives the courage and determination to open up paths of reconciliation. In each circumstance we can begin simply from where we are, with the poverty of what we are and the little that we understand, learning to walk forward in faith, allowing Christ's love and peace to remove our fear and point the way forward. Should it not be a priority in the formation and training of all Christians, ministers and laity alike, to nurture this vision and the practical abilities to know how to reflect on it and to act in the love of friendship?

At the beginning of my own research I saw the classical 'teleological' emphasis on virtue in the person whom we love as having constituted the original barrier to describing Christian love as friendship, because it makes friendship a particular love of what is already evidently good; and it risks restricting it in a selfish manner to those objects that are good for me. As I explored and lived with the issues, I was struck more and more by the positive aspect of this interest in goodness in the other, where goodness is seen not as a prerequisite but rather as the goodness that love itself creates. The outgoing love of friendship does care about goodness in the other, for their sake and that of God and the community and even also for my own sake. The content of goodness is outlined in Gal. 5.22–3, 1 Cor. 13, Rom. 12.9–21, Mt. 5–7. There will be limits, constituted by opposite behaviours, that cannot be condoned. But with its focus on the person and what they may become, Christ's friendship does not make the other's goodness a prior condition. The love of friendship is creative of personhood, rejoicing in each person's potential and suffering when that potential is missed or marred. Love is God's way of creating and revealing goodness.

Friendship-love is the exercise of goodness, so if we practise an ethic and spirituality of friendship-love we shall place emphasis on the formation of character, and on the practice of prayer so that character can come to its graced perfection. 'Tenderness' and 'passion' have been advanced as modern virtues that allow the wisdom of the heart to complement the more intellectual virtues. But the integrated person will also need courage and practical wisdom, balance and discernment, and will love not only with the attentiveness and compassion to which 'passionate friendship' points, but also with a mind that pierces to the truth and values justice.

We need, and delight in, close loving relationships that nurture us and model love, and we need smaller communities that support us within the larger world. But that means guarding against group selfishness and fear of other groups. Two things are disastrous: to have too high and narrow a doctrine of friendship, making it exclusive, or to forget friendship altogether in pursuit of universal neighbour-love. The dark side of friendship if taken exclusively is fear of strangers and enemies, dislike and hatred of those whom we suspect of not agreeing with us in all things human and divine. The world has these in plenty. In southern Africa the value of 'ubuntu', being-human-in-community, produces wonderful hospitality, generosity, availability and compassion. Yet a strong community sense, wherever it is found, can also be repressive of individual or prophetic gifts, and transmutes into ugly exclusiveness whenever some are deemed less human than others. Friendship is the overcoming of all its varied opposites: fear, strangeness and alienation, enmity and hostility, and indifference. To do this takes energy and work, and can be far from easy. But it opens up the new world of possibility. Peace is not just the absence of war, but the actual presence of freedom and friendship.

Ancient writers assumed friendship has practical limits because we are finite; and they were also much exercised about its moral limits. Both kinds of boundaries still raise issues for us. As finite creatures we must necessarily set practical bounds on loving, to maintain the quality of relationships and avoid burnout, so there will necessarily be a wide spectrum in the depth and duration of our actual concrete relationships on earth. In effect we apply Aristotle's principle of moderation, seeking the mean between deficiency and excess. As Cates rather starkly puts it, while we can exercise the positive regard of a friend towards all, in the exercise of practical compassion we may have to decide 'for how much of our time, with what intensity, and for how long we ought to regard *which* strange and even repulsive neighbors as we regard our friends'.[5] She reminds us too that while as friends of God we are 'called and empowered in charity to love all human beings, including the closest of our friends, as friends of God', that does not mean that all our closest and most vibrant relationships are reduced to 'a watered-down general benevolence'.[6] We still love those closest to us in more ways, and with even greater intensity. Grace, nevertheless, may intervene with its own law.

We are aware of living close together on a small planet where communication passes almost instantly between continents. We can conceive of the world rather as twelfth-century Cistercians conceived of the monastery, as the milieu in which the Kingdom of God must be made incarnate and where growth in love must replace the culture of violence in personal, social, and political life. The praxis of friendship requires that in addition to forming friendships with people close by, we should make efforts to cultivate a much wider network of deepening friendships in different continents and cultures, from which to gain understanding so that we may approach all people with respect and sensitivity. Where walls of division have been put up, we should ask ourselves and the others: what do friends do together? And start doing these things, at every level. Friendship is a strong and practical concept of love.

This study began with the simple purpose of discovering whether, and to what extent, there exists a view of Christian love that interprets it as the love of friendship. It shows that such a view, grounded in Scripture and practice, with a body of writing expressing it and a fund of experience in living it, does indeed exist and is alive and developing. Often those who contributed have not known, or were only obscurely aware, of each other's work. The material gathered here has been brought together for the first time, and has been presented in the form of an historical narrative. A full systematic analysis would be another book, but a simple analytical framework has emerged to link the material and to interpret this whole body of thought as a single system. Its elements are:

(i) All love concerns relationship, either actual or potential.
(ii) Friendship is the central case of relationship.
(iii) The love of friendship has three aspects:
  (a) ontological – it is grounded in shared being
  (b) deontological – it is goodness expressing itself in action
  (c) teleological – it is directed to the other (to God, or God's creature) with a view to fulfilment in mutual joy.

Love for every other person is always the love of friendship to the extent that it is an expression of our friendship with God. It is also the love of friendship in three further senses, corresponding to the three aspects listed above. (a) It is grounded in our shared nature, our likeness as creatures capable of being fulfilled by grace. (b) It is the self-giving of a friend on the pattern of Christ. God who commands love, also provides the power to love. Christian love is deontological in the sense that it springs from the inner imperative of God's goodness poured out in our hearts. (c) Equally on the pattern of Christ, it is a love of desire – an openness to the other that is also an undemanding but real and vibrant invitation to mutual joy.

Cicero's classical definition of friendship as perfect 'accord in all things human and divine, conjoined with mutual goodwill and affection' (*De amicitia* 20) has stood for centuries. Modern definitions may be subtly or quite radically different. Our understanding of interpersonal love has undergone multiple developments; and since Christian input into these changes has been significant, it will not be surprising if Jesus's transformation of friendship now speaks more immediately to us. 'Friendship is realized by sharing a table, and it comprises those who suffer under injustice. This stands on its head the whole ancient concept of friendship, as being between males of equal status.'[7] Recent decades have witnessed the most significant evolution in the concept of friendship since the New Testament itself. Current Western thought has become just as fascinated by the individual 'quiddity' of persons, as were ancient Greeks by similarity in virtue. Uniqueness is, perhaps, the newest virtue! For us, friendship sees each person in their particularity and loves each differently. Friendship is love between diverse people in dynamic interaction.

The love of friendship discovered in this study is love that sets people free to be and to become in their own individual uniqueness, and which is essentially directed towards, hopes for and invites, reciprocal love and the joy of fulfilment in mutual relationship: but without possessively demanding it. Friendship so understood is a fundamental attitude characterizing our whole approach to others. The word 'friendliness' conveys something of this sense but in a shallower way. Friendship cares about truth and justice, and has intensity and stability. Where friendliness would be rebuffed, friendship absorbs the hurt and remains committed. Such love can exist as an open offer without being reciprocated; but it is precisely its orientation towards the person of the other and towards mutuality, with goodwill and respectful interest, that distinguishes the love of friendship from possessive love on one hand, and an absolutely disinterested (or uninterested) altruism on the other. Having engendered a relationship, this same love remains within it, continually given and received.

God reveals what friendship is. In Christ our whole being becomes aligned with the universal friendship-love of God. Unity in such friendship is sacramental, an icon of the transcendent presence of God the Trinity. Friendship with God in prayer relates us with the whole human community and all creation as we look to the joy that Augustine's words express, the eternal 'enjoyment of God, and of each other in God'.[8]

'An enemy is a friend waiting to be made; that is the only hope for this conflict-ridden world.'[9]

' "I have called you friends . . . And I have appointed you to go and bear fruit, fruit that will last" ' (Jn 15.15–16).

Select Bibliography

Adkins, A. W. H., '"Friendship" and "Self-sufficiency" in Homer and Aristotle', *Classical Quarterly* 13 (1963) pp. 30–45.

Aelred [of Rievaulx], *Opera Omnia*, vol. 1: *Opera Ascetica* (ed. A. Hoste OSB and C. H. Talbot; Corpus Christianorum Continuatio Mediaevalis, I; Turnhout: Brepols, 1971).

—— [Ailred], *Christian Friendship*, trans. C. Hugh Talbot, O. Cist. (London: Catholic Book Club, 1942).

—— *L'Amitié spirituelle*, (trad. J. Dubois; Bruges: C. Bayaent, 1948).

—— *Treatises, The Pastoral Prayer* (CF 2; Spencer, Mass.: Cistercian Publications, 1971).

—— *Spiritual Friendship* (trans. Mary E. Laker, SSMD, intro. by Douglass Roby; CF 5; Kalamazoo: Cistercian Publications, 1977).

—— *Mirror of Charity* (trans. Elizabeth Connor, OCSO; intro. by Charles Dumont, OCSO; CF17; Kalamazoo: Cistercian Publications, 1990).

Albert the Great [Albertus Magnus], *Opera Omnia* (ed. A. Borgnet; 36 vols; Paris: Vivès, 1890–8).

—— *Super Ethica: Commentum et Quaestiones*, in *Opera Omnia* vol. 14 (2 parts) (ed. W. Kübel; Inst. Alberti Magni Coloniense, 1987).

Ambrose of Milan, *De officiis* (text, edited with introduction, translation and commentary by Ivor J. Davidson; 2 vols; Oxford: Oxford University Press, 2001).

—— (S. Ambroise), *Les devoirs* (texte établi, traduit et annoté par M. Testard; 2 vols; Corpus Christianorum Series Latina (Paris: Belles Lettres, 1984–92).

—*Some of the Principal works of St Ambrose*, including 'On the Duties of the Clergy'; 'On the Decease of Satyrus'; 'Concerning Virgins'; 'Concerning Widows' (trans. by H. de Romestin, in *A Select Library of Nicene and Post-Nicene Fathers*, 2nd series [NPNF 2], Vol. X; Oxford, etc., 1896).

'Amicus' (pseud.) *The Friendships of the Bible* (London 1853).

Andrews, Charlie F. (1932), *What I owe to Christ* (London: Hodder, 1932).

—— (1937) *Christ and Human Need* (London, 1937).

Anglund, Joan Walsh, *A Friend is Someone Who Likes You* (London: Collins, 1959).

Aquinas – see Thomas Aquinas.

Aristotle, *Complete Works* (revised Oxford translation ed. Jonathan Barnes; 2 vols; Princeton: Princeton University Press, 1984).

—— *The 'Art' of Rhetoric* (trans. J. H. Freese, Loeb Classical Library; London: Heinemann, 1926, repr. 1959).

Arnim, J. von, (ed.), *Stoicorum Veterum Fragmenta* (SVF) (4 vols; Lipsiae, 1903–24).

Aubrey, John, *Aubrey's Brief Lives*, ed.with intro. by O. L. Dick (London: Secker and Warburg, 1949).

Augustine, *The Works of Aurelius Augustine* (ed. M. Dods, trans. J. G.Cunningham; vol. VI: Letters, vol. I, Edinburgh 1872; vol. XIII: Letters, vol. 2, Edinburgh 1875).

—— *The Works of Saint Augustine: A Translation for the 21st Century* (ed. J. E. Rotelle; Hyde Park NY: New City Press, 1991).

—— *On Christian Doctrine*, [*De doctrina christiana*] (trans. D. W. Robertson, Jr.; Library of Liberal Arts; (Indianapolis: Bobbs-Merrill, 1958; repr. 1978).

—— *City of God* [*De civitate Dei*] (trans. H. Bettenson; Harmondsworth: Penguin, 1972).

—— *Confessions* (trans. H. Chadwick; Oxford: OUP, 1992).

Aulus Gellius, *Noctes Atticae* (trans. J. C. Rolfe; 3 vols; Loeb Classical Library; London: Heinemann, 1927, repr. 1948–54).

Bacon, Francis, 'Of Friendship', in his *Essays* (ed. J .M. McNeill; London: Macmillan, 1959) pp. 73–81.

Bailey, C., *Epicurus: the extant remains*, with transl. and notes (Oxford: Clarendon Press, 1926).

Barbour, Hugh, *The Quakers in Puritan England* (New Haven, London: Yale Univ. Press, 1964) p. 36.

Barr, James, 'Words for love in Biblical Greek', in *The Glory of Christ in the New Testament, essays in honour of George Caird* (ed. L. D. Hurst and N. T. Wright; Oxford, Clarendon Press, 1987) pp. 3–18.

Barth, Karl, *Ethics* (trans. G. W. Bromiley; Edinburgh: T.&T. Clark, 1981) (Original: *Ethik*, 1928–9).

Baxter, Richard, *The Christian's Converse with God* (ed. M. Silvester; London, 1693).

Bede, 'Life of Saint Cuthbert', in *Two Lives of Saint Cuthbert* (texts, transl. and notes by Bertram Colgrave (Cambridge: CUP, 1940) pp. 143–307.

Bennett, E. Arnold (1914), *Friendship and Happiness, a plea for the Feast of St Friend* (London 1914).

Benson, Robert Hugh, *The Friendship of Christ* (London: Longman's, 1912).

Bentley, Richard, 'Remarks upon a Late Discourse of Free Thinking' in *The Works of Richard Bentley D.D.* (ed. A. Dyce; 3 vols; London, 1836–8) vol. 3.

Berkeley, George (Bishop), *Works* (ed. A. C. Fraser; 4 vols; Oxford: Clarendon Press, 1901).

Bickel, Ernst, 'Peter von Blois und Ps. Cassiodor de Amicitia', *Neues Archiv* 45 (1924) pp. 223–34.

Black, Hugh, *Friendship* (London, new edn 1906) (1st edn 1897).

Bonhoeffer, Dietrich, *Ethics*, ed. Eberhard Bethge, trans. Neville Horton Smith (London: SCM, 1955, repr. 1960). Original: *Ethik* (Munich: Kaiser Verlag, 1949).

Booth, Mrs Bramwell, *Friendship with Jesus: Field Officers' Councils 1922* (London: Salvationist Publications 1924).

Boswell, James, *Life of Johnson* (ed. G. B. Hill, rev. L. F. Powell; 6 vols; Oxford: Clarendon Press, 1934).

Boswell, John, *Christianity, Social Tolerance, and Homosexuality: Gay People in Western Europe from the Beginning of the Christian Era to the Fourteenth Century* (Chicago & London: Univ. of Chicago Press, 1980).

Braithwaite, William C., art. 'Society of Friends', *Hastings' Encyclopaedia of Religion and Ethics* (Edinburgh, 1913) 6 pp. 142–7.

Bray, Alan, *The Friend* (Chicago, London: University of Chicago Press, 2003).

Brett, Jesse, *The Divine Friendship* (London: Longman's 1909).

Brown, P., *Augustine of Hippo* (London: Faber & Faber, new edn, 2000) (original 1967).

Brunner, Emil, *The Divine Imperative: A Study in Christian Ethics* (trans. O. Wyon; London: Lutterworth, 1937). (Original: *Das Gebot und die Ordnungen*, 1932).

Buber, Martin, *I and Thou* (trans. Roland Gregor Smith; Edinburgh: T&T Clark, 2nd edn 1959) (Original: *Ich und Du*, 1923).

Burnaby, John, *Amor Dei. A Study of the Religion of St. Augustine* (London: Hodder & Stoughton, 1938; reissued with corrections, Norwich; Canterbury Press, 1991).

Burridge, A. W., 'The Spirituality of St. Aelred', *Downside Review* 58 (1940) p. 225–47.

Burton, P. A., 'Aelred face à l'histoire et à ses historiens. Autour de l'actualité aelredienne', *Collectanea Cisterciensa* 58 (1996) pp. 161–93.

Cassian, John, Conference 16, 'On Friendship', trans. E. C. S. Gibson, *A Select Library of Nicene and Post-Nicene Fathers*, 2nd series, vol. X1 (New York, Oxford, London, 1894) pp. 450–60.

—— *The Conferences* (trans. B. Ramsey OP, Ancient Christian Writers, 57; New York: Paulist Press, 1997).

Cates, Diana Fritz, *Choosing to Feel. Virtue, Friendship, and Compassion for Friends* (Notre Dame: Univ. of Notre Dame Press, 1997).

Chadwick, Henry, *Augustine* (Oxford: OUP, 1986).

Cheyn, William, *The Friendship of Christ* (Edinburgh, 1718).

Cicero, M. Tullius, *De amicitia*, (trans. W. A. Falconer; Loeb Classical Library; London: Heinemann, 1923, repr. 1964).

—— *De officiis* (trans. W. Miller; Loeb Classical Library; London: Heinemann, 1913, repr. 1961).

—— *De finibus bonorum et malorum* (trans. H. Rackham; Loeb Classical Library; London: Heinemann, 1914).

—— *De natura deorum* (trans. H. Rackham; Loeb Classical Library; London: Heinemann, 1933, repr. 1972).

Clarke, E., *Jerome, Chrysostom, and Friends: Essays and translations* (New York: Edwin Mellen Press, 1979).

Coconnier, M. Th., OP, 'La charité d'après St. Thomas d'Aquin', *Revue Thomiste* 12 (1904) pp. 641–660; 14 (1906) pp. 5–31; 15 (1907) pp. 1–17.

Conner, Paul, *Celibate Love* (London: Sheed and Ward, 1980).

Cooper, Anthony Ashley, 3rd Earl of Shaftesbury, *Characteristics of Men, Manners, Opinions, Times, etc.* (ed. J. M. Robertson; 2 vols; London: 1900).

Coquart, André [Baudoin de la Trinité] OCD, 'Nature de l'amitié selon saint Thomas d'Aquin', Unpublished doctoral thesis, Faculty of Theology of the Discalced Carmelites, Rome, 1959. Borrowed with kind permission of the author from Casa Generalizia Carmelitani Scalzi, Corso d'Italia 38, 00198 Roma.

Corley, Jeremy, *Ben Sira's Teaching on Friendship*, Brown Judaic Studies 316 (Providence RI: Brown University, 2002).

Cousins, E., 'A Theology of Interpersonal Relations: Richard of St Victor's elaboration of the themes of interpersonal relations', *Thought* (Fordham Univ. Quarterly) 45 (1970) pp. 55–82.

Crossin, John W., OSFS, *Friendship: the Key to Spiritual Growth* (New York: Paulist Press, 1997).

Curtius, Ernst, 'Die Bedeutung der Freundschaft im Alterthum für Sittlicheit, Wissenschaft und Öffentliches Leben' *Protestantische Monatsblätter* 22 (1863) pp. 1–16. [Repr. as 'Die Freundschaft im Alterthume' (sic) in his *Alterthum und Gegenwart* (Berlin, 1882) I pp. 183–202].

D'Arcy, M.C., SJ, *The Mind and Heart of Love* (London: Collins Fontana Library edn, 1962) (1st edn 1945, 2nd edn 1954).

Davy, M.-M., *Un Traité de l'amour du XIIe siècle: Pierre de Blois* (Paris, 1932).

Derrida, Jacques, *Politics of Friendship* (trans. G. Collins, London: Verso, 1997).

Deverell, Mary, *Sermons* (Bristol 1774).

De Witt, N. W., *Epicurus and his Philosophy* (Minneapolis: Univ. of Minnesota Press, 1954).

Diogenes Laertius, *Lives of Eminent Philosophers* (R. D. Hicks; Loeb Classical Library; 2 vols; London: Heinemann, 1925).

Dubois, J. (1948) 'Introduction' in Aelred, *L'amitié spirituelle* (q.v.) p. ix–civ.

Dudden, F. Homes, *The Life and Times of St Ambrose* (2 vols; Oxford: Clarendon Press, 1935).

Dumont, Charles, OCSO, 'Aelred de Rievaulx' in *Théologie de la vie monastique* (Théologie 49) (Paris: Aubier, 1961).

——'Seeking God in Community according to St Aelred', *Cistercian Studies* 6 (1971) pp. 289–317. (Original: 'Chercher Dieu dans la communauté selon Aelred de Rievaulx' *Collectanea Cisterciensia* 34 (1972) pp. 8–35).

—— 'Personalism in Community according to Aelred of Rievaulx', *Cistercian Studies* 12 (1977) pp. 250–71. (Original: 'Le personnalisme communautaire d'Aelred de Rievaulx', *Collectanea Cisterciensia* 39 (1977) pp. 129–48.

—— 'Aelred of Rievaulx's *Spiritual Friendship*', in J. R. Sommerfeldt (ed.), *Cistercian Ideals and Reality* (Kalamazoo: Cistercian Publications, 1978) pp. 187–98.

Dunfee, Susan Nelson, *Beyond Servanthood. Christianity and the Liberation of Women* (Lanham: University Press of America, 1989).

Dutton, M., 'Aelred of Rievaulx on chastity and sex' Cistercian Studies Quarterly 29 (1994) pp. 121–96.

Edwards, Denis, *The God of Evolution* (New York: Paulist Press, 1999).

Edwards, Hubert Edwin, *The Friendships of Christ* (London: Nisbet 1919).

Egenter, Richard, *Gottesfreundschaft: Die Lehre von der Gottesfreundschaft in der Scholastik und Mystik des 12. und 13. Jahrhunderts* (Augsburg, 1928).

—— articles 'Gottesfreunde' and 'Gottesfreundschaft' in *Lexikon für Theologie und Kirche* (Freiburg 1960) 4, cols 1104–6.

—— *The Desecration of Christ* (London: Burns & Oates, 1967) Translation, with alterations, of *Kitsch und Christenleben* (Buch-Kunstverlag Ettal, 1958).

Egres, Odo, O. Cist., 'Mechtild von Magdeburg: Exile in a Foreign Land', in E. Rozanne Elder (ed.), *Goad and Nail* (Cist. Stud. Ser. 84;

Studies in Mediaeval Cistercian History 10; Kalamazoo: Cistercian Publications, 1985) pp. 133–147.

Epictetus, *The Discourses as reported by Arrian* (trans. W. A. Oldfather; 2 vols; Loeb Classical Library; London: Heinemann, 1925, repr. 1961).

Epicurus: see Bailey, *Epicurus*.

Fabre, P., *S. Paulin de Nole et l'amitié chrétienne* (Paris: Boccard, 1949).

Fénelon, François, *Christian Perfection* (ed. C. F. Whiston, trans. M. W. Stillman; New York: Harper 1947).

Festugière, André Marie J., OP, *Epicurus and his Gods*, trans. C. W. Chilton (Oxford: Blackwell, 1955) [*Epicure et ses dieux* (Paris, 1946; corrected edn 1968)].

Finnis, John, *Natural Law and Natural Rights* (Clarendon Law Series; Oxford: Clarendon Press, 1980).

——*Aquinas: moral, political, and legal theory* (Oxford: OUP 1998).

Fiske, Adele M., *Friends and Friendship in the Monastic Tradition*, CIDOC cuaderno 51 (Cuernavaca: CIDOC 1970).

Fitzgerald, John T. (ed.) *Friendship, Flattery, and Frankness of Speech, Studies on Friendship in the NT World* (Supplement to Novum Testamentum, vol. LXXXII; Leiden: Brill, 1996).

—— (ed.) *Greco-Roman perspectives on Friendship* (Atlanta: Scholars Press, 1997).

Florensky, Pavel, 'Friendship' in *The Pillar and Ground of Truth* trans. B. Joachim (Princeton: Princeton University Press, 1997) pp. 284–330. Original 1914.

Fraisse, Jean-Claude, *Philia: la notion d'amitié dans la philosophie antique* (Paris: J. Vrin, 1974).

Francis de Sales, *Introduction to the Devout Life* (trans. M. Day; London: Burns & Oates, 1962).

Fränkel, H., *Early Greek Poetry and Philosophy* (trans. M. Hadas and J. Willis; Oxford: Blackwell, 1975).

Furnish, Victor, *The Love Command in the New Testament* (London: SCM, 1973).

Gillon, L.-B., OP, 'Genèse de la théorie thomiste de l'amour', *Revue thomiste* 46 (1946) pp. 322–9.

—— 'A propos de la théorie thomiste de l'amitié', *Angelicum* 25 (1948) pp. 3–17.

Gregory of Nyssa, *The Life of Moses* (trans. and notes by A. J. Malherbe and E. Ferguson; CWS; New York: Paulist Press, 1978).

(Grosseteste, R.,) *The Greek Commentaries on the Nicomachean Ethics of Aristotle: in the Latin translation of Robert Grosseteste, Bishop of Lincoln* (critical edition with an introductory study by H. Paul F. Mercken; Vol. 3;

Leiden: Brill; Leuven Univ. Press, 1991). Latin text with commentaries by Aspasius (Bk VIII), Michael of Ephesus (Bk IX).

Hallier, Amédée, OCSO, *The Monastic Theology of Aelred of Rievaulx: An Experiential Theology* (trans. C. Heaney, OCSO, introduction by Thomas Merton, Cistercian Studies Series 2 (Shannon: Irish University Press, 1969) (Original: *Un Educateur Monastique: Aelred de Rievaulx* (Paris: Gabalda, 1959).

Häring, Bernard, CSsR, *Free and Faithful in Christ. Moral Theology for Priests and Laity* (3 vols; Slough: St Paul Publications, 1978, 79, 81).

Harnack, Adolf, '"Friends" (*hoi philoi*)', in *The Mission and Expansion of Christianity in the First Three Centuries* (trans. J. Moffatt; 2 vols; London: Williams & Norgate, 2nd edn 1908) I pp. 419–21.

Harrison, C., 'Marriage and Monasticism in St Augustine: the bond of friendship' *Studia Patristica* vol. 33, ed. E. A. Livingstone pp. 94–9 (Leuven: Peeters 1997) Papers presented at the 12th International Conference on Patristic Studies, held in Oxford 1995.

Harvey, T. Edmund, *Saint Aelred of Rievaulx* (London: Allenson, 1932).

Haseldine, Julian, (ed.) *Friendship in Mediaeval Europe* (Stroud: Sutton Publishing, 1999).

Hegel, G. F. W., *The Philosophy of Right* (trans. T. M. Knox; Oxford: Clarendon Press, 1942).

Henderson, Maureen, *Friends on the Way* (Peterborough: Epworth Press, 1999).

Heyward, Isabel Carter, *The Redemption of God. A Theology of Mutual Relation* (Lanham: University Press of America, 1982).

Hinnebusch, Paul, OP, *Friendship in the Lord* (Notre Dame: Ave Maria Press, 1974).

Holland, Lady Saba, *Memoir and Letters of the Reverend Sydney Smith* (2 vols, London, 4th edn 1855).

Hoste, Anselme, OP [later OSB Cam], 'The First Draft of Aelred of Rievaulx' *De Spiritali Amicitia*', *Sacris Erudiri* 10 (1958) p. 186–221.

Houston, James, *The Transforming Friendship* (Oxford: Lion 1989).

Hughes, H. Trevor, *The Piety of Jeremy Taylor* (London: Macmillan, 1960).

Humberstone, William, *The Friendship of Jesus* [a sermon] (London, 1875).

Hunt, Mary E., *Fierce Tenderness: A Feminist Theology of Friendship* (New York: Crossroad, 1991).

Iamblichus, *On the Pythagorean Life* (trans. with notes and intro. by Gillian Clark; Translated Texts for Historians 8; Liverpool: Liverpool University Press, 1989).

The Imitation of Christ (Imitatio Christi) Trans. L. Sherley-Price (London: Penguin, 1952).

Jay, Eric G., *Friendship with God; the way of the Anglican Communion* (London: Mowbray, 1959).

Joachim, H. H., *Aristotle: The Nicomachean Ethics: a commentary* (ed. D. A. Rees; Oxford: Clarendon Press, 1951).

Johann, Robert O., SJ, 'Meditation on Friendship', *Modern Schoolman* 25 (1948) pp. 126–131.

—— *The Meaning of Love. An essay towards a metaphysics of intersubjectivity* (London: Geoffrey Chapman, 1959).

John of the Cross, *Collected works of St John of the Cross* (trans. K. Kavanaugh and O. Rodriguez; Washington DC: Institute of Carmelite Studies, 1991).

Johnson, Elizabeth, *She Who Is: the mystery of God in feminist theological discourse* (New York: Crossroad, 1992).

Joly, Robert, *Le vocabulaire chrétien de l'amour est-il original? Philein et Agapan dans le grec antique* (Bruxelles: Presses Universitaire, 1968).

Jones, L. Gregory, 'The Theological Transformation of Aristotelian Friendship in the Thought of St Thomas Aquinas' *The New Scholasticism* vol. 61 (1987) pp. 373–99.

Jones, Richard, *Friendship with God: an Essay* (London, 1772).

Jones, Rufus M., *George Fox, Seeker and Friend* (London: Allen and Unwin, 1930).

Jowett, Benjamin, *Sermons Biographical and Miscellaneous* (ed. W. H. Fremantle; London, 1899).

—— 'Friendship', in his *Sermons on Faith and Doctrine* (ed. W. H. Fremantle; London, 1901) pp. 337–54.

Julian of Norwich, *Showings* (trans. E. Colledge and J. Walsh; CWS; Paulist Press: New York, 1978).

Kant, Immanuel, *Kant's Critique of Practical Reason and other works on the Theory of Ethics* (trans. T. K. Abbott; London, 6th edn, 1909).

—— *Lectures on Ethics*, trans. L. Infield (London: Methuen, 1930).

—— *The Doctrine of Virtue: Part II of The Metaphysic of Morals* (trans. Mary J. Gregor; New York and London: Harper Torchbooks, 1964).

Keaty, Anthony W., 'Thomas's Authority for Identifying Charity as Friendship: Aristotle or John 15?' *The Thomist* 62 (1998) pp. 581–601.

Kierkegaard, S., *Works of Love* (trans. H. V. and E. H. Hong; Princeton Univ. Press, Princeton, 1995).

King, Henry Churchill, *The Laws of Friendship, Human and Divine* (Haverford College Library Lectures; New York: Macmillan, 1909).

King, Martin Luther, *Strength to Love* (London: Hodder 1964).

Kirk, G. E., J. E. Raven, and M. Schofield, *The Pre-Socratic Philosophers: a critical history with a selection of texts* (Cambridge: CUP, 2nd edn 1983).

Knowles, David, OSB, 'The Humanism of the Twelfth Century', *Studies* 30 (1941) pp. 43–58. Repr. in his *The Historian and Character* (Cambridge: CUP, 1963) pp. 16–30.

—— *The Monastic Order in England, 940–1216* (Cambridge: CUP, 2nd edn 1963).

Konstan, David, *Friendship in the Classical World* (Cambridge: CUP, 1997).

Lambert, Anne Thérèse, Marq. de, 'A Treatise on Friendship', in *The Works of the Marchioness de Lambert* (English trans.; 2 vols; London, 1769) 1 pp. 140–75.

Lavaud, B., OP, 'La charité comme amitié d'après St. Thomas', *Revue Thomiste* 34 (1929) pp. 445–75. Based on Keller, 'De virtute caritatis ut amicitia quadam divina', *Xenia Thomistica* 2 (Rome, 1924) pp. 233–76.

Leclercq, Jean, OSB, 'L'Amitié dans les lettres au Moyen Age: autour d'un manuscrit de la bibliothèque de Petrarque', *Revue du Moyen Age Latin* 1 (1945) pp. 391–410.

—— *L'Amour des lettres et le désir de Dieu: initiation aux auteurs monastiques du moyen âge* (Paris: Cerf, 1957).

—— English translation of *L'amour des lettres*: *The Love of Learning and the Desire for God: a study of monastic culture* (trans. C. Misrahi; London: SPCK 1978).

—— art. 'Amicizia nella vita religiosa', *Dizionario degli istituti di perfezione* (ed. G. Pelliccia and G. Rocca; Rome: Edizione Paoline, 1974) I cols 516–20.

—— *Contemplative Life* (trans. E. Flunder, Cist. Stud. Ser., 19; Kalamazoo: Cistercian Publications, 1978).

—— 'Friendship and Friends in the Monastic Life', *Cistercian Studies* 24.4 (1989) pp. 293–300.

Lepp, Ignace, SJ, 'The Love of Friendship', in his *The Psychology of Loving* (trans. B. B. Gilligan; Dublin: Helicon, 1964) pp. 191–208.

—— *The Ways of Friendship* (trans. Bernard Murchland; New York: Macmillan, 1966) Original: *Les Chemins de l'amitié* (Editions Bernard Grasset, 1964).

Lewis, C. S., *The Four Loves* (London: Collins, 1983) (First pub. 1960).

Long, A. A., *Hellenistic Philosophy: Stoics, Epicureans, Sceptics* (London: Duckworth, 1974).

Lorde, Audre, 'Uses of the Erotic: the Erotic as Power' in *Sister Outsider* (Freedom, Calif.: Crossing Press, 1984) Paper delivered 1978, first published as pamphlet.

Lottin, Otto, OSB, 'Saint Albert le Grand et l'Ethique à Nicomaque' in his *Psychologie et Morale aux XIIe et XIIIe siècles* (6 vols; Gembloux: J. Duculot, 1960) 6 pp. 315–31.

Louth, Andrew, *Maximus the Confessor* (Introduction and texts; London: Routledge, 1996).

Luis de León, *The Names of Christ* (trans. M. Durán and W. Kluback; CWS; London: SPCK, 1984).

McEvoy, James, 'Notes on the Prologue of St Aelred of Rievaulx's 'de Spirituali Amicitia', with a translation.' *Traditio* 37 (1981) pp. 396–411.

—— '*Anima una et cor unum:* Friendship and Spiritual Unity in Augustine', *Recherches de théologie ancienne et mediévale* 53 (1986) pp. 40–82.

—— 'The sources and the significance of Henry of Ghent's disputed question, "Is friendship a virtue?" ' pp. 121–38 in W. Vanhamel (ed.) *Henry of Ghent* (Leuven University Press: 1996).

—— 'The Theory of Friendship in the Latin Middle ages: hermeneutics, contextualization, and the transmission and reception of ancient texts and ideas, from *c.* AD 350 to 1500' in Haseldine (ed.) *Friendship* q.v.

—— 'The other as oneself: friendship and love in the thought of St Thomas Aquinas' in *Thomas Aquinas: Approaches to Truth*, (ed. James J. McEvoy and Michael Dunne; Dublin: Four Courts Press, 2002).

McFague, Sallie, *Metaphorical Theology. Models of God in Religious Language* (London: SCM, 1983).

—— *Models of God: theology for an ecological nuclear age* (London: SCM, 1987).

McGoldrick, Terence A., *The Sweet and Gentle Struggle: Francis de Sales on the necessity of spiritual friendship* (Lanham: University Press of America, 1996).

McGuire, Brian P., *Friendship and Community. The monastic experience 350–1350* (Cistercian Studies Series, 95; Kalamazoo: Cistercian Publications, 1988).

McLynn, Neil B., *Ambrose of Milan. Church and court in a Christian capital* (Berkeley: Univ. of Calif. Press, 1994).

Macmurray, John, *The Self as Agent* (London: Faber, 1995).

McNamara, Sr. M. A., OP, 'Friendship in St Augustine', Doctoral Thesis (Fribourg: Studia Friburgensia, 1958)

Malherbe, A., *Social Aspects of Early Christianity* (Philadelphia: Fortress Press, 2nd edn 1983).

Malunowicz, Leokadia, 'Le problème de l'amitié chez Basile, Grégoire de Nazianze et Jean Chrysostome', *Studia Patristica* 16, ed. E. A. Livingstone (Berlin, 1985) pp. 412–17 (Paper presented to 7th International Conference on Patristic Studies, Oxford, 1975).

Martin, A, and O. Primavesi, *L'Empédocle de Strasbourg* (Berlin: de Gruyter, 1999).

Meilaender, Gilbert, *Friendship. A study in theological ethics* (Notre Dame: Univ. of Notre Dame Press, 1981).

Meyendorff, John, 'Introduction' in Gregory Palamas, *The Triads* (trans. N. Gendle; CWS; New York: Paulist Press, 1983).

Mitchell, Alan C., 'The social function of friendship in Acts 2:44–47 and 4:32–37', *Journal of Biblical Literature* 111.2 (1992) pp. 255–72.

—— ' "Greet the friends by name": NT evidence for the Greco-Roman *topos* on friendship' in Fitzgerald (ed.) *Greco-Roman Perspectives* pp. 225–62.

Moberly, Robert H., *The Great Friendship* (London: Hamish Hamilton, 1934).

Moltmann, Jürgen, *The Church in the Power of the Spirit* (London: SCM, 1977) (Original: *Kirche in der Kraft der Geistes*, Munich, 1975).

—— *The Open Church* (London: SCM, 1978). In USA: *Passion for Life* (Philadelphia: Fortress Press, 1978). A freely adapted translation by M. Douglas Meeks of *Neuer Lebensstil, Schritte zur Gemeinde,* (Munich: Chr. Kaiser Verlag, 1977).

—— *The Source of Life* (trans. M. Kohl; London: SCM, 1977).

Moltmann-Wendel, Elisabeth, and Jürgen Moltmann, 'Becoming Human in New Community' in Constance Parvey ed. *The Community of Women and Men in the Church* (Geneva: WCC, 1983) pp. 29–42.

Moltmann-Wendel, Elisabeth, *Rediscovering Friendship* (trans. John Bowden (London: SCM, 2000) (Original: *Wache auf, meine Freundin. Die Wiederkehr der Gottesfreundschaft*, Stuttgart, Keruz Verlag, 2000).

Montaigne, Michel de, 'De l'amitié', in his *Essais* (ed. P.Villey; Paris: Presses universitaires de France, 1965) pp. 185–95. First published 1580; first Eng. transl. 1603. Eng. transl.: *Essays* (trans. J. M. Cohen; Harmondsworth: Penguin Classics, 1958) pp. 91–105.

Moorhead, John, *Ambrose: church and society in the late Roman world* (London: Longman, 1999).

Murray, Andrew, *With Christ in the School of Prayer* (London: Nisbet 1886).

Nédoncelle, Maurice, *Vers un philosophie de l'amour* (Coll. 'Philosophie de l'esprit'; Paris: Aubier, 1946).

Neill, Stephen (1984), *The Supremacy of Jesus* (London: Hodder 1984).

Newman, J. H., Sermon: 'Beloved, let us love one another . . .', *Parochial and Plain Sermons* (8 vols; London, 1868) 2 pp. 51–60. First pub. in *Parochial Sermons,* 1835.

Nietzsche, Friedrich, *Human, all-too-Human* vol. 1 (trans. H. Zimmern, in vol. 7 of his *Complete Works*, ed. O. Levy; 18 vols; Edinburgh and London, 1909).

—— *Thus Spoke Zarathustra*, (trans. Walter Kaufmann; Harmondsworth: Penguin, 1978).

Noble, Henri-Dominique, OP, *L'Amitié avec Dieu : essai sur la vie spirituelle d'après saint Thomas d'Aquin* (La vie spirituelle: Collection dominicaine; Paris : Desclée Brouwer & Cie, 2nd edn 1932). First edn 1927.

Nygren, Anders, *Agape and Eros* (rev. transl. in one vol., trans. P. Watson; London: SPCK, 1982). Original, 2 vols, Stockholm 1930–6. First English translation 1932–9. This revised translation first published 1953.

O'Callaghan, Paul D., *The Feast of Friendship* (Wichita: Eighth Day Press: 2002).

O'Donovan, Oliver, *The Problem of Self-love in Augustine* (New Haven and London: Yale University Press, 1980).

Oppenheimer, Helen, *The Hope of Happiness. A sketch for a Christian Humanism* (London: SCM, 1983).

Origen, *Opera Omnia* (ed. K. Lommatzsch; 25 vols; Berlin 1831–48).

Osborne, Catherine, *Eros unveiled : Plato and the God of love* (Oxford: Clarendon, 1994).

Paton, H. J., 'Kant on Friendship', *Proceedings of the British Academy* 42 (1956) pp. 45–66.

Pelzer, A., 'Les versions latines des ouvrages de morale conservés sous le nom d'Aristote en usage au XIIIe siècle', in *Philosophes Médiévaux* vol. 8 (Louvain 1964) pp. 120–87. (Originally published in *Revue Néoscholastique de Philosophie* 23 (1921) pp. 316–41, 378–412).

Penn, William, *A Collection of the Works of William Penn. To which is prefixed a journal of his life* (2 vols; London, 1726).

—— 'Some Fruits of Solitude, in Reflections and Maxims Relating to the Conduct of Human Life', in his *The Peace of Europe, The Fruits of Solitude, and other writings* (with intro. by Joseph Besse, Everyman's Library; London: Dent, 1915) pp. 25–92.

Peterson, E., 'Der Gottesfreund: Beiträge zur Geschichte eines religiösen Terminus', *Zeitschrift für Kirchengeschichte* 42 (1923) pp. 161–202.

Pétré, H., *Caritas: étude sur le vocabulaire latin de la charité chrétienne* (Spicilegium Sacrum Lovaniense 22; Louvain, 1948).

Philippe, M.-D., OP, *Le Mystère de l'amitié divine* (Paris: Luf-Egloff, 1949).

Philippe, Paul, OP, *Le Rôle de l'amitié dans la vie chrétienne, selon saint Thomas d'Aquin* (Rome: Angelicum, 1938).

Philips, Katherine, *Poems*, to which are added M. Corneille's Pompey and Horace, with several other translations out of French (London, 1667).

The Philokalia (4 vols published to date; trans and ed. G. E. H. Palmer, P. Sherrard and K. Ware; London: Faber and Faber, 1979–1981).

Pinckaers, Servais, *The Sources of Christian Ethics* (trans. from 3rd edn by M. T. Noble; Edinburgh: T&T Clark 1995).

Plato, *Euthyphro, Apology, Crito, Phaedo, Phaedrus* (trans. H. N. Fowler; Loeb Classical Library; London: Heinemann, 1914).

—— *Lysis, Symposium* and *Gorgias* (trans. W. R. M. Lamb; Loeb Classical Library; London, rev. and repr. 1932, repr. 1953).

Plutarch, *Moralia* (16 vols, various editors and translators; Loeb Classical Library; London: Heinemann, 1939, repr. 1970).

Powicke, F. Maurice, *The Life of Ailred of Rievaulx*, Walter Daniel's text edited with introduction, translation and notes (London: Nelson, 1950). Introduction is Powicke's 1922 study of Aelred and his biographer, revised. Reprinted with new introduction by Marsha Dutton (Cistercian Fathers 57; Kalamazoo: Cistercian Publications, 1994).

Price, A. W., *Love and Friendship in Plato and Aristotle* (Oxford: Clarendon Press, 1989).

Quasten, J., *Patrology* (4 vols; Utrecht, etc., 1950–86).

Rader, Rosemary, *Breaking Boundaries: Male/Female Friendship in Early Christian Communities* (New York: Paulist Press, 1983).

Ramsay, Chevalier A.M., *The Life of François de Salignac de la Motte Fénelon, Archbishop and Duke of Cambray* (London, 1723)

Rawson, E., *Cicero: a Portrait* (London: Allen Lane, 1975).

Richard of St-Victor, *The Twelve Patriarchs, The Mystical Ark, Book Three of the Trinity* (trans. with intro. by G. A. Zinn; CWS; London: SPCK, 1979).

Ripple, Paula, FSPA, *Called to be Friends* (Notre Dame: Ave Maria Press, 1980).

Rist, J. M., *Epicurus: An Introduction* (Cambridge: CUP, 1972; p/bk 1977).

Robinson, D. (1990), 'Homeric *philos*' in E. M. Craik (ed.) *'Owls to Athens', Essays on Classical Subjects presented to Sir Kenneth Dover* (Oxford: Clarendon Press) pp. 97–107.

Rougemont, Denis de, *Passion and Society*, tr. Montgomery Belgion, (London: Faber & Faber, augmented edn 1956). First English edn 1940; original *L'Amour et l'occident* (Paris, 1939).

Rousselot, Pierre, SJ, *Pour l'histoire du problème de l'amour au Moyen Age* (Paris: Vrin, 1933). [Original in *Beiträge zur Gesch. der Philos. des Mittelalters*, Bd. 6, H 6: Münster, 1908].

Royden, A. Maude, *The Friendship of God* (London: G. P. Putnam's, 1924).

Russell, D. A., *Plutarch* (London: Duckworth, 1972).

Schilling, R., 'Aelredus van Rievaulx: Deus Amicitia est', *Cîteaux in de Nederlanden* 8 (1957) pp. 13–26.

Schüssler Fiorenza, Elisabeth, *In Memory of Her* (London: SCM 1983, 2nd edn with new intro., 1995).

—— 'Why not the category Friend/Friendship?' *Horizons* 2.1 (Spring 1975) pp. 117–18.

Scullard, H. H., *Early Christian Ethics in the West: from Clement to Ambrose* (London, 1907).

Seneca, L. Annaeus, *Ad Lucilium Epistulae Morales*, (trans. R. M. Gummere; 3 vols; Loeb Classical Library; London: Heinemann, 1917, repr. 1979).

Sheriffs, Deryck, *The Friendship of the Lord* (Carlisle: Paternoster Press, 1996).

Shillito, Edward (ed.), *The Purpose of God in the Life of the World: being some of the addresses delivered at a conference on international and missionary questions, Liverpool, Jan. 2–9, 1929* (London: SCM, 1929).

Smyth, Charles, *The Friendship of Christ. A Devotional Study* (London: Longman, 1945).

Squire, Aelred, OP, 'Historical factors in the formation of Aelred of Rievaulx,' *Collectanea Ord. Cist. Ref.* 22 (1960) pp. 262–82.

—— *Aelred of Rievaulx: A Study* (London: SPCK, 1969).

Stanford, Charles, *Friendship with God.* A sermon preached before the Bristol Association of Baptist Churches, held at Frome, 22 May 1850.

Sterling, G. E., 'The Bond of Humanity: Friendship in Philo of Alexandria', in J. T. Fitzgerald (ed.) *Greco-Roman Perspectives* pp. 203–23.

Stern-Gillet, Suzanne (1995), *Aristotle's Philosophy of Friendship* (SUNY Series in Ancient Greek Philosophy; Albany: State Univ. of New York Press, 1995).

Stuart, Elizabeth, *Just Good Friends: towards a lesbian and gay theology of relationships* (London: Mowbray, 1995).

—— *Gay and Lesbian Theologies: repetitions with critical difference* (Aldershot: Ashgate, 2003).

Swinton, John, 'Healing presence: reclaiming friendship as a pastoral gift' *Contact* 126 (1998) pp. 2–7.

—— *Resurrecting the Person: Friendship and the care of People with Mental Health Problems* (Nashville: Abingdon Press, 2000).

Tauler, John, *Spiritual Conferences* (trans. E. Colledge and Sr. M. Jane OP; St Louis: Herder, 1961).

Taylor, Jeremy, 'A Discourse of the Nature and Offices of Friendship, in a letter to the most ingenious and excellent M. K. P.' in Taylor, *Whole Works* (ed. R. Heber, rev. C. P. Eden; 10 vols; London, 1847–54) I pp. 71–98.

TePas, Katherine M. (Yohe), 'Spiritual Friendship in Aelred of Rievaulx and mutual sanctification in marriage', *Cistercian Studies* 27 (1992) pp. 63–72, 153–65.

—— 'Aelred's guidelines for physical attractions', *Cîteaux* 46 (1995) pp. 339–51.

Teresa of Avila, *Complete Works* (trans. and ed. E. A. Peers; 3 vols; London: Sheed and Ward, 1946).
The Theologia Germanica of Martin Luther tr. B. Hoffman CWS (Mahwah: Paulist Press, 1980).
Thomas à Kempis (attributed) – see *The Imitation of Christ.*
Thomas Aquinas, *Summa Theologica*, literally translated by Fathers of the English Dominican Province, 3 vols (London : Burns & Oates, 1947). First edn 1911, second edn rev. 1922.
——*Quaestiones Disputatae*, 2 vols (Turin: Marietti, 1949). (*Q.D. de Caritate* vol. 2, pp. 753–91).
——*Super Evangelium S. Ioannis Lecturae* (Turin: Marietti, 5th edn, 1952).
—— *In Decem libros Ethicorum Aristotelis ad Nicomachum expositio*, edited by R. M. Spiazzi, 3rd edition (Turin: Marietti, 1964) 1st edn 1949. Includes Latin text of *NE* with revisions ascribed to Moerbeke.
——*Commentary on the Nicomachean Ethics*, translated by C. I. Litzinger OP (Chicago: Henry Regnery & Co., 2 vols., 1964).
Thorold, Anthony W., *On Friendship* (Tavistock Booklets 9; London: 1896).
Torrell, J-P, OP, *Saint Thomas Aquinas*, vol. 1: The Person and his Work (Washington: Catholic University of America Press, 1996).
Traherne, Thomas, *The Way to Blessedness: Thomas Traherne's Christian Ethicks* (ed. M. Bottrall; London: Faith Press, 1962).
—— *Centuries* (Faith Press, London: 1963) (first published 1908).
Treu, Kurt, '*Philia* und *Agape*: zur Terminologie der Freundschaft bei Basilius und Gregor von Nazianz', *Studii Classici* 3 (Bucharest, 1961).
Tutu, Desmond M., *No Future Without Forgiveness* (London: Rider, 1999).
Vansteenberghe, E., 'Deux théoreticiens de l'amitié au XIIe siècle: Pierre de Blois et Aelred de Riéval', *Revue des sciences religieuses* 12 (1932) pp. 572–88.
Vansteenberghe, G., art. 'Amitié', *Dictionnaire de spiritualité* (Paris: G. Beauchesne, 1937) I cols 500–29.
Veach, Robert Wells, *The Friendship of Jesus* (New York, 1911).
Vischer, L., 'Das Problem der Freundschaft bei den Kirchenvätern', *Theologische Zeitschrift* 9 (Basel, 1953) pp. 173–200.
Voillaume, René, 'La Charité, amitié divine', *Lumière et Vie* 44 (1959) pp. 59–68.
Wadell, Paul J, *Friendship and the Moral Life* (Notre Dame: University of Notre Dame Press, 1989).
—— *Friends of God: Virtues and Gifts in Aquinas* (New York: Peter Lang, 1991).
—— *Becoming Friends: Worship, Justice, and the Practice of Christian Friendship* (Grand Rapids: Brazos Press, 2002).

Walter Daniel, *The Life of Ailred of Rievaulx*: see Powicke.

Weatherhead, Leslie D., *The Transforming Friendship* (London: Epworth, 1928).

Weil, Simone, 'Friendship' in her *Waiting on God* (trans. Emma Craufurd; London: Fontana, 1959) pp. 152–60.

White, Carolinne, *Christian Friendship in the Fourth Century* (Cambridge: CUP, 1992).

—— (trans.) *Early Christian Lives* (London: Penguin, 1998).

William of Auxerre (Gulielmus Altissiodorensis), *Summa Aurea* (ed. J. Ribaillier; 5 vols; Spicilegium Bonaventurianum 16–20; Paris and Rome: 1980–7).

Wilms, Jerome, OP, *Divine Friendship according to Saint Thomas* (trans. Sr. M. Fulgence, OP; London: Blackfriars, 1958; original 1933).

Wilson, Walter, *The History and Antiquities of Dissenting Churches* (4 vols; London, 1808–14).

Zizioulas, John D., *Being as Communion: studies in personhood and the church* (Crestwood: St Vladimir's Seminary Press, 1985; London: Darton, Longman & Todd, 1985).

Notes

Chapter 1: From classical friendship to New Testament love

1 Fraisse, *Philia* gives the fullest account of classical thought. Overview in White, *Christian Friendship* pp. 1–62. Reflections, continuing into the Christian era, in Osborne, *Eros unveiled.* Konstan, *Friendship*, examines only intimate friendship, a 'subset' (p. 91) of *philia* in its full sense.

2 Adkins, ' "Friendship" and "Self-sufficiency" '. A generally accepted analysis.

3 Robinson, 'Homeric *philos*' p. 101.

4 '*Hōs aiei ton homoion agei theos hōs ton homoion*', *Odyssey* 17.218. Author's translation. Cited by Plato, *Lysis* 214B4–5, *Symp.* 195B5.

5 '*kai kerameus keramei koteei kai tektoni tektōn, kai ptōchos ptōchō(i) phthoneei kai aoidos aoidō(i)*' 'Works and Days' l.25–6. Author's translation. Cf. Plato, *Lysis* 215D–E; Aristotle, *Rhet.* II.1381b16.

6 Fränkel, *Early Greek Poetry* p. 424.

7 I.31–8 (trans. Fränkel, *Early Greek Poetry* p. 403).

8 Tertullian (*c.* AD 160–*c.* 225) famously records pagan admiration for Christians: 'Look . . . how they love one another' (*Apol.* 39.7).

9 Iamblichus, *On the Pythagorean Life* 33.229–30 p. 96.

10 His poems survive only in fragments. Discussion and bibliography in Kirk, Raven and Schofield, *Pre-Socratic Philosophers*. A papyrus recently studied, attests the cyclical nature of his system (see Martin and Primavesi, *L'Empédocle*).

11 Aristotle, *NE* VIII 1155b4–7. Simplicius attributes two doctrines to Empedocles: likes retain a natural affinity because each element remains 'one' although its parts are scattered; and unlikes may be 'made like' by *philotēs* and be attracted to one another, until when *philotēs* reigns supreme, the harmonious mixture of likes and unlikes is complete (Simplicius, *In phys.* 160.26).

12 *Metaph.* I 985a5–7. Similarly Plutarch, *On Isis and Osiris* 48.

13 Dante, *Paradiso*, Canto 33; Lucretius, *De rerum natura* 1.1–43.

14 Quotations from Plato, *Lysis,* trans. Lamb.

15 Quotations from Plato, *Euthyphro, . . . Phaedrus*, trans. Fowler.

16 Quotations from Aristotle, *Complete Works* ed. Barnes, vol. 2. In accordance with current philosophical convention, Barnes translates *aretē*, 'virtue', as 'excellence'.

17 Against having many friends, Diogenes Laertius (V.21) claims one of Aristotle's favourite sayings was 'Whoever has friends can have no [true] friend (*hōi philoi, oudeis philos*)'; cf. *EE* VII1245b20; *NE* IX.1171a15–17.

18 Joachim, *Aristotle: The Nicomachean Ethics* p. 244.

19 To 'live together' perhaps in the same household, is a recurring expectation in classical friendship. It implies the free and leisured lifestyle that Aristotle considers prerequisite for acquiring virtue: 'no one can pursue the things pertaining to virtue who lives the life of an artisan or menial labourer' (*Pol.* III.1278a20, author's translation). If so, 'perfect' friendship would also be the preserve of the leisured.

20 Stern-Gillet, *Aristotle's Philosophy* pp. 123–45, discussion of self, 'other self' and self-actualization.

21 Finnis, *Natural Law and Natural Rights* p.142.

22 Nygren rejects Aristotle's love, despite its ostensible benevolence, as an upward striving 'built in the last resort . . . on self-love' (*Agape* p. 186). D'Arcy replies: 'if this be a doctrine of selfishness it is a very enlightened selfishness, for it is no more and no less than an exhortation to virtue' (*Mind* p. 142).

23 Cf. Aristotle's definitions in *The Art of Rhetoric:* 'A friend is one who exerts himself to do for the sake of another what he thinks is advantageous to him' (I.1361b36–7). 'Let loving (*to philein*), then, be defined as wishing for anyone the things which we believe to be good, for his sake but not for our own, and procuring them for him as far as lies in our power' (II.1380a36–8, trans. Freese). Aristotle's message in the *Rhetoric* is that a public figure who desires popularity and to have good friends, must act as a friend himself.

24 See O'Donovan, *The Problem of Self-love in Augustine.*

25 Price, *Love* p. 105.

26 Price, *Love* p. 108.

27 Stern-Gillet, *Aristotle's Philosophy* p. 76.

28 Stern-Gillet, *Aristotle's Philosophy* pp. 73–4.

29 Discussions in Fitzgerald (ed.) *Friendship, Flattery.*

30 Diogenes Laertius VII.33, citing Zeno's now lost *Republic.*

31 Long, *Hellenistic Philosophy* p. 205; Arnim, von, *SVF.*

32 Festugière, *Epicurus and his Gods* p. 32.

33 *Kyriai Doxai* (*KD*) 27, trans. Bailey, *Epicurus* p. 101.

34 *Vatican Sentences* (*VS*) 34, 52, trans. Bailey pp. 111, 115.

35 Diog. Laert. X.10–11, trans. Bailey p. 147.

36 Rist, *Epicurus* p. 158, citing Diels Frag. 84, l.14 p. 16 = Usener 386. See also Festugière, *Epicurus* p. 63, Peterson, 'Gottesfreund' pp. 165–7.

37 Epicurus' will for example, refers to his disciples solely as 'those who study philosophy together' (Diog. Laert. X.16–20). Harnack seems to have initiated a C20th trend, stating: 'the Epicureans like the Pythagoreans before them, simply called themselves "friends"' (*Mission* I p. 420). 'Epicurus virtually established a copyright on the topic of friendship' (De Witt, *Epicurus* p. 310). But the most that can accurately be said is, 'the combination of friendship and retirement was associated in a special way with the Epicureans and was one of the attractions the sect may have had' (Malherbe, *Social Aspects* p. 25 n. 58).

38 *Vatican Sentences* (*VS*) 23, trans. Bailey p.109.

39 Cicero, *De finibus* I.69 (cf. I.65–70, II.78–85).

40 *De off.* III.20.

41 *De am.* 62; *Mem.* II.iv.1; 4.

42 Then widely known, now lost, Theophrastus's *Peri Philias* was familiar to Jerome (*Comm. in Mich.* 6, PL.25.1219). Aulus Gellius (C2nd AD) says Cicero used it on friendship and wrongdoing (*Noctes Atticae* I.3.10f; *De am.*61). Seneca (*Ep.* 3.2) and Plutarch (*De frat. am.* 8) attribute the rule about judging new friends before trusting them (*De am.* 85) to Theophrastus.

43 Aspasius, *Ad NE* VIII 1158b (in Grosseteste, ed. Mercken, Vol. 3).

44 Quotations, with paragraph numbers, from Cicero, *De amicitia*, trans. Falconer.

45 Xenophon lists Achilles and Patroclus, Orestes and Pylades, Theseus and Peirithoüs (*Symp.* VIII.31). Cicero adds Damon and Phintias (*De off.* III.45; *De fin.* II.79), Plutarch a fifth pair (*Mor.* 93E). All are heroic males united in virtue and affection, willing to die for one another. Cicero himself wrote to Pompey that he hoped to play Laelius to his Scipio! (*Ad fam.* V.7).

46 The Stoic school 'emphatically rejects the view that we adopt or approve either justice or friendship for the sake of their utility ... In fact, the very existence of both justice and friendship will be impossible if they are not desired for their own sake' (*De fin.* III.70). On Cicero's insistence on the 'feeling of love' (*sensu amandi*), Fraisse (*Philia* p. 385) suggests Cicero's friendship, although also of the wise, is to be distinguished from the cool automatic unemotional friendship of the wise envisaged by the earliest Stoics.

47 Cf. Cicero, *De off.* II.29–31.

48 *De nat. deorum*, I.122–23.

49 Cf. *De off.* III.43–45.

50 Rawson, *Cicero* p. 5.

51 Cf. Xenophon *Memorabilia* II.iv.

52 Quotations from Seneca, *Ad Lucilium epistulae morales*, trans. Gummere.

53 Scullard, *Early Christian Ethics* p. 50.

54 Epictetus, *Discourses*, IV.iii.9 (cf. II.xxvii.29) trans. Oldfather.

55 Russell, *Plutarch* p. 6.

56 Quotations from Plutarch, *Moralia* (various translators).

57 E. N. O'Neil, 'Plutarch on Friendship', in J. T. Fitzgerald (ed.) *Greco-Roman perspectives* pp.105–22 (113).

58 Biblical survey in McGuire, *Friendship* pp. xvii–xxix; see also Corley, *Ben Sira's Teaching*; Johnson, *She Who Is*. On OT spirituality as exclusive inner-circle friendship with God: Sheriffs, *Friendship of the Lord* pp. 1–26.

59 Mk 12.29–31, Mt. 22.37–9, Lk. 10.27 (cf. Deut. 6.5, Lev.19.18).

60 The only direct evidence he cites from Greek literature consists of selected passages from the *Lysis* (Nygren, *Agape* p. 181 n. 3).

61 Nygren's table, slightly condensed, *Agape* p. 210.

62 Nygren dismissed Augustine's idea of love, *caritas*, as grounded in selfish Eros and having no proper place in Christianity; and while Aquinas and Aelred did introduce 'a certain counterbalance' when they saw God as mutually loving us with the love of friendship, human striving still crept in because 'friendship, therefore, is also the best heavenly ladder.' (*Agape* p. 655).

63 Nygren, *Agape* pp. 150–9.

64 Barr, 'Words for love' p. 4.

65 Oppenheimer, *Hope of Happiness* p. 104.

66 Vischer, 'Problem der Freundschaft' p. 174 n. 2; Treu, '*Philia* und *Agape*' p. 421.

67 Furnish, *Love Command* p. 226. Origen contrasts friendship/enmity with Christ/ 'the serpent' (*Hom. 20.7 in Jer.*, PG13.517A); Didymus the Blind (*c.*313–98) contrasts friendship/enmity for God/the world (*En. in ep. Jac.* 4.4, PG39.1754B–C).

68 Barr, 'Words for love' p. 14.
69 Mitchell, 'The social function' pp. 258, 272; see also ' "Greet the friends" '.
70 See 'Friendship language in Philippians', J. T. Fitzgerald (ed.) *Friendship, Flattery* pp. 83–160.
71 Barr virtually says this: '*agapan* . . . was already a normal and very natural term in the language and well established in the two connections that were most important, namely that of one person loving another like a child or close friend, and even more, that of a human loved by a god.' *Agapē* 'is no more than a nominalization of those same relations and emotions which in verb form were expressed by *agapan*'. No doubt, Barr comments, *agapē* could be used in 'bad' senses, but it happens that in the NT it never was (Barr, 'Words for Love' pp. 7–8; 12).

Chapter 2: Ambrose, Cassian and Augustine

1 Ambrose, *Expos. Evang. sec. Luc.* 1.12, PL15.1538C. Author's translation.
2 Peterson, 'Gottesfreund' p. 194.
3 Harnack suggested Christians had simply preferred the language of brotherhood as '*still more inward and warm*' (*Mission* I p. 421). He shows no antipathy towards friendship itself, but in adding that 'gnostics' seemed to have used the term *philoi* with greater ease than 'catholic' writers because they were more closely under the influence of Greek philosophy, he set the scene for anti-Hellenistic polemic. Half his evidence, however, depends on recruiting as 'gnostic' both Clement and the tomb-inscription of Abercius, C2nd Bishop of Hieropolis, Phrygia, now accepted as orthodox, which records that wherever Abercius went on his travels, faith 'set before me for food the fish . . . and gave this to friends to eat, always' (Quasten, *Patrology* I p. 172).
4 *Dialogue* 8, 28.
5 *Protrepticus* XII.122; Peterson, 'Gottesfreund' p. 186. Cf. Diog. Laert. VI.37,72, Philo *Mos.*156. By 'logos' Clement certainly means Christ, incarnate Logos and mediator of salvation (not merely 'reason' as in Konstan, *Friendship* p. 170).
6 *Sel. in Pss*, Ps. 22 [23], Origen, *Op. omn.* 12 p. 94; Peterson, 'Gottesfreund' p. 191.
7 See White, *Christian Friendship*; McGuire, *Friendship*; Clarke, *Jerome*; Rader, *Breaking Boundaries*.
8 Treu ('*Philia* und *Agape*') argued that Basil's greater use of *agapē*, against Gregory of Nazianzus's preference for *philia*, indicates Basil's greater degree of christianization. Against, Malunowicz, 'Le problème', and White, *Christian Friendship* p. 54, demonstrate the close synonymity of *philia* and *agapē* in these and other Greek theologians.
9 'For Philo it is axiomatic that *philia* extends to fellow Israelites, including proselytes . . . "It is necessary to regard everyone who has resolved to honour the Creator and father of the all . . . as the dearest friends and relatives" (*Virt.* 179).' In affirming 'that the worship of the one God is the basis for *philia*' (*Mos.* 2.171; *Spec.* 1.317; 3.155) and for kinship, Philo has 'redefined the boundaries of kinship and friendship along religious lines.' (Sterling, 'Bond of Humanity' pp. 217–18).
10 *In Cant. hom.* 13, PG 44.1044B-C, cf. Prov. 27.6; *Life of Moses* 320.
11 *Ep.* 168 cited by White, *Christian Friendship* p. 71.
12 Augustine, *Conf.* V.xiii.23. Quotations from *Confessions* trans. Chadwick.
13 'My ears were only for his rhetorical technique . . . Nevertheless together with the words which I was enjoying, the subject matter, in which I was unconcerned, came to make an entry into my mind' (*Conf.* V.xiv.24).

14 *De virginibus* I.60, trans. de Romestin, Ambroso, *Principal Works*, NPNF2, Vol. X.

15 McLynn (*Ambrose* p. 275) claims Ambrose's judicious *amicitia* in the political sphere 'should not be confused with friendship'. Moorhead (*Ambrose* p. 162) dismisses Ambrose's sentiments on friendship as Ciceronian borrowings: 'we may speculate whether they had any relevance to him at all, for there is scarcely any evidence for friendship in his life'. White (*Christian Friendship* p. 126) remarks that although Ambrose used friendship-language in his speech about love among Christians, 'human love is usually seen as potentially destructive of the all-important relationship between man and God'.

16 *Conf.* VIII.ii.3; V.xiii.23–xiv.24; VI.ii.3–4.

17 *Ep.* 37.2 to Simplicianus, PL16.1084.

18 *De ex. frat. Sat.* I. 39, 56.

19 'I do not feel any less love for you as children whom I have begotten in the gospel than I would if I had fathered you literally in marriage. Nature is no stronger than grace when it comes to love . . . You . . . are loved on the basis of deliberate judgment, and this adds to love's force the great weight of real affection (*caritas*).' One tests what one loves and loves what one has chosen. (*De off.* I.24; cf. Cic. *De am.* 85). Quotations are from Ambrose, *De officiis*, trans. Davidson, vol. I. By permission of OUP. (Note some anomalous paragraph numbering in older texts).

20 This fourfold division of virtue entered Greek philosophy in Plato, *Rep.* IV.427E–433B. Stoics in particular adopted it. Ambrose assured its continuation in Western moral theology, naming these virtues 'cardinal' (*Lib. V in Lucam*, Luke 5. 20–22; PL15.1649; *De ex. frat. Sat.* I.57; PL16.1366) or here 'chief', *principalis* (I.115).

21 Davidson in Ambrose, *De officiis*, 2 p. 39.

22 Dudden, *Ambrose* 2 p. 527.

23 The first rough Latin Bibles, which appeared in North Africa, used *caritas* and *dilectio*. *Amor* was not used, it covered the widest semantic field, comparable to 'love' in modern English, and also specifically designated erotic love. Jerome's revision, the 'Vulgate', featured *dilectio* throughout John's Gospel, and mainly *caritas* in the Pauline and Johannine correspondence.

24 Pétré (*Caritas*) studied words for love, notably excluding *amicitia*, in Latin writers before Augustine. She concluded that although influenced by scriptural usage, none had yet acquired a fully specialized Christian meaning. Ambrose still talks of selling corn during famine 'when it was dear (*in caritate*)' (*De off.* III.39).

25 Total occurrences in Ambrose's undisputed works in PL (rough count including headings and footnotes) compared with exact occurrences in his *De off.* [bracketed]: *caritas* 733 [16], *dilectio* 82 [5], *amor* 313 [11], *benevolentia* 68 [37], *amicitia* 113 [39], *amicus* 321 [64]. In *De off.* these words concentrate in four areas: Ambrose loves his clergy and urges their mutual love (I.24, II.134, II.155); *benevolentia* among friends (I.167, 171–3); clergy should attract people's love (II.29–40); on friendship (III.124–137).

26 I.167, cf. *De am.* 22.

27 I.167; cf. *De am.* 47.

28 I.172; cf. *De am.* 50.

29 Cic. *De off.* II.30–31.

30 Cic. *De off.* III.46. Quotations from Cicero, *De officiis*, trans. Miller.

31 Cf. Cic. *De off.* II.70.

32 In Athanasius's *Life of Anthony* the dying Anthony instructs his monks to avoid heretics as 'enemies of Christ', but to 'keep the Lord's commandments so that after your death the saints may receive you into the eternal tabernacles like

well-known friends (*quasi amicos et notos*). Angels arrive to fetch his soul, and 'he looked upon them as friends' (*Vita Ant.* 58–9, PL73.167B–C, trans. White, *Early Christian Lives* pp. 67–8).

33 *De Abraham* II.ii.5, PL14.458; *Expos. in Ps. 118,* 5.45; 6.36, PL15.1267, 1280.

34 *Unanimis*: a neologism first occurring in early Latin versions of the Bible (Pétré, *Caritas* pp. 326–9). Cf. *unus . . . animus fiat ex pluribus* (*De am.* 92); Acts 4.32, 1 Cor. 6.17, Gal. 3.28.

35 Dudden, *Ambrose*, 2 pp. 532–3.

36 White, *Christian Friendship* p. 126.

37 Compare the 'paraenetic' sections of epistles, e.g. Rom. 12, 1 Cor. 13, Col. 3. Testard even suggests Jesus' farewell discourse, Jn 13–17, as a parallel (Ambroise, *Les devoirs* 2 p. 227).

38 Benedict, *Rule* 73.

39 Quotations from the literal translation by Gibson (NPNF2 XI, 1894). Modern rendering in Cassian, *Conferences*, trans. Ramsey (ACW 57, 1997).

40 Cassian's sources appear to lie in the commonplaces of classical culture and in desert wisdom itself. His vocabulary and structure do not obviously reflect Cicero. Possibly he knew Theophrastus's *Peri Philias*, mentioned by Jerome (*Comm. in Mich.* 6.5–7, PL25.1219) with whom he almost coincided in Bethlehem.

41 The idea that Christ loved John for his virginity apparently originated in the apocryphal 'Acts of John' (*Acta Ioannis*, 113) and is mentioned by Jerome (*C. Iovin.* 1.26) and Augustine (*Tract. in Jo. Ev.* 124.7) (Cassian, trans. Ramsey, note to 16.14.3 p. 579).

42 Cf. Sallust, '*idem velle et idem nolle* (to will and refuse the same things)' (*Cat.* 20.4).

43 'God gave Solomon very great wisdom and discernment, and breadth of understanding (*latitudinem cordis*, largeness of heart) as vast as the sand on the seashore' (1 Kgs 4. 29).

44 Brown, *Augustine* p. 20.

45 *Conf.* II.ii.2. Augustine completed the *Confessions* by AD 400, after becoming Bishop. Of many studies on friendship in Augustine, see esp. McNamara, 'Friendship'; McEvoy, *Anima una*; White, *Christian Friendship* pp. 185–217.

46 *Conf.* II.ix.17.

47 *Conf.* IV.iv.7; vi.11.

48 *Conf.* IV.ix.14.

49 *Conf.* IV.vii.13, cf. *De am.* 68.

50 *Ep.* 130.ii.4, to Proba, dated AD 412. PL33.495, *Works* ed. Dods, XIII p. 145.

51 '*nemo nisi per amicitiam cognoscitur*' (*De div. quaest. 83*, q.71.5, PL40.82), AD 388–96.

52 Brown, *Augustine* p. 174.

53 *De civ. Dei* XIX.8, trans. Bettenson p. 862.

54 *De civ. Dei* XIX.9, trans. Bettenson pp. 863–4.

55 *Conf.* II.v.10.

56 *De am.* 20.

57 *Ep.* 258.4, PL33.1073. Paulinus comments (*Ep.*13.2) that the new ground of friendship, common commitment to Christ, needs no growth but is instantaneously present.

58 *Ep.*155.1 to Macedonius, PL33.667.

59 *Contra duas epistolas Pelagianorum*, I.i.1, PL44.551.

60 *Soliloquia* I.22.

61 *Conf.* IV.vi.11, cf. *De am.* 22, 92.

62 Brown, *Augustine* p. 52.

63 *Ep.* 82 to Jerome.

64 *De bono conjugali*; see Harrison, 'Marriage'. But on Eve he comments: 'how much better would two male friends live together, alike for company and conversation, than a man and a woman' (*De Gen. ad litt.* 9.v.9; trans. White, *Christian Friendship* p. 10).

65 *De div. quaest. 83* q.71.5–6, PL40.81–3.

66 *De catech. rud.* IV.7, PL40.314.

67 *Sermo* 87.x.12, PL38.536–7.

68 *De opere monachorum* 22.25.

69 *Conf.* IV.iv.7.

70 'This is the heart of Augustine's conception of friendship and his great innovation.' (McNamara, 'Friendship' p. 202).

71 *Ep.* 130.ii.4 to Proba, PL.33.494–5.

72 *Ep.*73.10 to Jerome, dated AD 404, PL33.250.

73 *Conf.* II.v.19; *Ep.* 243.4, PL33.1056.

74 *Tract. in Jo. Ev.* 10.5.3; 40.8.5.

75 *Tract. in ep. Jo.* 7.8.

76 *De doctr. christ.* I.xxviii.29; xxx.31.

77 *Ep.* 130.vi.13, to Proba, PL33.499; *Works* ed. Dods XIII pp. 151–2.

78 *ubi benevolentia, ibi enim amicitia.* (*De serm. Dom. in monte* XI.31).

79 '*amicitia quaedam benevolentiae*' *Tract. in ep. Jo.* 8.5 PL35.2038.

80 *Sermo* 357.1, 4. PL39.1584; *Works* ed. Rotelle, 10 pp. 184, 187.

81 *Tract. in ep. Jo.* 10.7 PL35.2059. Trans. McEvoy, '*Anima una*' n.80 pp. 90–1.

82 *Conf.* IV.ix.14.

83 *ordinatissima et concordissima societas fruendi Deo et invicem in Deo.* (*De civ. Dei* XIX.17).

84 *quis non desiderat illam civitatem, unde amicus non exit, quo inimicus non intrat . . . Erit ergo pax purgata in filiis Dei, omnibus amantibus se, videntibus se plenos Deo, cum erit Deus omnia in omnibus* (1 Cor. 15.28). *Enarr. in Ps.* 84.10, PL37.1076.

85 E.g., Moses, *amicus Dei*: *Trin.* 2.27, *Ep.* 36.13; John the Baptist, *amicus sponsi*: *Enarr. in Ps.* 35.9; 131.14; 133.1.

86 *Vita Antonii* XVII [33], PL73.142B, trans. White, *Early Christian Lives* p. 30.

87 Friendship with the devil: *De serm. Dom. in monte* I.x.31; with mortal things: *Conf.* IV.ix.14; friend of emperor or of God: *Conf.* VIII.vi.15.

88 *praedestinati amici*, *De civ. Dei* I.35.

89 On Jn 15.15, *Tract. in Jo. Ev.* 85. Cf: We the unjust are saved by Christ's death and, from being enemies, have been made friends (*ex inimicis amici facti sunt*), *En. in Ps.* 68.2; he loved enemies, so that we might be made friends, (*inimicos ille dilexit, ut amici efficeremur*), *Tract. in Jo. Ev.* 9.9.

90 *De Trin.* 5.xvi.17, PL42.924.

91 Burnaby, *Amor Dei* pp. 66, 256.

92 *Tract. in Jo. Ev.* 85 on Jn 15.14–15, *Tr.* 86 on 15.15–16. Dated c. 414–16.

93 Ambrose, *De fide* I.ii.18 (cf. Acts 4.32), 4.vii.74 (cf. Sallust *Cat.* 20.4), PL16.533, 631; *De Spiritu Sancto* 2.xiii.154, PL16.776. Discussion: White, *Christian Friendship* p. 127.

94 *De Trin.* 5.vi.7, 7.iv.7.

95 Johnson, *She Who Is* p. 195.

96 *At ipsa communio, consubstantialis et coaeterna: quae si amicitia convenienter dici potest, dicatur; sed aptius dicitur charitas. Et haec quoque substantia, quia Deus substantia, et Deus charitas, sicut scriptum est.* (*De Trin.* 6.vi.7, PL42.928).

97 *Caritas* is the term Augustine most commonly used, always in the 'good' sense of rightly ordered love and specifically as 'love of God', *amor Dei*. He says *amor* and *dilectio* are acceptable synonyms for *caritas* (*De civ. Dei* XIV.7, cf. '*caritatis, hoc est dilectionis et amoris*', XV.22) but he also uses them in the 'bad' sense, as synonyms for *cupiditas*, disordered love. Occurrences in Augustine's works in PL (rough count incl. chapter headings): *caritas* 4819, *dilectio* 1634, *amor* 1399, *amicitia* 254, *amicus* 1221, *amica* 57.

98 *De moribus ecclesiae catholicae*, written AD 388–90. Discussion in Burnaby, *Amor Dei* pp. 85–92. English text in NPNF Ser. 1, Vol. 4.

99 *De mor. eccl.* xiii.22.

100 *De civ. Dei* XIX.14.

101 *De mor. eccl.* xxvi.50.

102 *De mor. eccl.* xxvi.48.

103 *De doctr. christ.* III.x.16. Book III was written about AD 396. Quotations from Augustine, *On Christian Doctrine*, trans. Robertson.

104 *De civ. Dei* XIV.28, written in AD 418, trans. Bettenson p. 593. *Fecerunt itaque civitates duas amores duo; terrenam scilicet amor sui usque ad contemptum Dei, coelestem vero amor Dei usque ad contemptum sui*. PL41.436.

105 *De doctr. christ.* I.xxiii.22.

106 *De doctr. christ.* I.iv.4; cf. *De civ. Dei* XI.25.

107 *Sermo* 336.2. Author's translation.

108 *De doctr. christ.* I.xxii.20.

109 *De doctr. christ.* I.xxii.21.

110 *Ep.*130.13.

111 *De mor. eccl.* 25, trans. R. Stothert NPNF1, Vol. 4 p. 48.

112 *Ep.* 167.11 to Jerome, AD 415. 'Love, then, out of a pure heart, and a good conscience and faith unfeigned, is the great and true virtue, because it is "the end of the commandment" (1 Tim. 1.5)'. Trans. *Works*, ed. Dods XIII p. 326; PL33.737.

113 *De doctr. christ.* 3.x.16.

114 *De civ. Dei* XV.22.

115 Robertson, 'Translator's Introduction', Augustine, *On Christian Doctrine* p. x.

116 Brown, *Augustine* p. 153.

117 On 'Put no trust in a friend' (Mic. 7.5; 6.7 Vulg.) Jerome declaims that in these last days fidelity and true friendship are rare, betrayal and self-interest common. "Therefore do not put confidence in friends, that is, in these men who seek reward from friendships. If you wish to enjoy true friendship, be a friend of God, like Moses who spoke with God like friend with friend (Exod. 33.11). Be a friend like the Apostles to whom the Saviour said, "Now I do not call you servants" (John 15.15).' Jesus he adds, called his disciples 'friends' because they persevered with him in his trials (*Comm. in Mich.* 2.vii.517, PL25.1219C). In early letters Jerome had paraded the ideal of eternal faithful love of the other for their own sake, famously opining to his old school friend Rufinus, with whom he later fell out, that '*caritas* cannot be bought; *dilectio* has no price; friendship that can cease was never true (*amicitia quae desinere potest, vera nunquam fuit*).' (*Ep.* 3.6, PL22.336).

118 TePas, 'Spiritual Friendship' p. 65.

119 TePas, 'Spiritual Friendship' p. 64.

120 *De civ.Dei* XIX.19.

121 *Tract. in ep. Jo.* 6.10.

122 *De bono conjugali* 1.
123 *De bapt. con. Donat.* V.23.33, PL43.193.
124 McEvoy, *Anima una* p. 80.
125 McEvoy, 'The theory' p. 35. Konstan remarks on how Paulinus's stance of sinfulness rendered his friends' love unmerited, unlike classical friendship-love; he suggests Paulinus preferred other words for love so as to avoid classical friendship's association with pride in human excellence (*Friendship* pp. 158–60). The latter concern must indeed have played a role. But, as McEvoy well expresses, friendship itself is not thereby compromised but, transposed into a new context, finds fresh grounds in humility and grace.
126 McEvoy, *Anima una* p. 76.
127 'Maximus usually uses the word *agapē*, but sometimes the word *erōs*: I do not think we should make any great issue over his use of these words.' (Louth, *Maximus* p. 38).
128 Meyendorff, 'Introduction', *The Triads* p. 13.
129 Centuries I.1, in *The Philokalia* 2 p. 53.
130 *Ep.* 2, PG91.401C–D trans. Louth, *Maximus* p. 90.
131 Centuries I.13, in *The Philokalia* 2 p. 54.
132 *Ep.* 2, PG91.393B, trans. Louth, *Maximus* p. 85.
133 Florensky, 'Friendship'.

Chapter 3: Monastic friendship and Aelred of Rievaulx

1 Leclercq, *Love of Learning* p. 227.
2 Studies: Leclercq, *Love of Learning*; Fiske, *Friends and Friendship* (collected papers, perhaps a little over-enthusiastic!); McGuire, *Friendship*; Haseldine, *Friendship*.
3 Bede, *Vita Cuthberti* 28, *Hist. eccl.* IV.29 [27] (cited by McGuire, *Friendship* p. 94). Soon afterwards, '*spiritalis amicitia*' appears in the letters of another Englishman, St Boniface (Aelred, *Opera* I p. 290 n.).
4 G Arsenius 38, cited by McGuire, *Friendship* p. 12.
5 White, *Friendship* p. 171.
6 White, *Friendship* p. 78.
7 *Sermo asceticus* PG31.885/6A.
8 *Sermo de renuntiatione saeculi* 5, PG31.637/8B.
9 McGuire, *Friendship* p. xli.
10 McGuire, *Friendship* p. 55.
11 Chadwick, *Augustine* p. 58.
12 McGuire, *Friendship* p. 85.
13 In the West clerical marriage had been generally forbidden since about the year 306, but was only finally outlawed in 1139.
14 Laurence of Durham, monk, poet and friend of Aelred's family, dedicated a *Life of St. Bridget* to Aelred as a courtier, addressing him as 'my most dear friend', mentioning his piety and love of letters (Squire, 'Historical factors' pp. 272–3). Laurence left Cicero's *De amicitia*, perhaps the copy Aelred read as a boy, to the monastic library in Durham (Powicke, *Life* p. lvii n. 2).
15 Hoste, in Aelred *Opera* I p. viii. Bernard outlines this scheme, assuming his audience has completed its earlier stages, before commencing his exposition of the Song (*Serm. sup. cant.* 1.i.1–2).
16 Knowles, *Monastic Order* p. 223.

17 Moreover in Latin the Song connects directly to friendship. Aelred writes of contemplation: 'Then he who has been sought . . . invites to kisses: "Rise up, hasten, my friend *(amica mea)*, and come."' (Song 2.10; *De Iesu* III 22, Aelred, *Treatises* p. 30).

18 Letter prefacing *Speculum caritatis*, para. 3. From *c*.1543 until its ascription to Bernard was noticed by Harvey in a British Museum MS in 1932, this letter was ascribed to an obscure Abbot Gervase, thus contributing to Aelred's obscurity (Harvey, *Aelred* pp. 135–7).

19 Knowles, 'The Humanism of the Twelfth Century' (1941) p. 53.

20 Text in Aelred, *Opera* I pp. 3–161. Author's translation. For complete English translation see Aelred, *Mirror of Charity*, trans. E. Connor.

21 I.14, 24, 28. Patristic writers treated 'image' and 'likeness' (Gen. 1.26) as separable concepts; the image of God remains after the Fall, but its likeness is tarnished: 'the image now needs to be refashioned and brought to perfection, so to become close to him in resemblance'. (Aug., *De civ. Dei* XI.26).

22 Cf. Aug. *Conf.* 10.xxx.41–xli.66.

23 How the Cistercian life accomplishes this: II.65–78, cf. I.79, II.2–7; III.82–97.

24 See Lev. 23.25. For love's fulfilment as 'rest': Aug. *Conf.* 13.ix.10.

25 Dumont, 'Aelred of Rievaulx's *Spiritual Friendship*' p. 193, cf. *De spir. am.* III.127.

26 Compare Augustine: *Frui enim est amore alicui rei inhaerere propter se ipsam* (*De doctr. christ.* I.iv.4). Strictly, only God, Augustine goes on to state, can be 'enjoyed' for himself (I.v.5) while all else is to be 'used' to that end. Aelred is characteristically more open to the present enjoyment, in God, of created good. Augustine mentioned *ego te fruar in Domino* (Philemon 20, Vulg.) solely to emphasize that all enjoyment should be 'in the Lord' (*De doctr. Christ.* I.xxxiii.37). In the original Greek, Paul hopes for '*onaimen*' (benefit, help) from Philemon 'in the Lord'.

27 Cf. Aug. *De civ. Dei* XIX.27.

28 All, whether male or female, should aspire to this closeness to Jesus. Aelred exhorts his sister, an anchoress, to meditate on this scene and claim its 'sweetness'. He also points her to 'Bethany, where the sacred bonds of friendship are consecrated by the authority of Our Lord. For Jesus loved Martha, Mary and Lazarus. There can be no doubt that this was on account of the special friendship by which they were privileged to be more intimately attached to him.' (*De inst. inclus.* 3.31; Aelred, *Treatises* p. 85).

29 E.g. 'it is a solace in this life': *vitae huius solatium est* = *solatium . . . vitae huius est* (Amb. *De off.* III.132).

30 Dumont, 'Introduction' in Aelred, *Mirror of Charity* p. 35.

31 Prov. 27.6; cf Amb. *De Off.* III.128.

32 Egenter, *Gottesfreundschaft* pp. 234–5.

33 McEvoy, 'Notes' p. 410.

34 *Prologue* 6. Quotations are from Aelred, *Spiritual Friendship*.

35 The C13th Rievaulx catalogue lists no copy, but one showing C12th use belonged to nearby Byland Abbey (Squire, *Aelred* p. 101). Sustained parallels: *De spir. am.* II.11–18 = *De am.* 22–6; II 29, 40–61 = 35–51 (involving two changes of subject); III.14–30 = 62–5, 74; III.39–53 = 76–8. III.61–76 incorporates material not previously used from 62–85; III.72–82 = 86–8. Once, Aelred includes in a recapitulation, perhaps after checking the original, a Ciceronian passage previously omitted from his main development (III.90–7 = 69–73). Ciceronian allusions and quotations mostly retain their original sequence within these passages, although Aelred's more systematic approach occasionally results in rearrangement.

36 *De spir. am.* I.26 = 72, III.101 = 97 in L.A. Seneca, *Monita* (ed. E. Wölfflin; Erlangen, 1878).

37 Attributed: *De spir. am.* III.30 = Amb. *De off.* III.133; III.70 = III.134; III.83 = III.136; III.97 = III.129; III.106 = III.128. Unattributed allusions at: *De spir. am.* III.6, 7, 63, 70, 131.

38 *De am.* 20.

39 Cf. *Ad Dei vero dilectionem duo pertinent, affectus mentis, et effectus operis.* (*De inst. inclus.* 29). It is not the *utilitas* procured by a friend but their love itself that gives delight, *De Am.* 51. Aelred perhaps deliberately avoids saying the friend is 'dear' in themselves, on their own account. See note 72 below, and p. 65.

40 '*amicus enim quasi animi custos vocatur*', Gregory the Great on John 15 (*Hom. in Evang.* 27.4, PL76.1207A) similarly Isidore of Seville: '*Amicus, per derivationem, quasi animi custos*' (*Etymologiae* 10.5).

41 Possibly Aelred assumed that Ambrose's '*Virtus est . . . amicitia*' (*De off.* III.134) had philosophical antecedents. Cicero only said 'true friendships are eternal', being grounded in virtuous character which by nature is unchanging (*De am.* 32).

42 Jerome *Ep.* 3.6, quoted twice again: I.68; III.48.

43 Cf. Amb. *De off.* III.130, 132.

44 In terms of Augustine's threefold concupiscence (*Conf.* 10.xxx.41–xli.66, cf. 1 Jn 2.16) Aelred's 'carnal' friendships offer pleasures of the flesh while 'worldly' friendships offer material things and intangible goods to satisfy secular pride and ambition. Spiritual friendship rests on *caritas*. Although similar, Aelred's scheme does not derive from Aristotle's trio of pleasure, advantage, and virtue.

45 Aelred's Latin is closer to Sallust ('*idem velle atque idem nolle*', *Cat.* 20.4) than the variants of this proverbial saying in Cassian (*Confer.* 16.3) and Ambrose (*De fide* 4.74).

46 See II.57–9, III.87 on growing out of 'puerile' friendship. Cf. Bernard's *amor carnalis* as the first step of human growth in love (*De dil. Deo* VII.23).

47 Despite this Aelred teaches separation, and avoidance of friendship, between celibate men and women, to obviate temptation. A female recluse may speak to an elderly male confessor – but 'never allow messages to pass between you and any man, whatever the pretext, whether to show him kindness (*caritas*), to arouse his fervor (*affectus*), or to seek spiritual friendship and intimacy with him' (*De inst. inclus.* 1.7). No obvious misogyny here, but compare Walter's pronouncement: 'women, hawks and dogs . . . do not enter the gates' of Rievaulx! (*Vita* 5; *Life* 1950 p. 12; 1994 p. 97).

48 'The argument seems to be based now, not on the virtue of wisdom . . . but on Divine Wisdom. Friendship is said to possess the three essential characteristics of Divine Wisdom, eternity, truth and charity: and therefore, to be identified with it. This seems clear from his sudden identification of Friendship with God. Here again, to moderns, this seems far fetched.' (Talbot, in Ailred, *Christian Friendship* p. 137 n. 34).

49 Leclercq, 'Friendship and friends' p. 298.

50 McEvoy, 'Notes' p. 402.

51 Schilling, 'Aelredus' p. 22. Author's translation.

52 Hallier, *Un éducateur* p. 59. Author's translation.

53 Richard of St-Victor, *Book Three of the Trinity* p. 374.

54 Elsewhere Richard speaks of the bridal union of the soul and God as a 'bonding of friendship (*amicitiae confoederatio*)' (*Benjamin Minor* xi, PL196.8).

55 Henry suggests love is either simple *dilectio*, which we can have for ourselves, or *redilectio* when reciprocal, or *condilectio* among 'not less than three', to whom any number can be added (*Op. omn.* ed. Macken 1981 14 p. 278). Henry recognized Richard had made 'in a way a foundational statement on friendship', despite not using the word *amicitia*. (McEvoy, 'The sources . . .' p. 137).

56 Cousins, 'A Theology of Interpersonal Relations' p. 55.

57 Hoste ('First Draft') suggests the draft really existed and is the *Schedula de spiritali amicitia*, a collection of thoughts, mostly represented in the finished work, surviving in two Reading MSS and normally regarded as an abbreviation (text: Aelred, *Opera* I pp. 368–552).

58 Dumont, 'Seeking God in Community' p. 312.

59 Aelred's exegesis of the kiss is his own, independent of Bernard (cf. *Serm. sup. Cant.* 3, 4). Egenter (*Gottesfreundschaft* p. 236) notes an echo of Augustine, *De Gen. ad litt.* 12.7, on three kinds of vision: *corporale, spirituale, intellectuale.*

60 *De am.* 39.

61 Cf. *De am.* 40.

62 cf. Acts 4.32; Benedict's *Rule* 33.

63 *De am.* 45, 47–8.

64 *De am.* 30.

65 cf. Amb. *De off.* III.134. Ambrose's wording finds echoes throughout III.6–7.

66 Cf. Cassian on 'healing' the other's irascibility as well as one's own (*Confer.* 16.vii).

67 '*convicio, et improperio et superbia, et mysterii revelatione, et plaga dolosa*' (Sir. 22.27 Vulg). The Septuagint and NRSV list four faults: 'reviling, arrogance, disclosure of secrets, or a treacherous blow' (Sir. 22.22).

68 Cf. Cassian *Confer.* 16.xxvi–vii.

69 Cf. *De am.* 76–8.

70 *De am.* 78.

71 Cf. *De am.* 31, 51.

72 Amb. *De off.* III.136; Mt. 22.39; *De am.* 80. Cicero states we love ourselves 'for our selves', not for ulterior gain, and we love a friend 'as if another self' (*tanquam alter idem*). Again Aelred avoids saying a friend is loved 'for himself', true to Augustine's teaching that we love God alone for his own sake (*De doct. christ.* 3.x.16).

73 Amb. *De off.* III.134.

74 Amb. *De off.* III.136.

75 Cf. Augustine, *Conf.* IV.iv.7–vii.13.

76 Ps. 132/3.1; this verse used here in reference to close friendship is the same one previously applied to the ethos of the whole community (III.82).

77 Dumont, 'Aelred de Rievaulx' p. 534, author's translation.

78 Dumont, 'Seeking God in Community' p. 312.

79 Dubois in Aelred, *L'Amitié spirituelle* pp. lxxx–i.

80 Dumont, 'Aelred de Rievaulx' p. 536, author's translation.

81 *Serm.* 19.18–20; cf. *De inst. inclus.* 3.31 on Jesus' friendship with the Bethany family.

82 Powicke, Harvey and Knowles were content to hail Aelred as an affectionate personality, stressing his similarity to Augustine in longing 'to be loved and to love'. In 1969 Squire noted the intensity of the friendship at court mentioned at *Spec. car.* I.28.79 and described Aelred as bravely and successfully seeking solutions to 'problems' of love (*Aelred* pp. 14–15, 111). Roby cautiously agreed he may have experienced homosexual temptation in youth, perhaps not fully understanding it, and found escape in monastic life where he shows no emotional damage

(Introduction, Aelred, *Spiritual Friendship* 1977 p. 21). Boswell then assumed that Aelred had overtly homosexual relationships while at court (*Christianity, Social Tolerance* p. 222). Aelred's consequent acclamation as patron saint of gay people threatened to obscure all else. Subsequent investigations demonstrate the impossibility of establishing a definite answer concerning Aelred's sexual orientation, concluding that the question is anachronistic and suggesting that, since his behaviour conformed entirely to the expected moral standard, it has little point. See Dutton, 'Aelred ... on chastity'; TePas, 'Aelred's guidelines'; Burton, 'Aelred'. Burton (p. 192) hopes this 'parenthesis' in Aelred studies can now be closed. Cf. Bray's reflections in *The Friend* on mediaeval friendships as not necessarily being homoerotic.

83 Aelred was certainly aware of both hetero- and homosexual temptations among either sex as threats to chastity, and affirmed the traditional view that they must be avoided or overcome (*De inst. inclus.* 6, 15, 23; cf. his insistence on the control of passion, *Spec.* III.112). It is uncertain what he meant by his own loss of virginity (*De inst. inclus.* 32). Walter felt bound to admit that at court Aelred had 'occasionally deflowered his virginity' (*Ep. ad Maur.*, in *Life* trans. Powicke, 1950 p. 76; 1994 p. 154) but had homosexuality been involved it seems very doubtful that, in the C12th context, Walter would mention this so casually. Aelred thought virginity could be lost with a person of either sex, or 'without any commerce with another if the flesh is set on fire by a strong heat which subdues the will and takes the members by surprise' (*De inst. inclus.* 15). The passage about a young monk who immersed himself in cold water while singing psalms and praying, to overcome 'threats to his chastity from the promptings of nature' (*De inst. inclus.* 18), may be autobiographical (cf. *Life* lvii). Immersion was a mainly Celtic ascetic practice, common and admired.

84 See TePas, 'Spiritual Friendship'.

85 Aelred, *Opera* I pp. 171–240.

86 All thirteen extant MSS of the complete *De spiritali amicitia* appear of English or northern French provenance. At least six belonged to Cistercian abbeys, one or two to Benedictine. The many large Cistercian houses of Germany and Austria appear to have none (Hoste, in Aelred, *Opera* I pp. 281–5). Printed 1616, then in PL195.661–702. Critical text, plus the five abbreviations, in Aelred, *Opera* I pp. 279–634.

87 Text, with intro. and transl. in E. Vansteenberghe, 'Deux théoreticiens'. See also Bickel, 'Peter von Blois'; Davy , *Un Traité*.

88 Walter Daniel did write a (probably unremarkable) *De Amicitia* in five books which existed only at Rievaulx and has not survived (Powicke, *Life*, 1950 p. xviii).

Chapter 4: Thomas Aquinas

1 III *Sent.* d.27.1.1.

2 '*qui enim ponit animam pro amicis, ponit et pro inimicis, ad hoc ut et ipsi fiant amici*' (III *Sent.* d.29.3.2).

3 III *Sent.* d.30.1.1; Aug., *Ench.* 73.

4 '*Dilectio qua diligitur Deus propter se, et proximus propter Deum vel in Deo*' (III *Sent.* d.27 cap.2.1).

5 I *Sent.* d.17.

6 *SA* III.11.1.

7 *SA* I.2.4. Albert (*ST* II.4 q.14.4 a.2) credits this distinction both to William and an earlier Paris scholastic, Praepositinus of Cremona (d. 1210).

8 Abelard quoted Cicero, *Rhet.* 2.55, that friendship is willing good things to someone for their own sake, concluding that 'for their sake' distinguishes true from false friendship and *caritas* from *cupiditas* (*Int. ad theol.* I.1, PL178.982–3). Héloïse went further, proposing that ideal love, '*amicitia*', sacrifices even the enjoyment of its object. She reproached Abelard that '*concupiscentia* rather than *amicitia* joined you to me' (*Ep.* 2). Then, commenting on Romans, Abelard elaborated a brilliant but starkly theoretical doctrine of love for God absolutely without view to reward (PL178.891–3). But what, responded William of St-Thierry (d. 1148) could be more absurd or irrational than to be united to God by love but not in supreme happiness? (*De contemplando Deo* 8.16). The notion of 'pure' self-denying love resurfaces in various later forms, notably in the C17th French 'annihilation' of the self (*anéantissement*) and even in Nygren's Agape.

9 In I *Sent.* d.17 pars 1, a.1 q.2.

10 In III *Sent.* d.27 a.1 q.2 ob/ad.6.

11 Albert, *In Sent.* III d.27 a.4 (ed. Borgnet 28 p. 517).

12 *In Sent.* III d.28 a.2 (ed. Borgnet, 28 p. 537); cf. Albert's definition: *dilectio amicitiae* is directed to the other 'without *reflexio* to oneself'; *dilectio concupiscentiae* aims 'to enjoy them' (*ut fruatur illo*) (*Sup. Eth.* VIII, iii.ob.4, ed. Kübel 14(2) p. 599). On diversity, cf. Greg. Moralia 35.41 PL76.772C, '*haberi societas minus quam inter duos esse non potest*', ditto for *caritas* at *Hom.* 17.1 PL76.1139, cited by Albert *ST* II. Tract.4.q.14.

13 '*semper curva est in seipsa*' *ST* II Tract.4 q.14 (ed. Borgnet, 32 pp. 199–200).

14 *ST* II Tract.4 q.14 ad 6. Albert's concessive clause *etiamsi nihil debet sibi fieri* admits various interpretations depending on whether *sibi* refers to God or the creature. The reading we suggest is: 'even though nothing needs to be made/done for him [God]'.

15 Made by Robert Grosseteste, Oxford scholar and Bishop of Lincoln, complete with translated commentaries and Grosseteste's notes. Only partial translations had existed, of uncertain date, from one of which Albert had used passages from the early chapters of Book VIII in *De Quattuor Coaequaevis*: perfect friendship is between good men of similar virtue; bad friends seek only pleasure, good friends love a person for himself; and, perhaps significant for Thomas: the good are friends directly (*simpliciter*), the bad indirectly (*secundum accidens*) (ed. Borgnet, 34 pp. 488–9). See Pelzer, 'Les versions latines'; Lottin, 'Saint Albert' pp. 318, 325).

16 *Sup. Eth.* VIII.v, *Op.Omn.* ed Kübel 14(2) p. 609.

17 *Ethic. Lib.* VIII 1.1, ed. Borgnet 7 p. 515; cf. Dion. *Div. Nom.* 4.13.

18 *Ethic. Lib.* VIII 1.1, ed. Borgnet 7 p. 516.

19 *Ethic. Lib.* VIII 1.1 ed. Borgnet 7 p. 518; cf. *dilige, et quod vis fac*, Aug. *In ep. Jo.* 7.8

20 *videtur quod sit idem quod amicitia. Quia, ut dicit Philosophus in 9 Ethic., 'amicitia superabundantiae amoris similatur'. Sed caritas habet superabundantissimum amorem; unde et caritas dicitur, eo quod sub inaestimabili pretio, quasi carissimam rem, ponat amatum. Ergo caritas est idem quod amicitia.* (*In Sent* III, d.27, q.2 a.1, ag.1).

21 Aristotle suggested one can be said to have friendship 'for oneself' because (a) human nature has reflexive duality and (b) 'because the extreme (*hyperbole*) of friendship is likened to that which one has for oneself' (*NE* IX.1166b1). Grosseteste translates faithfully: '*quoniam superabundantia amicitiae ei, quae ad seipsum, assimilatur*' (Grosseteste, ed. Mercken 3 p. 235). Albert comments that friendship for oneself 'is like superabundance of friendship (*superabundantia amicitiae*) because one loves oneself greatly' (*Sup. Eth.* ed. Kübel 14(2) pp. 669–70). Thomas's (mis)quotation

most resembles Grosseteste's translation of the comment of Michael of Ephesus (died *c.*1120), which perhaps stuck in his mind: 'For whoever loves someone as themselves, loves superabundantly (*superabundanter amat*)' (ed. Mercken 3 p. 236).

22 *In Sent.* III d.27 q.2 a.1 ag/ad 8-12.

23 *NE* IX.1171a27–b.28.

24 *NE* VIII.1157b.28–9.

25 *In Sent.* III d.27 q.2 a.1.

26 *In Sent.* III.d.27.q.2 a.2.

27 Quotations are from Thomas Aquinas, *Summa Theologica* (literally translated).

28 *In Sent.* III.d.32 q.1 a.1-2.

29 *In Sent.* III.d.27 q.2 a.2.

30 *Sup. Ev. Ioh. Lect.* 15, lect.2.vii (p. 379). Author's translation.

31 *Cum ergo sit aliqua communicatio hominis ad Deum, secundum quod nobis suam beatitudinem communicat, super hanc communicationem oportet aliquam amicitiam fundari. De qua quidem communicatione dicitur 1 ad Corinth. 1,9:* Fidelis Deus, per quem vocati estis in societatem (*koinōnia*) Filii eius. *Amor autem super hanc communicationem fundatus, est caritas. Unde manifestum est quod caritas amicitia quaedam est hominis ad Deum* (II–II 23.1).

32 *NE* 1159b31–2.

33 Julian, *Showings*, Long text, ch. 41, p. 248.

34 Egenter, *Gottesfreundschaft*, pp. 62–3.

35 D'Arcy, *Mind,* pp. 106–7.

36 Coquart, 'Nature', pp. 111–12.

37 *Quaest. disp. de car.* a.1; II–II 23.2.

38 II–II 23.2 ad 1, ad 2, ad 3.

39 *In Sent.* III d.27 q.2 a.2.

40 II–II 23.3 con., cf. Aug., *De mor. eccl.* xi.19.

41 *In Sent.* III d.27 q.2 a.2, ag/ra.4.

42 *In Sent.* III d.27 q.2 a.2. ra.2.

43 II–II 23.4–5, cf. *Quaest. disp. de car.* a.5 ob/ad3.

44 II–II 23.6–8; *Quaest. disp. de car.* a.3.

45 I–II 2.8; I 60.2.

46 The four cardinal virtues, Thomas teaches, attune us to reason and are naturally attainable by ascetic effort. The theological virtue of *caritas* 'enlivens' and is 'the mother and the root of all the virtues, inasmuch as it is the form of them all' (*ST* I–II.62.4). The seven 'gifts of the Spirit' (wisdom, knowledge, understanding, counsel, fortitude, piety and fear of God, cf. Isa.11.2) presuppose the presence of the theological virtues and perfect our capacity to be prompted by God (*ST* I–II 68.4). General discussion in Wadell, *Friends*.

47 *In Sent.* III d.27 q.1 a.1.

48 I–II 28.1 ad 2; Aristotle, *Pol.* II.1262b11.

49 Aug. *De Trin.* VIII.8.

50 *In Sent.* III d.28 q.1 a.2.

51 *ST* I 20.2 ad 3; II–II 25.3.

52 *ST* II–II 25.3; *Quaest. disp de car.* a.7.

53 McEvoy, 'The other as oneself' pp. 24–5.

54 Bernard, *Serm. 2 in Purif.*; II–II 24.6.

55 II–II 24.10 cf. *NE* VIII.5.

56 *ordinavit in me caritatem* (Song 2.4), II–II 26.1; *De doctr. christ.* I.22; II–II 25.12.

57 Bernard, *De dilig. Deo* 1; II–II 27.6.

58 Lev.19.18; II–II 25.4 con.

59 *In Sent.* III d.28 q.1 a.6.

60 Cates, *Choosing to Feel* p. 101.

61 '"To love oneself" is a very ambiguous expression, because the self is a very ambiguous reality.' Virtues, knowledge of our inner self from the perspective of faith, and discernment about self-love, can only be developed through experience. (McEvoy, 'The other as oneself' p. 35).

62 Aristotle said: 'Friendly relations with one's neighbours, and the marks by which friendships are defined, seem to have proceeded from a man's relations with himself' (*NE* IX.1166a1–2). As we noted, he can be taken to mean either, or both, that love of others is an extension of the self's drive to self-preservation, or that neighbour-love is analogous to self-love. An influential study by Rousselot in 1908 argued that Thomas's friendship-love is merely an extension of the self-centred, centripetal concupiscence that is built into human nature ('*conception physique de l'amour*'): love is in the will, the will is specified by its end which is my happiness, hence all love, even love of the whole of which I am part, which is God, is inevitably reduced to self-love. Rousselot had no use for a '*conception extatique de l'amour*': for him, while 'disinterested' love is possible in a sense, 'ecstatic' love is impossible because there is ultimately no duality between subject and object. Most later commentators, however, interpret Thomas as placing self-love not in the context of the self as an isolated end, but in relation to God and the common good.

63 Burnaby, *Amor Dei* p. 269.

64 McEvoy, 'The other as oneself', p. 34.

65 Finnis, *Aquinas* p. 115. Already in 1980 Finnis made friendship his model in discussing community and common good. 'In friendship one is not thinking and choosing "from one's own point of view", nor from one's friend's point of view. Rather, one is acting from a third point of view, the unique perspective from which one's own good and one's friend's good are equally "in view" and "in play". Thus the heuristic postulate of the impartially benevolent "ideal observer", as a device for ensuring impartiality or fairness in practical reasoning, is simply an extension of what comes naturally to friends' (Finnis, *Natural Law* p. 143.)

66 Cf, 'to look upon the friend as another self' is 'a capacity derived from sharing in the good upon which the friendship is based' (Wadell, *Friendship* p. 130). McEvoy sees Dionysius's *extasis* as absolutely vital here: 'Love that dwells on the other breaks out, as it were, in a straight line from the self and remains within the term to which it attains, thus breaking the circularity of centripetal desire (what Aquinas calls *amor recurvus*), which goes out from the self, admittedly, but only to return to its own starting-point.' (McEvoy, 'The other' p. 31).

67 Cates, *Choosing to Feel* p. 102.

68 *NE* IX.1166a1–10.

69 Ps.10.6 Vulg.; II–II 25.7.

70 All people our 'neighbour': Aug., *De doctr. Christ.* I.31; II–II.25.6.

71 *Quaest. disp. de car.* a.4. Author's translation.

72 *In Sent.* d.28 q.1 a.4 a.1.

73 Mt. 9.11–13; II–II 25.6 ad 5.

74 *NE* IX.1165b.19–20.

75 *In Sent.* d.28 q.1 a.5.

76 II–II.25.9. Lk. 6.27, also imported into Mt. 5.44 in Vulgate and Authorised Version. Aug., *Ench.* 73.

77 *Quest. disp. de car.* a.8.

78 Mt. 22.30; II–II 23.1; ib.25.10.

79 Mt. 5.46; II–II 27.7 ob.1.
80 *In Sent.* III d.30 q.1 a.3.
81 1 Jn 4.21; II–II 27.8.
82 Johann 'Meditation' p. 130, cf. *ST* I.38.1–2 on the Holy Spirit as 'Gift'.
83 Wadell, *Friendship* pp. 122–3.
84 Jones, 'Theological Transformation of Aristotelian Friendship' p. 383.
85 McEvoy, 'The other' p. 28.
86 McEvoy, 'The other' p. 31.
87 On the '*amicitia seu affabilitas*' of Aristotle's *NE* IV.1127a9, Thomas affirms that the natural general friendship all humans have for others is a virtue: *omnis homo naturaliter omni homini est amicus quodam generali amore*' (*ST* II-II 114.1 ad 2). We show 'signs of friendship . . . by words or deeds' even to strangers, but do not show them the intimacy of perfect friendship. 'This virtue is a part of justice, being annexed to it as to a principal virtue. Because in common with justice it is directed to another person, even as justice is: yet it falls short of the notion of justice, because it lacks the full aspect of debt, whereby one man is bound to another, either by legal debt, which the law binds him to pay, or by some debt arising out of a favor received. For it regards merely a certain debt of equity, namely, that we behave pleasantly to those among whom we dwell, unless at times, for some reason, it may be necessary to displease them for some good purpose' (II–II 114.2).
88 Trent, Sess. 6 Cap. 7 and 10; Denzinger 799, 803.
89 Lavaud, 'La charité comme amitié' p. 464.
90 Examples, all by C20th Dominicans: Noble, *L'Amitié*; Wilms, *Divine Friendship*; P. Philippe, *Le Rôle de l'amitié*; M.-D. Philippe, *Le Mystère de l'amitié*.
91 Pinckaers, *Sources* p. 32.
92 Egenter, *Lexikon für Theologie und Kirche* 4 col. 1105.
93 Häring, *Free and Faithful* 1 pp. 76–80.
94 Häring, *Free and Faithful* 1 p. 209.
95 Pinckaers, *Sources* p. 21.
96 Wadell, *Friends of God*; *Becoming Friends*.
97 Cates, *Choosing to Feel* p. 2.

Chapter 5: Catholics, Anglicans, Reformers and Philosophers

1 *Serm.* 23, Tauler, *Spiritual Conferences* p. 107.
2 *Flowing Light* 6.21, trans. Egres, 'Mechtild von Magdeburg' p. 137.
3 *Theologia Germanica* p. 55.
4 *Showings*, Short text (*c.* AD 1373) ch. 20 p. 161; Long text (*c.*1393) ch. 76 p. 329.
5 Trans. Sherley-Price. On ambivalence see TePas, 'Spiritual Friendship'.
6 *Life* viii, *Complete Works* I p. 50, part of a passage on friendship with God.
7 *Life* vii, *Complete Works* I pp. 46–7.
8 *Way of Perfection* iv, *Complete Works* 2 p. 17.
9 II *Ascent* 16.9; III *Ascent* 28.2. *Collected Works* pp. 202, 318.
10 II *Night* 21.3; *Canticle* 27.4. *Collected Works* pp. 446, 582.
11 *Letter 26.* to Maria de la Encarnación, *Collected Works* p. 760.
12 Luis de León, *Names of Christ* pp. 329, 330–1.
13 Luis de León, *Names of Christ* pp. 333, 334.
14 Luis de León, *Names of Christ* p. 337.
15 Francis de Sales, *Traité de l'amour de Dieu* II.xxii. Author's translation.

16 Francis de Sales, *Traité de l'amour de Dieu* III.xiii.

17 McGoldrick suggests Francis de Sales also knew Aelred's *Spiritual Friendship*, albeit as the *Liber de Amicitia* attributed to Augustine and printed among his works in Paris in 1555 (McGoldrick p. 103). But the *Liber* does not as McGoldrick seems to suggest contain the complete text of *De Spiritali Amicitia*. De Sales may well have read it, but it is a non-dialogic summary, saying less than the original. (text: Migne PL40.831–44; Aelred, *Opera* I pp. 355–621).

18 *Introduction to the Devout Life*, 3.17–22; trans. Day pp. 140–1.

19 Fénelon, *Christian Perfection* pp. 183, 193.

20 Ramsay, *Fénelon* pp. 290–2.

21 Ramsay, *Fénelon* p. 295.

22 Lambert, *Works* 1 pp. 171, 173. Correspondence with Fénelon: 2 pp. 228–38.

23 *Christian Perfection*, ch. 28 pp. 106–110.

24 McGuire, *Friendship*, p. xliii. Cf. G. Vansteenberghe, 'Amitié'.

25 Thomas Merton, 'Introduction' in Hallier, *Monastic Theology* pp. xi–xii. Developments in, for example, Hinnebusch, *Friendship*; Ripple, *Called to be Friends*; Conner, *Celibate Love*; Crossin, *Friendship*; Leclercq, 'Amicizia'; 'Friendship'.

26 Leclercq, *Contemplative Life* p. 16.

27 Leclercq, 'Friendship' pp. 297–8.

28 'She was very religiously devoted when she was young; prayed by herself an hower together, and tooke Sermons verbatim when she was but 10 years old'; she had read the whole Bible by the age of four, and 'could have sayd I know not how many places of Scripture and chapters', and although highly intelligent she was 'very good-natured; not at all high-minded' (*Aubrey's Brief Lives* p. 242). Abraham Cowley's verse prefacing her *Poems* in 1667 confesses: 'We our old Title plead in vain: Man may be Head, but Woman's now our Brain'. She had died of smallpox, after the publication of some of her verse.

29 Poem 64, 'A Friend'. Subsequent stanzas explore sympathy, trust, wisdom and counsel, mutual correction, generosity and fidelity (*Poems* pp. 94–5).

30 Penn, *Fruits of Solitude*, Maxim 94 p. 37.

31 Holland, *Memoir* I p. 179.

32 Newman, Sermon ' "Beloved" ' p. 58.

33 Poem 71, on 2 Cor. 5.19 (*Poems* pp. 110–11).

34 Reprinted four times 1662–84, then in Taylor's *Works*, and as a monograph in 1920. Page references are to 'A Discourse' in Taylor, *Whole Works* I pp. 71–98.

35 Cf. Cic. *De am.* 20.

36 Hughes, *Piety of Jeremy Taylor* p. 146.

37 *Holy Living* ch. 3, sect. 2 'Rules for married persons' (*Whole Works*, vol. 3 p. 129).

38 'To the noble *Palaemon* on his incomparable Discourse of Friendship' (Philips, *Poems* pp. 14–15).

39 Cooper, *Characteristics* 1 pp. 67–8.

40 Meilaender, *Friendship* pp. 1, 54.

41 Meilaender, *Friendship* p. 35.

42 Meilaender, *Friendship* p. 52.

43 Meilaender, *Friendship* p. 30.

44 Meilaender, *Friendship* pp. 48, 61.

45 Taylor, *Whole Works*, 6 p. 664.

46 Traherne, *Christian Ethicks*, ch. XVIII p. 153.

47 Traherne, *Christian Ethicks*, ch. XVIII pp. 153–5.

48 Traherne, *Christian Ethicks*, ch. XIX p. 166.

49 Traherne, *Christian Ethicks*, ch, XXV pp. 212–13.
50 Traherne, *Christian Ethicks*, ch, XXV pp. 213–14.
51 Baxter, *Christian's Converse* p. 37.
52 Baxter, *Christian's Converse* p. 46.
53 Baxter, *Christian's Converse* p. 119.
54 Baxter, *Christian's Converse* pp. 133–5.
55 Baxter, *Christian's Converse* pp. 112–13.
56 Baxter, *Christian's Converse* p. 123.
57 Baxter, *Christian's Converse* p. 148.
58 Bentley, *Works* 3 pp. 418–9. Saying attributed to Aristotle in Diog. Laert. V.21.
59 Curtius, 'Freundschaft im Alterthum' (1863) pp. 4, 15. Author's translation.
60 Berkeley, *Works* 4 p. 190.
61 Berkeley, *Works* 4 p. 215.
62 Boswell, *Life of Johnson* 3 p. 289.
63 Barbour, *The Quakers* p. 36; R. M. Jones, *George Fox* p. 164.
64 Penn, *A Collection of the Works of William Penn*, I p. 121.
65 Fox, *Journal* I p. 317: quoted by R. M. Jones, *George Fox* p. 106.
66 Cheyn, *Friendship of Christ* p. 35.
67 Wilson, *History* I p. 356.
68 R. Jones, *Friendship with God* pp. 126, 113–14.
69 R. Jones, *Friendship with God* p. vii.
70 R. Jones, *Friendship with God* p. 1.
71 R. Jones, *Friendship with God* pp. 21, 24.
72 R. Jones, *Friendship with God* p. 56.
73 R. Jones, *Friendship with God* p. 95.
74 R. Jones, *Friendship with God* p. 29.
75 R. Jones, *Friendship with God* p. 107.
76 R. Jones, *Friendship with God* pp. 235–7.
77 Deverell, *Sermons* pp. 8–9.
78 Deverell, *Sermons* p. 14.
79 Newman, *Parochial and Plain Sermons* 2 pp. 51–60.
80 Squire, *Aelred* p. 99.
81 Newman, *Parochial and Plain Sermons* 2 p. 51.
82 Newman, *Parochial and Plain Sermons* 2 p. 52.
83 Newman, *Parochial and Plain Sermons* 2 pp. 52–3.
84 Newman, *Parochial and Plain Sermons* 2 p. 54.
85 Newman, *Parochial and Plain Sermons* 2 pp. 56–7.
86 Newman, *Parochial and Plain Sermons* 2 pp. 58–60.
87 Jowett, *Sermons on Faith and Doctrine* pp. 343, 351.
88 Jowett, *Sermons on Faith and Doctrine* p. 352.
89 Jowett, *Sermons Biographical* pp. 273–4.
90 Jowett, *Sermons on Faith and Doctrine* pp. 354, 157.
91 Jowett, *Sermons Biographical* p. 350; 1901 p. 372.
92 Stanford, *Friendship with God* p. 7.
93 Humberstone, *Friendship of Jesus*.
94 Edwards, *Friendships of Christ*.
95 'Amicus' *Friendships of the Bible* pp. 109, 111–12.
96 Murray, *With Christ* pp. 61, 57.
97 Andrews, *What I owe to Christ* p. 19.
98 Andrews, *Christ and Human Need* p. 12.

[99] Thorold, *On Friendship* p. 10.
[100] Black, *Friendship* p. 95.
[101] Brett, *Divine Friendship*.
[102] Veach, *Friendship of Jesus*.
[103] King, *Laws of Friendship* p. vii.
[104] King, *Laws of Friendship* pp. 4–5.
[105] King, *Laws of Friendship* p. 9.
[106] King, *Laws of Friendship* p. 29.
[107] Benson, *Friendship of Christ* p. 21.
[108] Bennett, *Friendship and Happiness*.
[109] Booth, *Friendship with Jesus*; Royden, *Friendship of God*.
[110] Weatherhead, *Transforming Friendship* p. 25.
[111] Ronald O. Hall, keynote address in Shillito (ed.) *Purpose of God* pp. 20–3. In 1944 as Bishop of Hong Kong, Hall ordained Florence Lee Tim Oi as the first Anglican woman priest.
[112] Moberly, *The Great Friendship* p. 24.
[113] Smyth, *Friendship* pp. 30, 45.
[114] Lewis, *Four Loves* p. 56.
[115] Lewis, *Four Loves* pp. 62, 81–2. R. W. Emerson, 'Friendship', in *Essays*.
[116] Neill, *Supremacy of Jesus* p. 131.
[117] Houston, *Transforming Friendship* p. 145.
[118] Houston, *Transforming Friendship* p. 155.
[119] Kant, *Critique of Practical Reason and other works* p. 38.
[120] Kant, *Critique of Practical Reason and other works* p. 47.
[121] Kant, *Doctrine of Virtue* pp. 140, 144–5. Discussion: Paton, 'Kant on Friendship'.
[122] Kant, *Lectures on Ethics* p. 209.
[123] Kierkegaard,, *Works of Love* 1995 p. 44. Page references in text are to this edition.
[124] Barth, *Ethics* pp. 188–90.
[125] Brunner, *Divine Imperative* p. 517.
[126] Brunner, *Divine Imperative* p. 518.
[127] Brunner, *Divine Imperative* p. 518.
[128] Bonhoeffer, *Ethics* p. 253 n. 1.

Chapter 6: God's friendship, ancient and so new

[1] René Voillaume (founder of the Little Brothers), 'La charité, amitié divine' pp. 64, 68. Author's translation.
[2] Burnaby, *Amor Dei* p. 18. Page references in text are to *Amor Dei*.
[3] Burnaby, *Amor Dei* p. 21. Welcoming Philia in this fully theological sense, Burnaby rejects as inadequate the account of friendship in the earthbound theology, as he sees it, of another 'anti-mystic', the personalist philosopher John Macmurray (1891–1976). Macmurray believed political structures should serve persons in community: 'All meaningful knowledge is for the sake of action, and all meaningful action for the sake of friendship.' (*Self as Agent* p. 15). Macmurray's thought, while not un-theistic, was deliberately 'practical' and anthropocentric. For him as Burnaby says, 'Christian love is Philia – a mutual relationship between persons and expressed by co-operation for the satisfying of other needs, but constituting in itself the highest of intrinsic values'; he gives supreme value to it, but only as inter-human love (*Amor Dei* pp. 19–20). Like Nygren but for different reasons,

Macmurray discounts the possibility that God may be loved directly. For him 'a true idea of God is reached, primarily if not exclusively, through the reflective universalising of those mutual relationships in which community is experienced. But it is only in loving one another that we can realise the value of personality . . . we cannot have Philia for Philia. Its only real object is the concrete human individual with whom and for whom we live and work.' (*Amor Dei* p. 20).

4 Burnaby, *Amor Dei* pp. 163–72; 312.

5 Lucretius, *De rer. nat.* iii, is nearest to his usage.

6 Rougemont, *Passion and Society*.

7 D'Arcy, *Mind and Heart* p. 37. Page references are to the 1962 edition.

8 Buber, *I und Thou* p. 11, quoted D'Arcy p. 156.

9 Nygren, *Agape* p. 92, quoted D'Arcy p. 77.

10 Buber, *I and Thou* p. 15, quoted D'Arcy p. 157.

11 Lepp, *Ways of Friendship* p. 127.

12 Weil, *Waiting on God* p. 115. Page references are to the 1959 edition.

13 Gillon, 'Genèse de la théorie thomiste' pp. 322–9 (325–7).

14 Johann, *Meaning* p. 9. Page references are to *Meaning*.

15 Johann, 'Meditation' p. 127.

16 Johann, 'Meditation' p. 128.

17 Nédoncelle, *Vers un philosophie* p. 28, trans. Johann, *Meaning* pp. 65–6.

18 Oppenheimer, *Hope* 1983 p. 74. Page references in text are to this work.

19 Barth, *Ethics* p. 189, quoted Oppenheimer p. 136

20 Brunner, *Divine Imperative* p. 518, quoted Oppenheimer p. 135.

21 Address to Peru Support Group, Oxford, 4 March 1989. Author's notes.

22 Moltmann, *Source of Life* pp. 1–9.

23 'In the friendship of Jesus' in *The Church in the Power of the Spirit* (1977) pp. 114–21. In a more popular form, ch.4, 'Open Friendship' in *The Open Church* (1978) pp. 50–63.

24 Anglund, *A Friend is Someone Who Likes You*; cited in *Open Church* p. 50.

25 *Open Church* p. 50.

26 *Open Church* p. 51.

27 *Open Church* p. 51.

28 *Church in Power* p. 115; *Open Church* p..51. Kant, *Doctrine of Virtue* pp. 140–5. The connotation Moltmann gives to 'respect', a free respect and acceptance of the person based on the fact *that* they are, is personalist rather than Kantian; Kant's view is classical: virtue commands respect, and the human person has dignity in so far as s/he embodies duty, i.e. is virtuous and under rational control. Kant's respect is primarily for the moral law, and for *what* a person is, or can potentially be, in relation to it.

29 Brecht, *Gesammelte Werke* 12 p. 389, trans. and quoted in *Open Church* p. 51.

30 *Church in Power* p. 115.

31 *Church in Power* p. 116.

32 *Open Church* p. 53.

33 *Church in Power* p. 115.

34 *Open Church* p. 52. For Hegel a 'concrete concept' ('*konkrete Begriff*') is a 'thought which does not remain empty but which is self-determining and self-particularizing', it is Hegel's philosophical equivalent of the creative word of God (translator's foreword in Hegel, *Philosophy of Right* pp. viii–ix). Moltmann quotes from notes taken at Hegel's lectures, printed in *Rechtsphilosophie*, which report him as saying that the 'concrete concept of freedom' comes into being when the will 'posits itself

as an **other** and ceases to be the **universal**' – and this already happens in Friendship and Love, for example (Hegel, *Philosophy of Right* p. 228).

35 *Open Church* p. 52.

36 *Church in Power* p. 115.

37 *Open Church* p. 52.

38 Moltmann quotes Nietzsche: 'Fellowship in joy, and not sympathy in sorrow, makes people friends' (Nietzsche, *Human* p. 499); quoted in *Church in Power* p. 377, n. 86). Of the faith as it had been presented to him Nietsche had expostulated bitterly: 'Christianity arose for the purpose of lightening the heart; but now it must first make the heart heavy in order afterwards to lighten it. Consequently it will perish.' (*Human* p. 126).

39 *Church in Power* p. 114.

40 *Open Church* p. 52.

41 *Open Church* pp. 52–3.

42 *Open Church* p. 54.

43 *Church in Power* pp. 115–16.

44 *Church in Power* p. 119.

45 Moltmann-Wendel and Moltmann, 'Becoming Human' p. 40.

46 *Open Church* p. 55. Attacking sentimentality in German piety, Egenter defined kitsch as 'artistic miscarriage' (p. 15) in which 'the true nature, importance and intrinsic value of the chosen theme are either not understood or not made manifest; instead we are offered its superficial aspect only' (Egenter, *Desecration* pp. 15, 53). A number of classic English hymns however demonstrate a genuine use of 'friend'.

47 *Church in Power* p. 117. Cf. Luke 7.34.

48 *Church in Power* p. 116.

49 *Church in Power* p. 117.

50 *Church in Power* p. 117.

51 *Church in Power* p. 118.

52 Smyth, *Friendship* p. 35.

53 *Open Church* p. 61.

54 *Church in Power* p. 121.

55 *Church in Power* p. 121. The phrase 'festival of the earth', which Moltmann fills with his own exuberant meaning, comes from Nietszche who decried 'love of neighbour' as merely hypocritical self-love, saying it was better to accept love openly through the friend: 'I teach you not the neighbour, but the friend. The friend should be the festival of the earth to you and an anticipation of the overman (Übermensch) . . . I teach you the friend in whom the world stands completed, a bowl of goodness – the creating friend who always has a completed world to give away . . . in your friend you shall love the overman as your cause' (*Thus Spoke Zarathustra* pp. 61–2.

56 *Church in Power* p. 121.

57 *Church in Power* p. 118.

58 *Church in Power* p. 119.

59 *Open Church* p. 58.

60 *Church in Power* p. 116.

61 *Church in Power* p. 121.

62 *Church in Power* p. 121.

63 'Why not . . . Friend/Friendship?' cited by Dunfee, *Beyond Servanthood*, p. 163, n. 75.

64 McFague, *Metaphorical Theology* p. 179.

65 *Metaphorical Theology* p. 180.

66 *Metaphorical Theology* p. 181.
67 *Metaphorical Theology* p. 184.
68 *Metaphorical Theology* p. 186.
69 *Metaphorical Theology* p. 190.
70 McFague, *Models of God* p. 162.
71 McFague, *Models of God* p. 165.
72 McFague, *Models of God* p. 167.
73 McFague, *Models of God* p. 178.
74 McFague, *Models of God* p. 179.
75 Schüssler Fiorenza, *In Memory of Her* p. 344.
76 Schüssler Fiorenza, *In Memory of Her* p. 345.
77 Schüssler Fiorenza, *In Memory of Her* p. 132.
78 Schüssler Fiorenza, *In Memory of Her* p. 344.
79 Schüssler Fiorenza, *In Memory of Her* pp. 346–9.
80 Dunfee, *Beyond Servanthood* p. 137.
81 Dunfee, *Beyond Servanthood* p.xiii.
82 Dunfee, *Beyond Servanthood* p. 138.
83 Dunfee, *Beyond Servanthood* p. 157.
84 Dunfee, *Beyond Servanthood* p. 158.
85 Macmurray in E.Shillito (ed.) *Purpose of God* pp. 167–8.
86 Macmurray in E.Shillito (ed.) *Purpose of God* p. 170.
87 Heyward, *Redemption of God* pp. 167–8.
88 Hunt, *Fierce Tenderness* p. 2.
89 Hunt, *Fierce Tenderness* p. 78.
90 Hunt, *Fierce Tenderness* p. 4.
91 Hunt, *Fierce Tenderness* p. 22.
92 Hunt, *Fierce Tenderness* p. 29.
93 Hunt, *Fierce Tenderness* p. 105.
94 Hunt, *Fierce Tenderness* p. 151.
95 Hunt, *Fierce Tenderness* p. 9.
96 Lorde, 'Uses of the Erotic'pp. 55, 53, 59.
97 Hunt, *Fierce Tenderness* pp. 19, 9.
98 Hunt, *Fierce Tenderness* pp. 165–9.
99 Aristotle, *NE* 1166b33. Cates, *Choosing to Feel* pp. 88–9.
100 Stuart, *Just Good Friends.*
101 Lepp, *Psychology* pp. 191–2. Lepp's writings predate current changes in attitude to homosexuality, but this comment seems to me undated and useful.
102 Stuart, *Gay and Lesbian Theologies* p. 89.
103 Stuart, *Gay and Lesbian Theologies* p. 110. Stuart states 'there is something eschatological about same-sex friendship; it anticipates the kingdom of heaven in a way marriage cannot because marriage ends at death.' (p. 110). This assumes marriage cannot express friendship. If, as we would argue, it does, and all Christian friendship is eternal whether expressed through marriage or not, this conclusion is incoherent.
104 Moltmann-Wendel, *Rediscovering Friendship* p. 5.
105 Moltmann-Wendel, *Rediscovering Friendship* p. 5.
106 Moltmann-Wendel and Moltmann, 'Becoming Human' pp. 29, 34.
107 Moltmann-Wendel, *Rediscovering Friendship* p. 12.
108 Moltmann-Wendel, *Rediscovering Friendship* p. 37.
109 Moltmann-Wendel, *Rediscovering Friendship* p. 46.

110 King, Martin Luther, sermon on 'Love your enemies' (Mt. 5:43–5) in *Strength to Love* pp. 50–1, 54. King distinguishes reciprocal *philia* from the *agape* of God towards all, which however creates friendship.
111 Tutu, *No Future Without Forgiveness*, ch. 11 pp. 206–30.
112 Moltmann-Wendel, *Rediscovering Friendship* p. 41.
113 Moltmann-Wendel, *Rediscovering Friendship* p. 6.
114 Moltmann-Wendel, *Rediscovering Friendship* p. 123.
115 Moltmann-Wendel, *Rediscovering* pp. 68–84.
116 Moltmann-Wendel, *Rediscovering* pp. 95–6.
117 Moltmann-Wendel, *Rediscovering* p. 102.
118 Johnson, *She Who Is* p. 216.
119 Johnson, *She Who Is* p. 217.
120 Johnson, *She Who Is* p. 145.
121 Johnson, *She Who Is* p. 217.
122 Johnson, *She Who Is* p. 218.
123 Johnson, *She Who Is* p. 235.
124 Johnson, *She Who Is* p. 236.
125 Zizioulas, *Being as Communion* p. 46.
126 Zizioulas, *Being as Communion* p. 102.
127 Zizioulas, *Being as Communion* p. 49.
128 O'Callaghan, *Feast of Friendship* p. 138.
129 O'Callaghan, *Feast of Friendship* pp. 80, 138.
130 Edwards, *God of Evolution* pp. 16, 28.
131 Edwards, *God of Evolution* p. 30.
132 Edwards, *God of Evolution* p. 31.

Chapter 7: Conclusion: living friendship

1 Henderson, *Friends on the Way* pp. 15, 46.
2 Swinton, 'Healing presence' pp. 4–6.
3 Swinton, *Resurrecting the Person* p. 39.
4 Swinton, *Resurrecting the Person* p. 167.
5 Cates, *Choosing to Feel* p. 128.
6 Cates, *Choosing to Feel* p. 128.
7 Moltmann-Wendel, *Rediscovering Friendship* p. 25. Derrida seems to convey a similar hope: for an ideal friendship beyond all previous homo-fraternal schemata, in the future democracy that always eludes our grasp! (*Politics of Friendship* p. 306).
8 *De civ. Dei* XIX.17.
9 Archbishop Desmond Tutu, speaking in the Anglican Communion Office, London, Ash Wednesday 2004.

Indices

Index of Subjects

Index of Names

Index of Biblical References